# The Which? Guide to Computers for Small Businesses

## About the author

After a decade in the software industry Richard Wentk now works as a freelance writer, computer trainer and consultant, with a particular interest in making computer technology accessible to non-technical people. He is also the author of *The Which? Guide to the Internet* and *The Which? Guide to Computers*.

## Acknowledgements

The author would like to thank Christina Carson, Liz Barker, Marcus Austin, and everyone who contributed to the case histories.

# The Which? Guide to Computers for Small Businesses

*Richard Wentk*

CONSUMERS' ASSOCIATION

Which? Books are commissioned and researched by
Consumers' Association and published by
Which? Ltd, 2 Marylebone Road, London NW1 4DF

Distributed by The Penguin Group:
Penguin Books Ltd, 27 Wrights Lane, London W8 5TZ

First edition April 1999
Copyright © 1999 Which? Ltd

*British Library Cataloguing-in-Publication Data*
A catalogue record for this book is available from the British Library

ISBN 0 85202 755 9

No part of this publication may be reproduced or transmitted in any form or by any means, electronically or mechanically, including photocopying, recording or any other information storage or retrieval system, without prior permission in writing from the publisher. This publication is not included under licences issued by the Copyright Agency.

> For a full list of Which? books, please write to Which? Books, Castlemead, Gascoyne Way, Hertford X. SG14 1LH, or access our web site at http://www.which.net

Cover and text design by Kyzen Creative Consultants
Cover photograph by Pictor International
Illustration *External and internal parts of a computer* by Peter Harper

Typeset by ensystems, Saffron Walden, Essex
Printed and bound in England by Clays Ltd, Bungay, Suffolk

# Contents

|    | Introduction | 7 |
|---|---|---|
| 1 | What can a computer do for my business? | 9 |
| 2 | Computers and the very small business | 18 |
| 3 | Sharing information | 45 |
| 4 | Managing money | 63 |
| 5 | Working with information | 78 |
| 6 | Advertising and promotion | 94 |
| 7 | Buying for business | 112 |
| 8 | Choosing the right hardware | 136 |
| 9 | Buying and using software | 148 |
| 10 | Safeguarding your investment | 158 |
| 11 | Business and the Internet | 175 |
| 12 | E-commerce and the electronic economy | 214 |
| 13 | Dealing with the Year 2000 problem | 240 |

## Appendices

|    |    |    |
|---|---|---|
| I | Making sense of specifications | 257 |
| II | Choosing options and extras | 280 |
| III | Operating systems | 306 |
| IV | Internet addresses explained | 319 |
| V | Useful addresses | 327 |
| VI | Further reading | 333 |
|    | Glossary | 337 |
|    | Index | 345 |

# Introduction

As computer systems have become ubiquitous, a firm understanding of the technology, as well as the opportunities it creates, is almost essential for the successful running of a business. It is now as important as the ability to prepare a business plan or deal with the VAT office. As recently as the late 1980s, computers were used only for simple business work – preparing letters, helping with accounts, invoicing, sales and stock control, and sometimes creating promotional materials. While they still perform these functions, they also offer unprecedented challenges and opportunities for small businesses. In terms of opportunities, the most exciting development for business is the arrival of e-commerce – electronic trading on the Internet. It is now possible for small companies to trade successfully in markets that were previously available only to large multinationals. According to a September 1998 survey by British Telecom, more than 8 million companies in Europe are likely to be using e-commerce facilities by the year 2003. Some 40 per cent of all shopping and business transactions will be electronic, forming part of a new sector of the economy worth more than £2 billion a year. Many of these companies will be small enterprises that have taken advantage of gaps in this new market to create distinctive business niches. E-commerce offers the interesting possibility of a company that runs an almost completely computerized business, trading at all hours of the day or night, 365 days a year, with minimal human intervention.

The challenges come from the technology itself, which remains badly designed and unreliable on more occasions that it should. Users are often forced to find ways around these limitations and can waste time with poorly designed products that could easily be improved. A good example of this is the Year 2000 (Y2K) problem or 'millennium bug'. The bug's effects may yet prove to be extremely serious, although informed management and technological forethought could easily have avoided the whole issue. Rumour and hearsay about the bug remain widespread, especially from those who have a product to sell. Businesses that fail to understand what is involved will either lose money chasing problems that do not exist or – worse still – wake up on 1 January 2000 to find that none of their computer systems work properly.

Finding a way to exploit the opportunities fully and avoid the pitfalls of technology requires a ready source of explanation and information. Sources of information are not as plentiful as they might be. Consultants are expensive, and many computer magazines seem obsessed with technology for its own sake and unaware of the practical implications for business users. Computer dealers are often more interested in making a sale than explaining the technology that is most suitable for their customers' needs. This can result in, for example, the purchase of a new piece of software that simply will not work on an older machine; or of a printer which, though cheap to buy, costs more to run and is also significantly slower than a more expensive model, which would be a better long-term investment. Both beginners and experienced users can be left wondering where to turn when they need to make informed decisions about buying new systems or improving and updating old ones.

This book is a practical introduction to computers for small businesses, covering everything from the simplest and most straightforward technology to the most advanced and speculative products and possibilities. It will help business people without a technical background to find a way through the maze of jargon and discover the different ways in which information technology can support their work. Whether you are just starting out, already running a small enterprise or expanding an existing business, you will find all the advice that you need here to buy and use computer products cost-effectively and with confidence.

# Chapter 1

# What can a computer do for my business?

A computer is the perfect tool for working with information. Fifty years ago a business might have employed a small army of clerks, accountants and errand boys to process facts and figures and pass them around an organisation. Today's technology can do the same kind of work faster, more efficiently and, when wisely chosen and properly installed, more cheaply.

To a computer, 'information' can be almost anything that is not a physical object. Words, photographs, faxes, sounds, mathematical formulae, video clips, musical compositions, financial summaries and cartoon animations are just some of the kinds of information with which a computer can work. In some cases it can even translate certain kinds of information into useful equivalents – for example, the sounds of spoken English can be converted into words that appear on the computer's screen exactly as if someone had typed them in.

A computer also makes it possible to store very large amounts of information in a small space. In business use, computer systems sometimes pay for themselves by removing the need for large amounts of paper storage and so allowing lower premises costs. It can also be much easier and quicker to find information inside a computer (if it has been filed correctly) than it is in a paper-based filing system.

Computers are very good at distributing information. A useful way to look at them is as the successors to the humble telephone handset. Where a handset is used to transmit one kind of information – the sound of the human voice – a computer connected to a telephone line, or some other electronic link, can transmit any kind of information to almost anywhere in the world very quickly. A simple example is the sending and receiving of faxes. Computers can take the place of paper faxes, and information can be sent straight from one computer screen to another without having to be printed out and run through a fax machine first. A slightly more complex example is electronic mail – email – whereby information can be sent as text, or even pictures and video, directly from one computer to another.

In an office environment, this kind of technology can help save paper, make communications more efficient and sometimes even lead to new ways of working. Internal phone directories, newsletters, employment contracts and even technical or business help (including answers to frequently asked questions) can be made available on demand on screens, rather than printed pages in binders. Information can be updated from a central location, and the changes will be visible to everyone immediately. Expensive reprints and paper copies, which are sometimes out of date almost immediately, are no longer necessary.

The Internet and the mobile-phone networks (some of which now offer true global coverage) have made it possible to expand facilities beyond the confines of a company and out to the rest of the world. Information can now move between individuals, businesses and countries almost instantly. Customers can read information about product lines and prices at any time of the day or night, from any country. Electronic discussions can take the place of face-to-face negotiations. Similarly, employees no longer need to be tied to a desk at the office. Working from home – 'teleworking' – can often be more cost-effective for businesses, and less stressful for employees who do not need to waste time and money commuting.

Internet technologies have also created completely new commercial opportunities for businesses, allowing them to develop new products and services, or to sell old products and services in new ways. The result has been a true gold-rush for some new businesses, which have suddenly found that they can compete on equal terms with much larger and more established companies.

## A first look at computer technology

A computer system has two components. **Hardware** describes the parts of a computer that you can touch. It is rather like the chassis and engine of a car – it provides the raw power that supports everything, but is not particularly useful in itself. **Software** is the name given to the tools that give a computer its flexibility. In effect software adds a body, seats and a steering wheel. Software products are technically known as 'software packages', but are often referred to as just 'packages' or 'applications'.

A computer can have many different kinds of software installed. Each kind of software does a specific kind of job. If you want to use your computer for something new – for example, accounts – you simply buy and install accounts-related software for it. There are many thousands of different software tools on the market today, designed to help with a range of tasks. It is probably fair to say that almost anything people do for a living has suitable software available that can help with it.

Since the start of the 1990s, the cost of buying a computer has fallen spectacularly, and this has made it possible for businesses to buy tools – software – for work that they might not have been able to afford before. An example of this is video editing. Systems good enough for professional use are currently available for a couple of thousand pounds, while those for more modest applications are available for a few hundred. Equivalent technology at the start of the 1990s would have cost six figures or more. This has meant that small businesses can now produce their own simple videos in-house. Video professionals, who were once essential to the process, are now hired only when their advanced directing and editing skills are required.

## Tools of the trade

When buying a computer system, a good first step is to become familiar with the different kinds of work that a computer can perform. As a rule of thumb, for business use it is best to buy a computer as a *specific solution* – in other words as a tool, or toolbox, that will be used to do very specific kinds of work. It is worth noting that this is unlikely to be the way in which computers are advertised. In much of the computer press, the latest and most impressive hardware specifications are bandied about with a cheerful disregard for whether or not they make any practical difference to a real user.

Of course, the speed and power of a system matter, but the second rule of thumb to remember is that for typical office work, computers are completely over-specified. Today's simple, cheap machines are far more powerful than they need to be. (Ironically, computer games make the greatest demands on hardware, and if you want to get the best from these, you will need the biggest, best and most expensive model you can buy.) This rule of thumb makes buying decisions simpler. The plain truth is that for a typical very small business any modern computer will do, and Megahertz, Megabytes and other hardware jargon can be conveniently forgotten. However, other less tangible and rarely mentioned qualities, such as reliability and support from dealers, are much more important (see page 116). Larger businesses need to consider other options, which are discussed in later chapters. For anyone who wants a simple office tool to help with the chores while starting up a business, hardware specifications are far less significant than the advertising would have you believe.

The third rule of thumb is that, whether you are buying for use in a home office or running a company with tens of employees, software has by far the greatest impact on usefulness and productivity. For a business, it is especially important to choose software carefully, and the first step towards doing this is to understand the kinds of business tools that are available. What follows is an overview of the different types of software that are available to help with work that computers can do in a business setting – from the simplest and most basic to the more challenging and commercially speculative.

## The bare essentials

The bare essential software products are designed to help with the everyday chores that any small business needs to do in order to survive. You can do all of this work the old-fashioned way with pen and paper (or fingers and typewriter), but computers can make it easier to correct mistakes, or, in the case of financial calculations, to ensure that you get the right answer in the first place.

**Basic money management** Every business needs to know what its costs are, to whom it owes money, and who has not yet paid. A rough idea of how much capital is in the bank is also very useful. Keeping track of such information is child's play for a computer. Simple accounting systems are cheap and easy to use, and some can be linked to the home-banking services now offered by many banks. These make it possible to get an up-to-the-minute electronic statement for an account (or accounts, if there is more than one) at any time of the day or night. It is also possible to pay bills electronically or arrange transfers.

**Word processing** Letter-writing is still by far the most popular use for computers, and many businesses now find word processing essential. A word processor is a software tool that turns a computer into a sophisticated typewriter. Words are typed on to the screen instead of directly on to paper, which means they can be checked and changed before being printed out. Word processors can also check spelling, make suggestions for the layout of a letter on the page, and help you file your outgoing correspondence more efficiently. With a word processor, printed copies become redundant. You can file old letters inside your computer and look at them on the screen whenever you need to see them again.

**Address book and appointment diary** The electronic versions of these do not suffer from the 'diary scrawl' that develops when changes have to be made in the tiny space left by the crossed-out original entry. If someone you know moves, or if an appointment time is changed, you can change electronic entries much more easily than paper ones. Some electronic address books also have facilities for dialling phone numbers automatically.

## More advanced tools

Advanced tools are suitable for slightly larger businesses, which need to keep track of more information about staff, products, expenses and income than very small companies. They are also helpful for small businesses that are looking to expand and would like to plan and analyse their growth more formally.

**Advanced money management** Payroll calculations, VAT, and cheque and invoice printing are slightly more advanced financial tools that businesses need to consider once they start to employ more than one or two people. Computers can easily automate these chores. Some VAT software will produce a single quarterly printout that can be sent directly to the United Kingdom's Customs and Excise with a cheque. Similarly, some invoice and payment tracking systems will produce letters of complaint for overdue accounts, or will print a complete cheque run.

**Financial planning and business development** A **spreadsheet** is a general-purpose tool for working with numbers and formulae. At its simplest it can be used to work out very simple credit/debit accounts, or to calculate loan repayments. However, a spreadsheet can also be used for much more complex work, such as answering 'what if?' questions when preparing a business plan. For example, what happens to profitability if the interest rate on a business loan goes up? What happens if loan repayments are made over two years instead of five?

**General information management** A **database** is rather like an intelligent filing cabinet. It provides a central store for all kinds of records, and can select records according to different criteria, making it easier to analyse information. Databases have many, many uses. They can be used for employee records, as address books, stock-control systems, computer-based catalogues, and sales analysis tools (which can, for example, check which items sell well, and also track seasonal and regional variations).

**Electronic Point-of-Sale (EPOS) systems** These are used by shops to create a direct link from tills to a central computer. Items are identified to the computer as they are sold (for example, by scanning a bar code, typing in a code, or pressing a button that specifies the product on the till). The till works in the usual way, and the computer keeps track of stock and stores sales records, which can be used to create accounts.

## Utilities: optional extras

Specific tools for jobs that are not essential for the main activities of a business are known as utilities. For most businesses they are useful optional extras. Many of these tools are available for less than £100.

**Internet tools** Electronic mail (email), and access to the World Wide Web and the international newsgroup network make it possible to communicate with certain customers very quickly and cheaply, to research information, get support from people with similar personal or business interests, and (in some cases) to advertise goods and services and take orders electronically after office hours.

**Photo and image editing** If you ever work with photographs or images, perhaps for brochures or advertising, then good image-editing tools are very useful. At their most basic you can use them to correct photographic mistakes, including over- and under-exposure, colour balance, brightness and contrast. More creatively, you can generate an almost infinite range of special effects, and assemble photomontages that would take hours in the darkroom using traditional methods.

**Desktop publishing** This can be used to produce brochures, posters, newsletters, business cards, and even T-shirts and promotional mug designs. Most desktop publishing (DTP) packages include sample page layouts, which make it easy to produce professional-looking results with minimal effort.

**Graphic-design tools** These can help with the creation of logos and other graphics, such as posters and advertising designs, or with more general illustration work.

**'Mail merge' software** This creates personalised letters by merging a list of names and addresses (and perhaps some other personal details) with a form letter. Some software packages can also print appropriate address labels. Mail merge software is ideal for mail shots. Mail merge features are often supplied as part of a word processor.

**Route plotters** Anyone who spends a lot of time driving will appreciate these electronic navigators, which can plot the shortest or quickest set of roads between any two points, or combine all of those criteria to suggest the ideal compromise. With the help of suitable extras, some route plotters can even display your current location on a map (see page 84).

**Voice dictation** The computer listens to words spoken into a microphone and converts them into words that appear in a word processor, where they can be edited further, sent to someone as a message or faxed.

**Legal boilerplate and form letters** Many legal contracts are simply copies of 'boilerplate' legal jargon that can be applied to the relevant legal situation. It is possible to buy copies of boilerplate contracts in computer-editable form and create usable, professional-looking contracts simply by filling in the blanks. There will be situations, of course, where a lawyer's professional contribution will still be required, but for many everyday business situations these packages provide a useful, money-saving shortcut. Business form letters can also be bought and used in a similar way.

**Project management** Formal project-management systems can easily be automated with a computer. Dependencies can be tracked and calculated on complicated projects that would be time-consuming to manage by hand.

## Larger systems

As well as providing specific tools to help with certain kinds of work, you can also buy software that provides a complete all-in-one business solution with a large range of facilities. These systems are general-purpose business development tools, rather than individual tools designed to do a specific task. They can be an attractive choice because they do a complete job 'out of the box'. These systems are always designed to work with groups of computers that are linked together.

Some of the most popular larger systems include:

**Financial-management packages** A complete set of facilities for a working business, including stock and inventory control, job costing, and sales and invoice ledgers.

**Groupware** Industry jargon for tools that help people work together in groups. It comes into its own during collaborative projects that involve small to medium-sized groups of people. At its simplest it enables people to send messages from one desk to another (electronic mail), arrange meetings, allocate tasks electronically and share information when working on a project. More complex systems allow for electronic discussions, for the posting of information that is relevant to the company (which in practice can mean anything from price lists to product colour schemes, to standard terms and conditions of employment), and even for 'document management', which is the ability to set up a database of all the most important documents in a company.

**Enterprise systems** Complete all-in-one trading packages that control orders, track their assembly and delivery, and maintain accounting records. In some cases they can accept orders from the

Internet and send messages to various global banking networks to transfer money from one account to another. While this level of service may seem ambitious for a small company, electronic commerce, or **e-commerce**, technology is rapidly levelling the playing field. E-commerce is expanding the catchment area of small businesses.

**Business-specific solutions** Specific off-the-shelf software that handles the needs of one particular kind of business, for example, a garage, a farm or a doctor's surgery, are also available. They sometimes have the advantage of being easier to learn and use because they use terms and language that are specific to a given profession. Moreover they can offer a convenient all-in-one way to do certain kinds of work, which will sometimes save on the planning needed for a business computer system.

Having looked at the possibilities in general, you will find it useful to consider the various options in more detail. Chapter 2 starts this process by looking at the needs of a typical very small business.

Chapter 2

# Computers and the very small business

This chapter is for sole traders, home workers and anyone who wants to buy the simplest possible computer system to help with their work. Buying a computer is now relatively straightforward because, as mentioned in Chapter 1, any modern computer, technically speaking, is suitable for office work. Choosing software is slightly more complicated, although the ways to make it easier to decide which software to buy are discussed below.

## What does a business need?

Most computers are used for office chores, and the two most common kinds of chores are creating documents and book-keeping. Slightly less common tasks include maintaining address books and diaries and creating publicity. Currently rare, but rapidly increasing in business popularity is an Internet connection. Finally, computers can help with taking messages and sending and receiving faxes.

### Creating documents

Writing letters and other documents is still by far the most popular use for computers. The software used to do this is called a **word processor.** Relatively few offices still use typewriters, because the advantages of word processing are so obvious. The biggest difference between word processing and typing is that word processing gives you the chance to make changes and corrections before committing any words to paper. Paragraphs and sentences can be moved around, words can be rearranged, and the page layout can be checked on the screen before text is printed. This is useful enough in its own right, but word processors have even more powerful facilities to offer:

**Automated corrections** of spelling errors, including common errors such as mistyping 'teh' for 'the'. Errors that are unique to different typists can be remembered and corrected.

**Control over text size and style** allows the use of different lettering styles (known as fonts), while letter sizes can be scaled from tiny lettering to poster-sized giant letters.

**Automated layout** ranges from automatic indentation of paragraphs, to automated numbering of sub-headings, to so-called style sheets, which use pre-defined letter styles and sizes for different parts of a document. For example, paragraph headings may be in **bold** or *italic* styles.

**Form letters** can be written once with blanks, and then the blanks filled in each time the letter is needed. There is no need to retype the whole letter or use a clumsily modified photocopied version.

**Mail merge facilities** can print personalised form letters automatically when provided with a blank form letter and a list of recipients' names, addresses and other personal details.

**Advanced options** include the ability to create tables, list information in alphabetical or numerical order, add ('import') pictures and other information from other software, and convert documents so that they will work with a different make of word processor. All of these can make documents more useful or visually appealing. For example, quotes for a project can be prepared in a spreadsheet (see below), and a summary of the quote, which lists the most important figures, can be copied straight into a word processor, ready for printing.

**Electronic publishing** facilities can convert documents into a form that is suitable for presenting on the Internet, or for distribution on home-made CDs (see page 107).

---

This is 9 point Times New Roman
**This is 12 point Arial Black**
**This is 14 point Claredon Condensed**
This is 16 point Tahoma

---

The above gives some indication of the range of fonts and sizes (measured in points) that are available in most word-processing packages.

## Publicity

Word processors can be used for simple publicity, including flyers and posters. Their ability to work with different lettering styles and sizes, and to include images and graphics, make them ideal for simple posters. A business that produces very occasional publicity may well find that a word processor – or even old-fashioned transfer lettering, cut-and-paste page layouts and photocopying – may be enough.

There are occasions, however, when a more sophisticated page-design tool is required. A **desktop publishing** (DTP) package can produce professional effects, such a block of text across different areas on a page, or complex backgrounds made of grids and other graphics, or text and images at unlikely angles. Businesses that find themselves producing a lot of promotional materials should consider investing in some DTP software, as it makes it possible to produce much more impressive results very quickly. A more comprehensive discussion of DTP is included in Chapter 6.

## Book-keeping

Computers are perfect for book keeping. They do not make mistakes with calculations, they can keep years of information in a small space, and they produce useful summaries of trading results very quickly and easily. The three kinds of tools that can help with book-keeping are personal finance managers, accounts packages and spreadsheets.

### Personal finance managers

Although designed for home finances, personal finance managers may be adequate for the needs of a very small business. They are very simple, cost less than £100, and make it easy to do elementary budgeting and book keeping. Regular income and outgoings can be automated to keep track of regular payments such as loans, bills and building society interest. They can also help with statement reconciliations, and, on occasion, with the preparation of simple balance sheets. Other typical features include:

- user-defined lists of credits and debits by category
- multiple accounts to keep track of credit card payments, mortgage payments, savings accounts and investment portfolios
- invoice preparation and printing

- cheque printing
- summaries of useful information, such as total income and outgoings, graphs, tables and charts.

Some personal finance managers can cope with VAT calculations, and will even deal with all the different VAT codes that apply to products and services. Their main disadvantage is that they often include samples and examples for domestic rather than business use, and so may need quite a bit of work to reset. However, the better packages, such as Intuit's Quicken, offer very good value for money, and can provide all that a small business needs for its books.

## Accounts packages

Specifically designed for business use, the accounts packages lack 'domestic' features, such as investment portfolio summaries and mortgage calculations, but add more comprehensive book-keeping tools that reflect the way that accountants work. A typical package includes:

- a sales ledger, where sales are noted
- a purchase ledger, where outgoings are listed
- a cash book, which lists cash transactions
- a nominal ledger, which keeps a running total of credits versus debits
- invoice printing, during which invoice totals are automatically included in the sales ledger
- cheque printing
- statement printing for creditors
- analysis tools that show which items sell well, which customers place the most orders, and which items are most profitable, etc.
- the ability to calculate and print VAT returns.

With prices between £100 and £1,000, accounts packages may represent a significant investment for a very small business, and the extra features may only become essential when business is brisk. They may be unnecessarily complex for someone who trades sporadically or does long-term contract work with a single company. The same applies to any other situation that involves only one or two creditors, one or two suppliers and a relatively small number of transactions.

For this kind of work a good personal finance manager is a better choice.

However, any business that plans to grow, or has dealings with tens of customers and regular suppliers, or is likely to need extra facilities, such as payroll calculations and stock control, can benefit from investing in a true accounts package. The best packages can be upgraded with new features, including payroll facilities, which slot neatly into the existing system. If your business falls into this category you may need to consider the more advanced tools discussed in Chapter 4. Buying a cheap package that will be unable to grow with your needs can be a bad mistake. It is best to avoid the possibility of re-keying five years of financial records into a different and incompatible system.

## Spreadsheets

Spreadsheets are the ultimate financial tool. Completely free-form, they offer no pre-prepared facilities to help with calculations. Users have to create their own accounting and financial management tools by specifying lists of facts and figures and defining the relationships between them.

Spreadsheets work by providing a grid of cells. Each cell can contain a number, other information (such as a word or date) or a formula. Formulae can be very simple, such as the sum of a collection of cells, or very complex, such as the monthly repayment on a loan. Averages, statistical calculations, scientific and mathematical functions, and a wide range of financial calculations are available. The result of a formula can be used in other calculations, which in turn can be used in another formula and so on indefinitely. When one number is changed, all the numbers that depend on its value are re-calculated automatically.

Spreadsheets are very useful for advanced work, but their flexibility makes them daunting for beginners. In theory, a spreadsheet can do anything an accounts package can, although in practice the time required to set up spreadsheets for this kind of work makes them less than ideal for any but the simplest accounts. Their main advantage is that they are sometimes supplied 'free' with a computer. Someone with very simple needs may find that, with a little work, they may be all that is required.

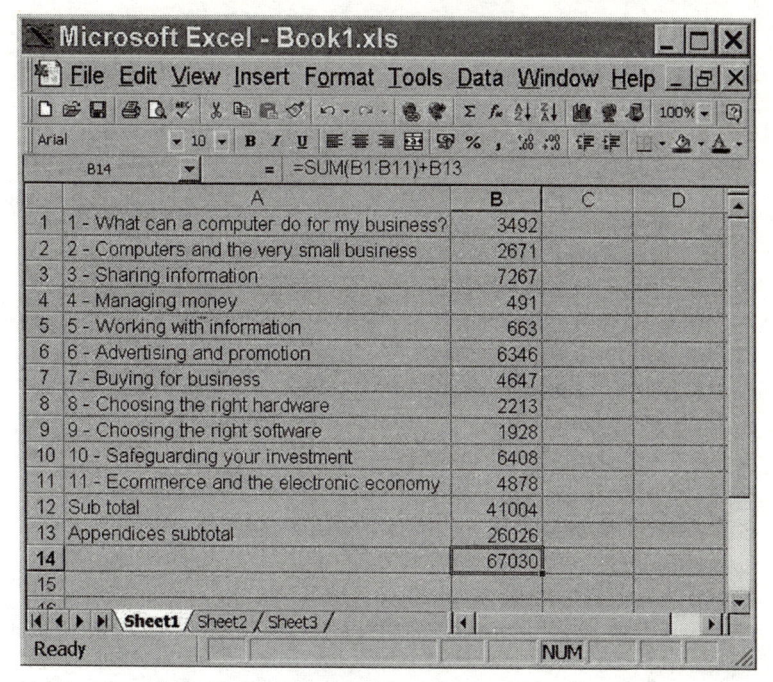

| | A | B | C | D |
|---|---|---|---|---|
| 1 | 1 - What can a computer do for my business? | 3492 | | |
| 2 | 2 - Computers and the very small business | 2671 | | |
| 3 | 3 - Sharing information | 7267 | | |
| 4 | 4 - Managing money | 491 | | |
| 5 | 5 - Working with information | 663 | | |
| 6 | 6 - Advertising and promotion | 6346 | | |
| 7 | 7 - Buying for business | 4647 | | |
| 8 | 8 - Choosing the right hardware | 2213 | | |
| 9 | 9 - Choosing the right software | 1928 | | |
| 10 | 10 - Safeguarding your investment | 6408 | | |
| 11 | 11 - Ecommerce and the electronic economy | 4878 | | |
| 12 | Sub total | 41004 | | |
| 13 | Appendices subtotal | 26026 | | |
| 14 | | 67030 | | |

Using a spreadsheet to calculate word counts for the different chapters in an early draft of this book. In this case '=SUM(B1:B11)+B13' is the formula for cell B14, which shows the grand total.

## Transferring money

A useful tool that has appeared relatively recently is **on-line banking**, which connects a home or business computer to a bank's computer through a telephone link. The service can be used to check balances, pay bills and make many other standard bank transactions. Statements can be printed out directly.

On-line banking can be a terrific time-saver for small businesses, and indeed for anyone who has to work during office hours and has too little time at lunch to get to a bank. The number of banks and building societies that offer this service is growing all the time.

To use the service, a computer needs to be fitted with an optional extra called a **modem** (see page 276), which in turn needs to be connected to a telephone line. This line can be shared with an ordinary telephone by fitting a simple and inexpensive two-way adaptor plug to a wall socket, or installing an extension socket in the office. Two lines are not necessary.

23

On-line banking is very easy to use. The bank provides suitable software, and a password or pin-like number is used to ensure that the connection is secure. Once connected, the service provides much of the information that is available to personal bankers in branches. Statements appear on-screen very quickly, and can be printed out for reference. Transfers and other transactions can be done with a few keystrokes. When contemplating this kind of service, consider the following:

- **banking charges** How much does the service cost? Is there an extra charge for transactions?
- **telephone charges** Is a low-cost number used, which charges at the local-call rate?
- **customer support** Is there a number to call if there are problems? Is it open 24 hours, or only at set times?
- **business banking** Is the service available for limited companies and those with business accounts?
- **software** Which software is used? Will the service work with any finance manager or accounting packages?

## Tax calculators

Tax and VAT are the bane of many businesses. The arrival of self-assessment has made the tax situation even more complicated. Tax calculators can help those who do not wish, or cannot afford, to hire an accountant. These tools take business people through the ins and outs of a tax return step by step, explaining what each section on the form is for and providing extra background information to make it easier to fill in.

They are not a substitute for an accountant, whose main job should be to advise on all the available tax breaks. They have no facilities for dealing with more advanced questions, such as the pros and cons of limited companies versus sole trading, payment by dividend instead of PAYE, or off-shore tax havens. However, for about £30 they do offer a reasonably inexpensive and pain-free way to help avoid late-filing and late-payment penalties, and also to estimate tax liabilities.

## Address books and diaries

Diaries and address books are usually combined in a single tool known as a **contact manager** (CM) or a **personal information manager** (PIM). Contact managers are ideal for anyone who spends a lot of time talking to people and would need relevant personal information, including notes from previous conversations, to hand. PIMs are more general purpose, but overall there is a large degree of overlap between the two kinds of products. Both PIMs and CMs typically include other facilities, such as a 'to do' list of important tasks, an 'infinite' (or near-infinite) calendar, and perhaps the computer equivalent of sticky-notes for free-form note-taking and memory jogging.

Electronic address books offer a number of advantages over their paper equivalent, including:

- easier and neater corrections and changes
- grouping people together more easily by category
- speedier access to someone's details
- the transfer of useful information (such as email addresses, or lists of people who might be interested in a product or service)
- automatic printing of addresses
- the facility (with some packages) to dial telephone numbers if the computer has a modem
- easy free-form note-taking (about people or the details of telephone conversations), which can be used in the future.

The case for electronic diaries and appointment books is less clear-cut, and there is still a lot to be said for using pen and paper. Paper diaries are cheap, convenient, quick, easy to use and portable, and for many people they are a perfectly sensible way of organising their time.

Electronic diaries offer only a slight improvement over the pen and paper approach. The main advantages are their ability to automatically remember anniversaries such as birthdays, to provide audible and visual alarms and reminders of other important dates and times (sometimes before they happen), and to connect with other features, such as a 'to do' list of important tasks, or an address book. For example, an appointment can easily be linked to someone's personal details, so they can be studied before the meeting. They are also neater and less prone to scrawled changes, and, of course, appointment details can be changed an indefinite number of times and still look neat and comprehensible. Finally, they do not need to be renewed every year, but will continue working until they are obsolete (usually not till well into the twenty-first century).

For those who want more complex facilities, software tools called **databases** are available. While these can be used to create an address book and diary system to any specification, they are really general-purpose information management tools, which can do many kinds of work, and are a rather complex way to keep track of names, addresses and appointments (see page 86).

## The Internet

Internet usage is set to explode in the first few years of the twenty-first century, and this alone makes it something for a business to consider. However, in the late 1990s Internet facilities are still quite crude. Connections are slow, information can be hard to find, and the transmission of such things as video clips are of very poor quality. However, for work such as journalism, or other home-based work, an Internet connection is very useful, and using a connection adds a nominal amount to existing monthly expenses. In the late 1990s the Internet offered cheap, near-instant communications with approximately 75 million people (the exact number seems to double annually). Many businesses, large and small, now use electronic mail (**email**), which is often a more successful and convenient way of communicating than a letter, phone call or fax. There is no extra cost for sending messages overseas, and, when compared to a fax, the savings are considerable.

A vast library of information on every subject imaginable is found on the Internet. This includes answers to questions about computer use, the ins and outs of a particular trade, or being in business in general. It also provides catalogues and perhaps stock listings from suppliers; general background information, including news and weather from almost any city in the world; share prices; magazine features that are not available in print; and fact summaries from a professional field, such as legal precedents or drug side-effects. Hard-to-find books and other information from abroad can also be ordered over the Internet.

The Internet also provides a chance to discuss business with people involved in related work, and to find inspiration for new business ideas and trading possibilities (see Chapter 11).

## Getting 'on-line'

To use the Internet, a computer has to have a **modem** installed and connected to a phone line. Some modems are available for less than £50 and can be purchased from a huge number of sources. Many computer suppliers will include a modem for a nominal extra charge.

As with the on-line banking facility (see page 23), a phone line can be shared with an ordinary telephone. One disadvantage of this is that when the computer is connected to the Internet, the line will produce a 'busy' signal for anyone trying to call. A better, if more expensive, option is a separate phone line. An existing fax line is suitable, although, again, faxes will not be able to get through if the Internet is being used. Some businesses go as far as to install a line that is exclusively for the Internet, although this is an expensive and possibly unnecessary luxury.

To use the Internet, a connection has to be 'hired' from an Internet access company. This company will provide suitable (if perhaps very basic) software, details of a phone number for the modem to call, and Internet facilities at the other end of the line. Once someone has 'dialled in' they can send and read email messages, 'surf' the World Wide Web (see below), and generally use the Internet as if they had a direct connection to it. When they have finished they break the connection, and the phone line reverts to its usual function. While on-line (connected to the Internet) phone charges accumulate in the usual way.

There are two sorts of Internet companies. **Internet Service Providers** (ISPs) offer a simple connection with no frills. They leave the ins and outs of exploring the Internet's facilities to their customers. **On-line services** provide a 'value-added' service with extra features. These include magazine-like features, convenient access to the latest news and weather, and the ability to have typed conversations with complete strangers, either individually or in 'chat rooms', which are grouped according to people's interests. In general, on-line services are a better choice for complete beginners, because they make using the Internet very simple. Experienced users will prefer the more direct connection available from an ISP, which offers more choice about which software can be used.

Connections via an ISP can be very cheap indeed. In fact some companies are now offering a completely free service (the only charges are for telephone time). On-line services tend to be significantly more expensive. For example, in the United Kingdom the major on-line service provider, America Online (AOL), currently charges £16.95 per month for unlimited connection time. CompuServe, another on-line service provider (which is effectively owned by AOL), charges the UK equivalent of $9.95 per month, with complicated additional charges accruing for each minute spent using its 'Premium Services'.

For fairly light use, perhaps involving ten email messages a day and half an hour spent on the web looking for information, the total cost is likely to be somewhere between £50 and £100 a quarter. Even heavy business users will find it hard to run up a bill of more than £300 a quarter. This is not quite so true of on-line services, where the vast number of options and the ease with which people can make new friends on the Internet can be addictive. Some users find themselves with £500 or more to pay each quarter, although this is very rare, and a little measured restraint should be enough to prevent this.

### Internet software

On-line services supply their own proprietary software, which will do everything you need. It is sometimes possible to use an alternative web browser (see below) with an on-line service, but email and other features are typically built into the software and cannot be changed.

ISPs typically offer a starter-pack of generic Internet-ready software, which includes some or all of the following:

**Email facilities** Electronic mail sends a message directly from one computer to another. Usually this is a simple text message; only the words are sent, with no details of lettering styles or page layout. However, it is also possible to send, in decreasing order of convenience, formatted documents, photographs and pictures, sounds, and video clips.

**News reader** In spite of the name, this software has very little to do with the kind of news available from newspapers, radio and television.

Instead it provides access to **newsgroups**, which are free-for-all discussion areas, devoted to tens of thousands of different topics. Many newsgroups are, quite frankly, a waste of time; personal invective and name-calling have replaced any semblance of useful debate. However, a handful can offer the chance to meet people who share similar personal or professional interests, or provide informal technical, or other, support from experts in their field.

**Web browser** The World Wide Web is the main Internet information resource. It is rather like a magazine that has no editor and millions of contributors. Articles are cross-linked together, so that you can jump from one piece of information to another as you follow a train of thought. Information includes text, photographs and graphics, although special effects, such as animation and music, are increasingly being used. Web browsers make it possible to view this information and to follow links between articles.

Web browsers often include email and newsgroup facilities and can be used for reading and sending email and news messages. However, these features are very crude and inefficient. Software specifically designed for email and news is much more effective, and can save time and money too. Many ISPs supply a web browser and expect their customers to use it for everything. Fortunately, better software is available for free on the Internet, and can be copied to your computer very easily. For details of suggested products see the list at the end of this chapter. For information about how to copy free software to your computer see page 37.

## Messages and faxes

If a computer has a modem modem fitted, it will, as a matter of course, be able to send and receive fax transmissions without using any paper. A word-processed document can be 'printed' to the modem instead of to a printer, and the message will be faxed to a remote fax machine, or another computer, in the usual way. Incoming faxes will be stored in the computer's filing system, and can be viewed on the screen or printed to paper. Using a modem is much cheaper than buying a separate fax machine, although it means that the computer has to be left on all the time, or turned on specially whenever a fax is due. Frequently faxed numbers can also be organised more intelligently, or copied from an electronic address book. The other major advantage is that faxes are printed on plain paper. This is more durable than fax paper, which can crinkle and fade.

Answering-machine 'voice' facilities are available on the latest modems. These turn the modem into an answering machine. A greeting can be recorded via a microphone plugged into the computer, and messages are played back via the computer's loudspeakers (if it has any) or via the telephone handset. More advanced voice modems include record and play buttons on the modem itself, and the modem will continue to work as a fax and answering machine even if the computer to which it is connected is turned off.

Again, this is a cheap way to provide answering-machine facilities. Unfortunately recording quality on these models is poor compared to a tape-based answering machine, which prevents this approach from being the ideal solution that it might otherwise be.

## Other needs

There is more to buying a computer than buying hardware and software. A computer is a *system*, which needs to be maintained as a whole. This means considering other factors when buying, and allowing for extra expenditure once the system is working. Some of these, such as security and technical support, deserve a fuller treatment than is possible here, and are covered in detail in other chapters.

### Protecting information

The most important extra consideration is making sure that business information can survive accidents and technical problems. **Backup** (safety copy) facilities are essential for business use, but are not usually included with computers. For more details see Chapter 10.

### Getting help

Computer users face two kinds of problems. Hardware failure, in which some or all of the computer stops working, can be dealt with under warranty, or by using a repair engineer (see Chapter 10 for further details). Software problems, which include 'How do I . . .?'

and 'Why is it . . .?' questions, can either be forestalled with training through courses and books or dealt with by asking an expert (see Chapter 9 for further details).

## Other considerations

Floor space and extra furniture may need to be considered when buying a computer. Computers can take up a surprisingly large amount of room, although 'workstations' (desks with built-in shelves for screens, printers and other extras) can sometimes minimise this. A computer-ready desk and a typist's chair at the lower end of the price range can easily cost upwards of £150, while more expensive and robust office furniture can cost two or three times this.

Furniture is advertised in computer magazines and sold in some computer stores. In general this furniture tends to be functional rather than inspired, so it can be a good idea to look further afield, for example in proper office-supply catalogues, to see if better alternatives are available. Good furniture is a worthwhile investment. Not only will it last indefinitely, it also helps to make the user's time on the computer more productive.

## Buying for a very small business

Buying a computer does not have to be hard. With a few caveats and a little research it is possible to make a good choice without the need to become an expert on computer technology. This DIY approach is by far the cheapest, and should only take a week or so. General advice is given below, but see Chapters 7 and 9 for more details.

Friends can be a source of buying advice, although their comments are usually based on their own needs and experiences, which may be quite different to yours. In fact comments from friends who are computer experts may need to be avoided altogether, as many experts are interested in technology for its own sake. They may not appreciate how the needs of a very small business are not technology-centred.

## Buying hardware

As emphasised earlier in the book, any new computer will probably be adequate for a very small business. Prices are coming down rapidly, and now start at around £500 for a slightly outdated (but still usable) model, rising to around £800 for an 'average' machine, to more than a £1,000 for a machine that is significantly faster and more powerful than average. Unless you plan to play games or do more complex work, such as design, computer animation, or sound and video editing, most of the extra power will be wasted. A good printer may, rarely, be included with a computer, but is more likely to cost an extra £150 or so. Places to research possible computer purchases include:

- high-street stores
- specialist 'superstores'
- supermarkets, which are increasing their stock of computers
- newspaper advertising
- computer magazines.

The last of these is the best place to start. Magazines are written for a more experienced audience, which is less likely to be impressed by persuasive selling tactics, either on paper or face to face. They also offer a much wider range of products and manufacturers.

A problem for newcomers is that both articles and advertising in computer magazines can seem like total gobbledegook. Appendices I and II in this book have been written to help provide a way through the jargon. For those who prefer a less technical approach, a number of indicators distinguish reputable manufacturers from cowboys. A good starting point are magazine awards for reliability and service, which are a good indication that a manufacturer is likely to offer a trouble-free product and will deal with problems efficiently if something goes wrong. Another good source of information is the surveys on reliability and user satisfaction from the Consumers' Association, as these are based on the experiences of real users rather than computer journalists. A useful survey appeared in the October 1998 issue of *Which?* magazine. These indications do not guarantee that a computer will work reliably, or that a manufacturer will be prompt and professional when dealing with problems, but they do make it far less likely that you will be sold a problem-prone white elephant at an inflated price.

## Buying extras
When buying a computer it makes sense to include any extras you think you may need, such as backup facilities (see page 166). It is often possible to get extra or improved hardware, for example a larger screen, for much less than it would cost later.

**Upgradeability**, the ability to add new filing space or new hardware extras, or to improve performance, is something of a red herring for small-business computers. It can take as little as three months for a computer to become technologically obsolete, but in practice this is an irrelevance for a very small business. As long as a computer can produce letters and do the accounts, it does not need to be replaced or enhanced, and some businesses are quite happily using computers that are a decade old. (Home computers, in contrast, need to be replaced or improved regularly to make them suitable for the latest games.) It is possible that improvements in the Internet will demand a completely new breed of machines in the early years of the twenty-first century, but until then simple business computers can expect a working life of at least five years.

One exception to this is filing space. In rare circumstances, it is possible to run out of filing space fairly quickly, although this can be remedied easily and fairly cheaply on even the cheapest new machine by adding a new hard-disk drive, a process that takes an hour or two and costs about £150 (see page 302).

## Buying software
The number of ways to try out and buy software is surprisingly large. Indeed, some of the methods can provide useful software for no outlay at all, or can provide significant discounts.

### 'Free' software included at purchase
Many computers are supplied with a selection of software when they are bought. When buying such a computer, check that paper manuals and 'disks' for the free software are included. If the disks are missing, you will need to spend the best part of a day or two making safety copies of your free software. Otherwise if your computer has

problems your software may vanish. Sometimes disks and manuals will be included only on payment of an extra sum, which may be as much as £80. Free software typically includes one or more of the following:

**'Office suite'** This is a collection of business-oriented software from a single manufacturer that is designed to work together, and usually includes a word processor, spreadsheet, database, address book and diary, and perhaps email software. Office suites are always worth having, even if some of the included software may not be the best that is available for a given job.

**Selection of games** These are unlikely to be among the better games available and are more likely to be examples of what is sometimes known as 'shovelware' – a collection of relatively cheap products used to make a computer appear more appealing.

**'Family multimedia' software** These include encyclopedias, dictionaries, cookbooks and children's software. Again, these are usually shovelware.

**'Home productivity' software** Simplified versions of an office suite, these will typically include a simple and cheap word processor and a home finance manager instead of a spreadsheet. Again, this is an extra worth having. The software may lack the more powerful features of an office suite, but its simplicity may make it a better choice for beginners.

**'Utilities'** Some of these optional extras are useful – for example, the 'anti-virus' software that helps keep computer viruses at bay. Some are less useful, and are best considered interesting extras that are likely to prove disappointing in practice.

### Free magazine offers

Huge amounts of software are given away free with computer magazines each month on their **cover disks**, which are disks that are attached to the front of the magazine. CD-ROMs are most commonly used for this. Floppy disk offers are rare now, so unless your computer has a CD-ROM drive, you will be missing out. The software available is often quite useful, and very popular software, such as the latest web browser, is regularly included.

Free offers take three forms. **Shareware** is usually relatively simple software produced by individuals and small companies. It is offered on a trial basis. If you like the software, you send the author(s) a payment in return for the right to use the software legally. This is known as 'registering' the software. Payment can be made by post, or over the Internet with a credit card. The former can be a problem if authors live abroad, because money will need to be sent as a money order rather than a cheque.

Because many people are happy to use shareware without paying for it (something of a shame, as shareware authors are a valuable resource and deserve to be cultivated), most shareware includes features that make payment more likely. The software may stop working after a month, or there may be an annoying 'nag' screen, which appears as a reminder to register. Finally, the software may be crippled in some way. For example, an address book may only hold ten addresses. 'Crippleware', as it is sometimes known, is not popular.

**Trial versions** of professionally produced software are similar to shareware, and may also stop working after a set period, or may be limited in some other way. If you want to use the proper version of the product you will need to buy it from a store or, in some cases, order it directly from the magazine. Trial versions are sometimes used by manufacturers to 'hook' customers on their products, and it is worth remembering that just because a product comes with a three-month free trial period it may not necessarily be the best choice. Further shopping around is always advisable.

**Full working versions** are simply free copies of an existing product. There are no time limitations, and the software works exactly as it would if you paid for it. Software given away in this way is sometimes older than the most up-to-date version currently for sale, and usually there is no supporting documentation, although this is sometimes available for a small fee, or it may be supplied in electronic form as part of the software itself. This kind of software is often given away as a 'teaser', intended to persuade you to buy the current product. However, an old version will often do everything you need of it, and in effect you will be getting free useful software.

## Outright purchase

This is the most obvious, if not necessarily the cheapest, way to buy software. Here you simply order the software, pay for it and, if buying by mail order, have it delivered. There are two problems with this approach. The first is that some pricing schemes are decidedly eccentric. If you buy a single product, a word processor, for example, you may find yourself paying more than if you bought the same product sold with a selection of other products as a 'bundle'. As an example, Microsoft has sold its Word package (a word-processing system) individually for £230 exclusive of VAT. However, a bundle called Home Essentials costs £80 and includes the full version of Word as well as an atlas, a games collection, and Works, which is a simplified version of Microsoft's Office collection of useful business software. It is well worth looking out for these kinds of offers rather than simply buying a product without shopping around.

Another cheaper alternative to outright purchase of software is **competitive upgrade**. This is a marketing ploy that encourages people to switch from one brand of software to another, by offering a sizeable discount on the full purchase price. The disadvantage is that the software can only be bought if you have access to a competing product.

Fortunately the definition of 'competing product' is usually rather broad, and you may well find you already have something suitable on your computer. If not, magazine cover disks are good sources for competing software, and it may be cheaper to buy a competing product outright together with a competitive upgrade than to pay the full price. Alternatively, some companies that advertise in the trade magazine *Micromart* sell, for very low prices, outdated versions of software, which will usually still count as a competing product. (Technically the Home Essentials package mentioned above is really a competitive upgrade, which is why it is comparatively cheap.)

Finally, **student offers** are a good way to buy certain software made by Microsoft (currently its Office business suite, various versions of Windows, and its computer-programming tools) at a hugely reduced price. The discounts are only available to students and teachers, but Microsoft defines a student as anyone in full-time education, including primary- and secondary-school pupils. Parents can, of course, buy these packages for their children. However, buying software this way is much more complex than buying it directly. The packaging includes a certificate, which has to be signed by a teacher or department and then sent to Microsoft. Once authorised, the software is delivered within two or three weeks. No paper manuals are included, although comprehensive electronic manuals are available.

## Software from the Internet

The Internet can be an excellent source of free software or shareware. Many magazines copy software from the Internet for free inclusion on their cover disks. The problem with getting software from the Internet is that it can take a long time to copy it to your computer. A small program will take a few minutes, but a full-featured web browser may take a few hours. Phone costs mount up steadily while this is happening. This makes the Internet a good source of simple packages, and obscure software that would not normally be given away free with a magazine. More mainstream software, such as a web browser, is best copied from a cover disk.

## Other sources of information

Some manufacturers are happy to send demonstration or trial versions of their software if asked, along with brochures and other publicity. If these are available they are usually listed in magazine advertising (another good reason to use computer magazines for research). Magazines also run regular software reviews in which the pros and cons of competing products are summarised. Reviews are not infallible, and experienced journalists may find it hard to put themselves into the shoes of non-specialist users. However, they do offer a good starting point for further research, if only by listing all the different products that are available for a specific kind of work.

### CASE HISTORY: Judith

Judith Holmes works from home as a freelance technical writer. Her needs were very simple and she bought an all-in-one package that did everything she wanted.

'I used to work as a manager at one of the big agencies in London, but I decided I wanted a change of pace so I moved out to the countryside in Buckinghamshire. I've kept all my old contacts, so getting steady work hasn't been too much of a problem.

'I couldn't have made the change without a computer. When I was about to move I asked a friend's advice and he suggested getting a machine from one of the larger mail-order companies. We looked through some computer magazines, compared prices and decided on a Dell Pentium system. This came with Microsoft Office pre-installed, so I didn't need any other software. It includes a word processor and a spreadsheet, which were all I needed. The only hardware extra I needed was a modem for the Internet, which turned out to be included in the package too.

'I ordered the computer from Dell's web site, and had it delivered to my new address. Going for a big name like Dell might not have been the cheapest deal overall, but I've had no problems with it, and that counts for a lot, so I'm told.

'For my Internet connection, I use an ISP that another friend used to work for. They supplied some basic software for email and the web, and that's been enough to get me by. I don't get hundreds of messages, so there doesn't seem any point in buying better software. I never use newsgroups, so again there's no point in me spending any extra there.

'For the writing work I'll be sent faxes, emails or a CD-ROM (if there's lots of it), with details of what's needed. I use a separate fax machine, as it means I don't have to leave the computer turned on with the modem listening for incoming calls. I also prefer working with a paper print-out, and if I used the modem for incoming faxes I'd only have to print them out anyway.

'I use Microsoft Word to produce the work. I then email it, or fax it off to the clients. For me, Word is just a glorified typewriter. I never use the more advanced facilities. I have done mail shots on a couple of occasions when looking for new work. I know Word can do mail merge, but I took one look at the Help file and decided it would be quicker and easier to do it the hard way.

'I don't have many expenses. Apart from office odds and ends like paper for the fax, it's really only heat and light, occasionally travel, stationery for mail shots, and monthly Internet charges. I keep track of all those and my income using the spreadsheet Excel. I'm not VAT registered, so it's just a case of typing in what comes in and what I spend, and then sending it all off to my accountant. There doesn't seem any point in buying proper accounting software when what I have now does it all for me.

'The computer has been very reliable. The software has been fine too. I don't keep proper backups of my work, as once something is sent off, it gets used by the client very soon afterwards. As for software backups – I have so little software installed it would be just as quick to reinstall it all from scratch.

'If I shopped around I could probably improve things, but I don't think it would be worth the time. What I have now doesn't get in the way, and that's all you can ask of a computer.'

## Other options

Not every business wants or needs a large computer system. Other options are always worth considering. Some of these are significantly cheaper or more convenient than a complete computer system.

### Stand-alone word processors

Stand-alone word processors are next-generation typewriters. They offer a simplified collection of word-processing facilities (and in some cases simple spreadsheet, address book and calculator features) in a small and relatively cheap package. Desktop word processors are in fact very slow, cheap and old-fashioned computers that typically use technology that dates back to the mid-1980s. They offer quite poor value for money, because much more powerful computer systems are now available for only a slightly higher price. Word-processing facilities are very basic, and there is relatively little software available for them. Anyone thinking about one of these machines is perhaps better advised to get a new computer that will do much more and will probably be easier to work with too.

These machines are likely to disappear in the near future. For example, by the late 1990s production of Amstrad's PcW16 model – which was originally sold for more than £300 but was later reduced to £99.99 – had been put on hold. At the new price it is something of bargain for anyone who wants a basic letter-writing machine with a built-in basic spreadsheet, address book and calculator. However, at the original price it was competing with cheap and only slightly outdated recent technology, which offers far more overall.

Portable word processors offer basic word-processing facilities in an easily moveable, if not quite lightweight, package. They include a built-in screen and a bubble-jet printer. The latter is good enough for occasional correspondence and simple reports, but print quality is rather rough and letters do not look very smooth or sharp.

These models are relatively easy for beginners to master. Some beginners find their first encounter with a computer system overwhelming, and the amount of learning required to start producing useful work can be considerable. Word processors are much simpler. The manuals for them are written with beginners in mind, and the basics can usually be picked up within an hour or so.

A good example of a portable word processor is Canon's StarWriter 500. This offers features like foreign-language support, variable letter sizes, a very small selection of lettering styles, spellcheck and form-letter facilities, and the ability to exchange text with other computers by way of floppy disks.

## Laptops

Most computers are desktop models. They cannot be used away from a power source, and are far too cumbersome to travel with. Laptop computers are much smaller – slightly larger than an urban phone directory – and can run off batteries as well as mains power. They are designed for travel and can be used almost anywhere.

Apart from portability, laptops offer few advantages. They are much more expensive than desktop models (the most expensive models cost around £6,000, although good machines start at around £1,500) and are usually less powerful. However, even the designs under £1,000 are adequate for light office work. They are also slightly harder to work with, as the keyboards are fiddlier, and sometimes the displays are smaller or less clear. The latest models with Thin Film Transistor (TFT) displays have overcome the last handicap, and can actually be more pleasant to work with for long periods than desktop screens.

Whether to buy a laptop or a desktop model is very much a matter of finances and personal preference. Functionally they are more or less identical, and from a business point of view any kind of work that can be done on one can be done on another. However, laptops are not usually suitable for more demanding work, such as design or advanced scientific calculations. Laptops can be connected to the Internet, using a mobile-phone link, although the connections are much slower and very much more expensive than those possible with a desktop computer and a modem.

Overall, portability is a very expensive feature, and from a business point of view laptops only offer significant advantages for very specialised kinds of work, such as on-site costings or coffee-shop novel writing.

## Palmtops

Palmtop computers are small enough to fit into a jacket pocket, briefcase or handbag, and are usually lighter than a paper-based organiser. They are much slower than desktop or portable models. Facilities typically include basic word processing and note-taking, address and diary features, and either a spreadsheet or a tool for listing expenses. Advanced models include a screen that responds to the touch of a finger or pen; handwriting-recognition facilities (although these are usually fairly error-prone); the ability to add extra software and work as a 'digital dictaphone' (albeit with a very limited recording time); and perhaps even a very simple Internet connection. All palmtops can exchange information with larger computers, although some do this more simply than others.

Palmtops can be a very good choice for someone who wants some simple business-oriented facilities without the price or clumsiness of a full-sized computer. They are much easier to use, although keyboards are usually quite poor, and it is impossible to touch-type at reasonable speeds. When looking at palmtops, ask the following questions:

- What is the keyboard like to type on?
- How clear is the display?
- What other software is available?
- How long do the batteries last?
- Is a mains adaptor included?
- Are extras for exchanging information with a larger computer included in the purchase price?
- Can the information be copied straight into the word processor, spreadsheet, etc., of a larger computer?

## Do you need a computer at all?

Computers are not for everybody, and there is certainly no need to buy a computer just because they are currently fashionable things to own. In a business, the outlay has to justify itself, and for some businesses a computer system simply fails to do this. A computer is unnecessary if a business:

- produces very few letters
- has simple accounting needs
- only has a small number of customers, with limited repeat sales
- already has efficient paper-based systems.

---

**CASE HISTORY: Mavis and Brian**

Mavis and Brian Hill run a small village store and post office in Hampshire. They looked into using a computer, but decided it was not for them.

'We thought about getting a computer a few years back, but when we looked into it, it just didn't make sense. We don't write many letters, so it would have been mainly for the books. The thing is I don't *like* computers. I don't understand them. As I said, we don't write lots of letters, and the ones we do I can do by hand, and no one complains. We have a book-keeper that comes in and looks after the basic accounts. She's not expensive, and we do our tax returns ourselves from the figures she leaves us, so we don't pay an accountant anything. We're not VAT registered, which does make it easier.

'So why should I spend £1,000 on something that's going to take years to pay for itself, and which I don't want to use? This is only a little business and it's not going to get any bigger while we're alive. So, no, I don't think we need a computer.'

---

## Networks

For many people a computer working on its own will be all they will ever need. But slightly larger businesses may require a number of computers, and these are much more productive when linked together. A collection of linked computers is called a network, which is discussed in Chapter 3.

### Products to watch for

**Office suites**
Microsoft Office 2000
Lotus Smartsuite Millennium
Corel WordPerfect Office 2000

**Word processing**
Microsoft Word
Lotus WordPro
Corel WordPerfect

**Financial management**
Pegasus Capital Series
Sage Line 50 Series
Intuit Quickbooks
Intuit Quicken
Microsoft Money
Megatech TAS Books
Best Mind Your Own Business

**Desktop publishing**
Adobe Pagemaker
Microsoft Publisher
Serif Pageplus

**Spreadsheets**
Microsoft Excel
Lotus 123

**PIMs and CMs**
Symantec ACT!
Lotus Organizer
Inprise (Borland) Sidekick
Microsoft Outlook

**Databases**
Microsoft Access
Lotus Approach
Inprise (Borland) Paradox

**Popular Internet software and palmtops**

**Email software**
Eudora Lite (free)
Eudora Pro

**Internet news software**
Forte Free Agent (free)
Forte Agent
Newswatcher (for Macs only)

**Web browsers**
Netscape Communicator (free)
Microsoft Internet Explorer (free)
Opera

**Palmtop computers**
Psion Series 3
Psion Series 5
Philips Nino
3Com Palm IV
Hewlett Packard 620LX

**Internet Services**
Which? Online
AOL
Dixons Freeserve (free)
Direct Connection (Dircon)
Demon Internet

# Chapter 3

# Sharing information

In an office environment, linking two or more computers together creates a **network**, a tool that is greater than the sum of its parts. Networks offer a small business a range of possibilities that are not possible with a single machine, and can significantly help productivity. The disadvantage of networks is that they are more complex to install and maintain and, because there are more machines involved, so there are more potential problems. If a network fails, it may even prevent a company from trading, as anyone who has called a business when its computer network is 'down' (not working) can testify.

However, you should consider a network if any of the following apply:

- you regularly exchange information with co-workers by copying it on to a floppy disk and carrying it to their computer
- you would like to exchange information with co-workers, but floppy disks have too little space for the job
- you have a printer, fax modem, scanner, or other useful extra which it would be useful to share within the office
- copying and printing paper memos takes up a lot of time, and paper costs are starting to become significant
- you would like to set up a central store of information (customer records, for example) that a group of employees can access
- you would like to extract summaries from a central information store without having to collate information from different computers by hand.

Networks offer two very simple advantages: they make it possible for a number of users to share extras, such as a printer or a fax machine, and they help people share information so that they work together more efficiently. A further option is a **network application** – a specific business-oriented system that either streamlines the flow of information within a company, or makes completely new kinds of commercial activities possible. Finally, some networks also offer **remote-access** options. These make it possible to use a computer from a distance. For example, you can set up the office desktop computer so that you can use your laptop to copy information to and from the office computer when you are miles away.

## Sharing extras

Sharing a printer is a very popular and simple task for a network. Without a network, sharing a single printer between a number of staff in an office is cumbersome and impractical. Documents have to be copied to floppy disk and taken over by hand to the computer that has the printer attached. If someone else is working on it, they will have to stop what they are doing while they print whatever is on the disk. If there is a lot of printing from different people to do at once, they may even be prevented from doing any useful work altogether for a while. If a document is long and complex, it may not fit on to a floppy disk at all.

Connecting all the computers in an office together solves these problems. Everyone can print exactly as if the printer were connected to their own machine. The person using the computer with the printer attached can carry on working because the network controls the printer automatically. He or she may notice that their computer slows down while it is printing for someone else, but this is preferable to being interrupted and distracted. The network is clever enough to separate print jobs from different people, so they appear in the order that they were requested and pages are never mixed up or scrambled.

Networks are not limited to sharing printers. In fact almost any extra can be shared, although for certain kinds of work extra software may be required. One possibility is sharing a fax modem. Faxes can be sent through a single modem from any computer on the network. Modem-sharing software also makes it possible for the one modem to be connected to the Internet, so that a number of people can send and receive information through it at the same time.

## Printer switches

For those who want to share a printer, but have no need for other network facilities, a printer switch is worth considering as an option. They simply create or break a connection between two items. They do not make it possible to 'queue' one set of information for printing while another set is being printed, however. Passive printer switches are small, cheap (about £15) boxes that can connect two or more computers to two or more printers. Switching is done by hand, using large switches on the front panel of the box. Active switches, which cost slightly more (about £50), monitor the printer link from a computer and connect the printer to it automatically if they see any activity. A *modem switch* or *serial switch box* will do the same for a modem.

## Networked extras

In many networks, a printer is usually connected via someone's computer. While this works perfectly well, it can sometimes cause performance problems because the computer may appear to slow down or even stop completely when something is being printed. Certain specialised printers, modems and other extras can be connected directly to a network.

A common example is the **network printer**, which connects to the network directly. It works as a completely independent item, and so does not require any computer time. A **network modem**, for example those supplied by a company called Shiva, works in the same way. Everyone on the network can use the modem as if it were connected to their computer directly, even though it may be on the other side of the office or even in a different room altogether. Networked products are usually very much more expensive than their non-networked siblings, but are significantly more convenient in an office.

# Efficient information-sharing

A network makes it possible to access and work with information filed in one computer while using another machine. All the information, including all the software, that is available on one machine

47

can be made available to every machine on the network. In more complex systems, access to certain information can be deliberately restricted. For example, James in marketing may be able to see all the information shared among his co-workers, but is unable to see the information held by Christina in accounts. However, there may be a 'public' area on the network where they can exchange information if they need to. This level of sharing is relatively easy to arrange.

More complex are pieces of software that are specifically designed to work on a network so that they can be used by many people at the same time. A good example of this would be a networked accounts package. All the information is kept in a central location, but people working at different desks can work with it and change it, and everyone else will see those changes. Information held in the accounts system can also be summarised centrally, so that management can keep track of the overall financial state of the company. Networked versions of many of the larger and more popular accounting packages, such as Sage Accounting, are available.

## Groupware

Beyond this level, products start to become more explicitly focused on helping people work together and on passing useful information around the company. Software that can do this is sometimes known as groupware. Although a slightly nebulous marketing concept, the term groupware typically covers products that make it easier to do some or all of the following:

**Electronic mail** The ability to send messages directly from one person's computer to another is invaluable in a business setting, and email has replaced paper memos, phone calls and even fax messages in many situations. The advantages are obvious: there are no printing, photocopying or paper costs, and the information is delivered instantly to all the addressees. The medium is also relatively unobtrusive and not as distracting as a phone call. Non-urgent email can be ignored or even deleted at the reader's whim.

**Document sharing** Information stored on one computer can easily be made accessible to another on the network. For example, in the magazine publishing trade 'raw' text from writers, copy-edited text, photographs and illustrations and page outlines can all be shared between the staff of a publication. Although each works on copy editing, page layout and artwork on their own computer, the way the information is shared means that all their contributions are held in a single location.

**Document and data filing** By making it easy to share documents, it also becomes easy to create a central collection of useful information. For example, an office can keep single copies of often-used form letters on a server, where anyone can read them. This also makes it easier to distribute work. Employees can become more flexible, because they have more information to hand.

Some businesses use larger document filing systems. These can hold electronic images of paper documents, as well as documents that have been created electronically. Examples include engineering blueprints, architect's diagrams and product specifications. By keeping a central library of these it becomes possible to reuse information and techniques in subsequent projects. It is also easier to find information about old projects when queries are made.

**'Bulletin boards' and information distribution** Networks can be very useful in disseminating company information. An electronic bulletin board works rather like its physical equivalent, as information can be posted on the board for anyone to read. This may include low-priority news of interest to employees and staff. However, it is also possible to use bulletin boards to pass facts, figures and proposals from one department to another, and to make useful information more widely available. Cannondale, a company that makes mountain bikes, saved itself a fortune and improved efficiency by making new paint schemes available on its internal network. Previously schemes would be printed and bound and then sent to its factory. Once a networked system was available, schemes could be updated electronically, which meant that changes were immediate, and wasteful printing and binding costs were eliminated.

**Conference and discussion groups** Discussion groups have both serious and frivolous uses. Netscape, the company that makes the popular Communicator web browser and also sells various other Internet-related services, has a number of internal discussion groups for the use of its own staff. Two of these, 'Bad attitude' and 'Really bad attitude', are used solely to let off steam, and staff can use them to complain about anything that annoys them without fear of censure. Creating such discussion areas is a good, if slightly unconventional way, for managers to monitor morale and also look out for any part of the business that is not working smoothly.

More seriously, discussion groups can sometimes take the place of formal face-to-face meetings. Staff can make comments about the pros and cons of different approaches to a project whenever they are free. Used this way groups can create a level playing field where all the staff involved can contribute equally, without the kind of time-wasting, political manoeuvring or one-upmanship that can distract formal meetings away from functional discussions and effective decision-making.

**Scheduling meetings** In some companies the job of the departmental secretary has been replaced by electronic meeting-scheduling tools. When a meeting is needed, the electronic diary of every participant is checked to find a time that is suitable for everyone. If such a time exists the meeting is booked and the participants are informed. If conflicts occur, participants may be asked to reschedule existing commitments. If there are no conflicts the process happens entirely automatically; the first the participants hear of it is when they receive a message detailing time and place.

**Project scheduling** Networked project-management tools can make it easy for a supervisor to manage and delegate contributions from different staff members. The supervisor keeps track of the interdependencies between different work that needs to be done, and schedules work accordingly. For certain kinds of work, for example the preparation of end-of-year accounts or a large computer programming project, contributions can be collated over the network. For work that deals with objects rather than information, such as engineering or architecture, the network can be used as a way of reporting progress.

**Electronic meetings** Although there are still situations where face-to-face meetings are desirable, electronic meetings can now take the place of some physical discussions. These are possible at different levels of sophistication (and expense). At the lower end of the scale, participants can type to each other, with everyone's comments distributed instantly and simultaneously to all the participants' screens. The next level of complexity is a shared 'electronic whiteboard', which displays diagrams and annotations that are also duplicated on every screen. Telephone-like voice-conferencing and live video conferencing are the most complicated options. All the options can be combined, so that a video conferencing system may also offer whiteboard facilities.

**Workflow management** The distribution of email messages and other documents can be automated so that when one person has finished their work the results can be sent automatically to another person, who will add his or her own contribution.

**Centralised network management** Companies that create and sell groupware are working hard to create systems where a single network manager can keep tabs on all the computers on a network and deal remotely with problems in the way that software has been set up or installed. However, this is more wishful thinking than reality at the moment.

## Intranets

Intranets use Internet-like tools to make a network more manageable. Information is distributed on an 'in-house web site' that looks and works like an ordinary web site, but is only available on the company network and not on the Internet itself. Internal email looks like Internet email (and uses the same software), and discussion groups look like Internet newsgroups.

The advantage of using an Intranet is that it can make life very much easier for users. Many people now have some experience of using the Internet, and will suffer less from culture shock with an Intranet than with some other approach to networking. The disadvantage is that Intranets can require more work to set up and run. Designing proper web pages, with graphics and logos, can take much longer than simply presenting a simple list of documents and leaving people to find what they need. However, they have proven benefits for certain kinds of work, especially if there is existing expertise in web design within the company. Intranets make the distribution of information much more convenient. For example Future Publishing, a large technology magazine publishing company, has contact details for all of its freelance contributors available on its Intranet. Editors can check the central records for contact information instead of having to duplicate effort by keeping their own personal lists. When a freelance contributor moves, their details can be updated and made available to everyone from a single location.

## Intranet and groupware products

The huge range of groupware products vary in price and performance from systems (at about £1,000) for up to around 25 users, to huge 'enterprise' systems that can be used by hundreds of people at once. The two largest groupware product manufacturers are Lotus and Microsoft. Sample products include:

**Microsoft BackOffice Small Business Server** This allows up to 25 users to exchange email and faxes using a single modem or Internet connection, to look at and design web pages on a company Intranet, to access the network from a remote location using a temporary telephone link (for example, from a hotel room), and to share information.

The Small Business Server is a subset of a Microsoft's BackOffice Suite, which is a collection of network-ready tools that can be used for anything from routing email around an office to creating a product database, putting it on the web and allowing people to buy products from it directly. BackOffice includes:

- the Exchange email server, which can handle the email needs of a medium-sized office
- a Proxy server, which acts as a secure entry doorway between a company network and the Internet, and also keeps copies of frequently viewed Internet information locally so that an Internet connection is used as efficiently as possible
- a Site Server, which forms the basis of a company Intranet
- a Systems Management Server, which allows a network manager to keep track of how well the network is functioning, which computers are connected to it, and also to solve problems and to distribute new software from a central location.
- a SQL server (pronounced 'sequel'), which is a solid and reliable network-ready database system.

**Lotus** offers a similar range of products for business use, albeit with a slightly different slant. It includes Notes, which is rather like a 'super-email' system, offering extra intelligence over and above that offered by a simpler email system. Lotus also provide Domino, a range of products for business use that are based on a World Wide Web-like system. The details of the full range are too complex to list here, but as an example, the **Domino Intranet Starter Pack** includes the following components:

- **Contact Management**, which keeps track of useful customer, vendor and would-be customer details
- **Customer tracking**, which collects and manages information on customer accounts
- **Employee phone book**, a centralised company phone list
- **Company forms**, a library of pre-prepared administrative paperwork
- **Job postings**, an electronic in-house job-skills exchange, where project leaders and employees can advertise their skills and services
- **Document library**, a centralised document store
- **Discussion groups**, a way to exchange opinions and discuss work projects and other topics
- **Project management**, which makes it easy to manage projects and tasks
- **F.A.Q.**, which is a central store of frequently asked questions about products and the company itself
- **Home page**, a custom-made company web site for the Internet
- **Registration**, which collects information about people and companies that visit the company's web site
- **Product catalog**, a detailed product or service catalogue, again for the company web site.

Lotus Instant!TEAMROOM is a smaller, simpler and much more affordable groupware product designed to make project management and group discussions easier on a company Intranet.

## Researching Intranet and groupware products

Compared to everyday software, groupware products are not so widely advertised. This is partly because these products are *much* more complex than something like a word processor. They are also sold in a more complex way. Instead of a single product, there is likely to be a whole range of related tools from which to choose. These are likely to include a simplified 'small business system' at one extreme, and a set of full-sized 'enterprise' tools at the other. The latter are powerful enough – and expensive enough – to be used by a major multinational corporation that can afford vastly superior and exotic computer hardware.

A first step to making sense of what is available is simply to contact the relevant manufacturers and ask for as much information as possible, telling them that you are a small business with small-business needs. Paper brochures and Internet research should produce a minimum list of options and features outlining the different products on offer. The next step is to decide which of these are really relevant to you. You may feel that a company Intranet is too complex for you, and you are simply looking for a way to share information held in different computers and perhaps exchange email messages. If so, then you may discover that the network facilities built into Windows 98, for example, are already adequate for your needs. On the other hand you may feel you need the power and complexity of a larger system.

Once you have a rough idea of what you would like the product to do for you, consider your future needs, and look at any possible limitations of the different products, which may cause you problems in the future. For example, BackOffice Small Business Server is limited to 25 users. If you are likely to need more than 25 users, you should start with a larger and more expensive version of BackOffice from scratch. Otherwise you will have to throw away your investment in Small Business Server at a later date and risk the disruption of a major software upgrade after your network is up and running.

Finally, consider the costs. Network software is licensed on either a 'per user' or a 'per seat' basis. With the former, you are allowed to have a fixed number of people using the software simultaneously. With the latter, you pay for a fixed number of copies irrespective of whether or not they are actually being used.

The former is usually cheaper as you are likely to find that there are never more than two people working with a certain piece of software at the same time, even though five people may need to use it altogether. Apart from the basic product cost, you should also check on the cost of extra licenses. Again, you may find that if your company is likely to grow rapidly then spending more initially is a better choice than spending less now and more later.

## CASE HISTORY: Adrian

Adrian Allan and his wife Tricia run a property rental service in North London. They started with no technology at all, but ended up with a networked system because it seemed like a logical progression for them.

'We actually started with a card index because we were doing this on a shoestring. We'd keep properties on the cards and do it all from memory, which worked better than you'd think, but obviously wasn't what you'd call professional.

'So we started with one PC and put all the details from the cards on a database, an early version of Access. That made it a lot easier to match customers to properties. When someone came in we could do a search on a price or location, and we'd find them something much more quickly. It also meant that we could print out lists and send them to people. Although this was more work, we got more turnover that way, so it paid for itself quicker than we'd been expecting.

'But there was still only one PC in the office, and three of us. So one person did the searches, and the other two were really just glorified receptionists. The obvious thing to do was to get another couple of PCs and link them together, but we weren't sure about how to do that.

'In the end a friend helped us out. Although not a computer whiz, he knew more about computers than any of us. He called lots of places and talked to the sales and tech people and eventually got an idea. So we bought the PCs with the extra bits he ordered, and he came in one day and plugged it all together, and there it was.

'Now we share the database, which means we can see people individually and also find things right away, while on the phone, instead of having to call people back later. This obviously makes it easier to get a sale, and our turnover has gone up.

'We also found other things that the network could do, which we hadn't thought of before. If you take a message for someone while they're at lunch or out showing someone round, it's much more convenient to send them an email about it from your desk than to write a sticky note and stick it to their screen, where they're probably going to lose it anyway. It was those little touches that made the difference. It also means that we can share the one printer now, even though there are three of us who need to print things. I'm not sure how it works, but all the things to print get queued up and come out in the right order for us, even though they're coming from different machines.'

## Practical networking

Physically, networks come in two types: Local Area Networks (LANs) link computers in a single building or office, while Wide Area Networks (WANs) create links between offices in different buildings, different cities or even different countries. Bespoke (tailor-made) WANs are more complicated and more expensive to set-up than LANs, and will be beyond the scope of most small businesses. However, the Internet provides a convenient public-access WAN, which, with a little thought, can be used to provide many of the facilities of a custom-built network for a tiny fraction of the cost. Some of the groupware products listed above include facilities for creating a Virtual Private Network (VPN), which uses the Internet as a WAN, but hides all the information on the network (using a secret code) so that unauthorised users cannot make sense of it. VPN technology is still in its infancy, but this facility is likely to become increasingly popular as the Internet grows and develops.

### Looking at LANs

**Peer-to-peer networks** connect two or more similar computers together. All the computers are considered equally important. This is the simplest and cheapest scheme, and you will almost certainly be able to create a peer-to-peer network without needing to spend a lot on extra hardware.

**Client-server networks** are built around a large and powerful computer called a server, which offers very fast access to a central store of information. There are a number of different client-server schemes. In some schemes, only information is stored centrally. The software (to work with the information) is kept on individual client machines, which are usually standard desktop computers that have a fitted network connection. In other client-server networks, software is also stored internally and has to be copied to the client machines before they can work with it. With this system, software is only available for as long as it is needed. It disappears when the client machine is switched off at the end of the working day.

The final approach is known as the **application server**. Here the server stores information and software, and does all the work too. The client, which may be known as a **terminal**, simply provides a way to type in information and display the results. (This is actually the way that large business computers were used originally, but the cost and complexity of application-server systems has made them less popular in the 1980s and 1990s.) Application servers are usually a bad choice for smaller businesses. The main server has to be extremely fast and powerful, which makes it very expensive, while the terminals are not usually much cheaper than ordinary desktop computers.

## Network hardware

Physically, LANs use a selection of extra hardware over and above that supplied with a typical computer. (WAN hardware is more complex and may require specially leased connections, satellite links and other options which are beyond the scope of this book.) Although it is possible to link two computers together using the same connections that are used to plug in a modem, it is far more common to install **network cards** or **network adapters** inside computers when building a network. These provide a link between the insides of a computer and the rest of the network along which information can pass at high speeds in both directions. Network adapters are usually connected together with fixed cabling, although wire-less systems can be bought at a high price.

Cables are distributed by plugging them into a central **hub**, which is essentially a central meeting point and 'telephone exchange' for the cabling. This usually works completely automatically. Certain kinds of work, especially tasks that require the fast movement of very large amounts of information such as video and animation, can benefit from a **switch**, which subdivides the network to prevent bottlenecks.

If two or more networks have to be connected together, they are linked using a **bridge**, which acts as an intermediary between the networks and keeps track of all the machines on the network, so that information can be passed between them. A more sophisticated option is a **router**, which is often used on WANs, and is clever enough to be able keep track of where all the computers on a network are so that it can send information to them very efficiently.

## Network nuts and bolts

At the level of cables, cards, and connectors, there are a number of different types of networking systems. The most widely used today are Ethernet and Fast Ethernet, although others are still sometimes installed. The list that follows introduces the most popular types, with some of the terms used in advertising and the recommendations made by network consultants.

**Ethernet** works at a maximum speed of 10Mb/s, which usually means around 7Mb/s in practice for technical reasons. (As a rough guide, you can copy the entire contents of a floppy disk across the network in around a second and a half.) Cheap, widely available, and reliable, it is suitable for small, simple networks where a faster speed is not required.

**Fast Ethernet** is similar to Ethernet, but ten times faster. As many network cards offer both standard and fast Ethernet options, the cost saving involved in choosing the former may be minimal, although Fast Ethernet hubs are between two or three times the cost of their standard Ethernet equivalents. This is the system most widely used today. However, for a very small business standard Ethernet will be adequate. The speed advantage of Fast Ethernet only becomes obvious once a lot of information needs to be transferred rapidly – for example in a very busy sales department.

**Token Ring** is an antiquated network technology, originally designed to connect larger computers made by IBM (International Business Machines) to smaller ones. The top speed is 16Mb/s. Network cards and other extras are much more expensive than either variety of Ethernet. The system is not recommended unless it has to be used for compatibility with an older existing network.

**FDDI (Fibre Distributed Data Interface, or 'Fiddy')** is a system that runs at the same speed as Fast Ethernet but uses a clever fault-tolerant technology, which means that it will continue working even if a connection is cut. In spite its name, FDDI will work over standard cables (fibre-optic connections are not essential). Although very reliable (it avoids the electrical problems that can make other networks unreliable), at between £150 and £500 per computer it is too expensive for most businesses.

**Gigabit ethernet** is an experimental next-generation Ethernet system with top speeds of 1Gb/s, but is not widely available yet.

**ATM (Asynchronous Transfer Mode)** has a theoretical top speed of 622Mb/s and as such is used on large company networks for video and voice communications as well as the exchange of other information. A typical network costs tens of thousands of pounds and requires very advanced technology, and this makes it far too complex and expensive for a small company.

**ARCnet** is an older networking system, with a top speed of 2.5Mb/s, which was popular in the late 1980s and early 1990s. It is now too slow to consider seriously, although still very cheap.

## Network cables

Most networks use one of two kinds of cabling system. **RJ45 cables**, which are widely advertised, are essentially US-style telephone cables. Technically this cable system is known as an **unshielded twisted pair** (UTP) because it is made of a pair of wires twisted together (although the wires are hidden by a thick plastic sleeve). Different-quality UTP cables are available, distinguished by category ('Cat') numbers. The only type worth considering is 'Cat 5' cable as anything cheaper is a false economy. Connectors are simple telephone-style click fittings. A network that uses the Ethernet system and twisted-pair cables is sometimes known as a **10Base-T** network. Similarly, a Fast Ethernet system using twisted pairs is known as **10Base-TX**. Twisted-pair systems are connected using a 'star' connection pattern, where all the cables lead into and out of a central point. Problems with one cable will remove only one computer from the network, and the other computers will continue to work properly. The star system uses more cables, and therefore costs more, but the enhanced reliability makes this worthwhile.

**Coax** (pronounced 'co-axe' not 'coax' and short for 'coaxial') cables use larger, locking metal plugs and sockets (known as BNC connectors) and cable that looks very much like the cable used to connect an aerial to a television. Older networks used a type of coax known variously as ThickNet, Thick Ethernet and 10Base-5. This is still available and offers the advantages of improved resistance to electrical interference and suitability for long cable lengths (up to 500m). However, ThickNet is too expensive and cumbersome for most business applications.

**ThinNet** (also known as 10Base-2) is more affordable, but is only recommended for situations where there is a lot of electrical noise, for example where cables have to be run around heavy machinery, or close to fluorescent light fittings. For most situations twisted-pair cables are a better choice. The biggest difference is that coax is not fault tolerant. Computers are connected in a long line, and if the cable is cut at any point, or if the connectors suffer from problems (which they do, with monotonous regularity), the network stops working.

**Fibre-optic cables** are the best choice if money is no object. You can expect to pay about £300 to £500 to connect each computer to the network, compared to less than £100 (and perhaps as little as £50) for a twisted-pair system. On the other hand, fibre-optic cable is totally immune to electrical interference and will also work over a much greater range (up to 2km). It can be worth considering these expensive cables if you are linking two buildings together.

**Wire-less systems** are just starting to become available, but currently only at prices that are beyond the reach of small businesses. A true standard has yet to emerge, although a system known as Bluetooth offers connection speeds of up to 1Mb/s. So far most wire-less systems are based on mobile-phone technology and are really intended for use with portable computers rather than as substitutes for a traditional network. Moreover, there are technical problems involved in creating wire-less systems that can work fast enough or reliably enough. However, the advantages of offering a system where computers can be sited anywhere, cable is eliminated, and email and assignments can be picked up on a laptop simply by taking it into the office, are obvious. Affordable systems are likely to become available some time after 2001.

## Network software

Network software can be extremely confusing to newcomers because it consists of a number of different related systems, all of which contribute to the way the network functions. There are effectively four layers involved.

At the top level are one or more **network applications**. These are the software tools, such as accounts and database systems, with which users work directly. Most applications hide away the technical details of the network, so that all people see is the information they need to do their work. Examples include the groupware applications listed above.

Network applications are supported by a **network operating system (NOS)**. This keeps track of where information is kept and provides a framework in which network applications can do their job. Novell's Netware is an example of a network operating system. Once the only serious choice for network applications, it now faces competition from various versions of Microsoft's Windows, all of which include network-operating-system facilities. The Windows NT (New Technology) Server (also known as Windows 2000) is specifically designed to run a network. Windows 95 and 98 (Win 95/98) can also be used as the basis of a network, but they are less secure, less efficient and less robust. On the other hand they are very much cheaper and will work with a much wider variety of computer hardware. For a small network of perhaps no more than five computers Win 95/98 is the better choice. For larger networks Windows NT or Netware becomes the more viable option. A commercial battle is anticipated between the suppliers of the next version of Windows NT (NT5), which is due early in 2000, and the current version of Netware, which offers a number of advanced facilities, such as the ability to keep track of every single computer, printer and other extra on an extremely large WAN. From the point of view of a small business each system has its pros and cons, but realistically either will do the job for a small company. The decision about which to go for should perhaps depend more on pricing schemes and the availability of support than on the technological differences between these two products.

Beneath the NOS level is the **network protocol**, the system that determines exactly how information is sent across the network, and how all the computers on the network are distinguished from each other. Most users do not need to worry about this level of detail at all, as they will never come across it in daily use. Usually this level is only of interest to the people who set up and maintain the network. However, it helps to be familiar with the system that your network uses even if you do not want or need to know exactly what the technical differences are between the various systems available.

Popular protocols include IPX/SPX (Internet Packet eXchange/Sequenced Packet eXchange), originally designed by Novell for its Netware range of products; TCP/IP (Transmission Control Protocol/Internet Protocol), which is also used as the foundation of the Internet; NetBEUI (NetBIOS Extended User Interface), a simple, fast protocol that does not work with Novell's Netware; and, for Apple computers, AppleTalk. It is possible to change from one protocol to another as a network grows. NetBEUI is a good choice for a smaller network, but TCP/IP is a better choice for a more complex network with sub-networks connected to it. As long as every computer on the network is changed at the same time, it should be possible to change the protocol with no problems.

Finally, at the lowest level of the network, there is the distribution mechanism or **network driver**. This will be one of the hardware types mentioned above, such as Ethernet or Token Ring. Again, most users do not need to know exactly which system is being used, but the person installing and the person maintaining the network will have to be familiar with the way that your particular network works.

# Chapter 4

# Managing money

Computers are excellent tools for managing money. They excel at the simple and repetitive calculations required to keep track of income, outgoings and profit. They also provide a convenient way to keep information about a business in a relatively compact space. Apart from basic 'bread-and-butter' calculations, computers are also good at financial planning. They can easily provide financial forecasts for a business plan, or make it possible to work out how external financial conditions will affect a business. Finally, computers can also provide up-to-date financial summaries that estimate how well a business is doing, providing early warnings of problems or suggesting when it is practical to expand.

## Money-management basics

Even a simple accounting package can save money in the long run. Both the Inland Revenue and HM Customs and Excise require that complete and up-to-date records be kept and summaries made readily available if a business is 'investigated'. An accountant can help with this, but it is much cheaper simply to have all the information to hand. This means keeping receipts and organising them so that they can be found and referred to quickly, but it also means providing up-to-date book-keeping records. Failure to do so could lead to a range of problems, ranging from fines to an unexpected and unjustifiably high tax bill. Simple **accounts packages** have the following features:

**Customer details** These keep track of customer contact details. Very simple packages simply list transactions by customer and provide an up-to-date summary. More advanced packages include a credit-control facility, which sets a limit for each customer and raises a query if they try to go over it. This feature only applies to certain businesses – for example, someone working as a freelance writer or other consultant is likely to be paid on a per-contract or per-project basis, and the idea of customer credit is not quite so relevant.

**Supplier details** Included in the supplier details is a list of people you owe money to, how much you owe, and when you should pay them.

**Invoice details** This part of the accounts package lists all the invoices raised. Invoices can be tracked for age (30 days, 60 days, and so on) to see when payments need to be chased.

**Nominal ledger** This is the heart of the package, and provides a current working balance based on the information held elsewhere.

**Bank statement reconciliation** This element makes sure that all your transactions have been recorded on your statements accurately.

**VAT report** This looks at VAT-related information and summarises it on-screen. Some packages can print out these numbers and send them in as an official VAT return. With other packages the numbers have to be copied by hand into the relevant boxes on a paper return.

**Other reports** These typically include a balance sheet, which lists all your debts and assets, and a profit-and-loss account, which shows you how much money the business is making overall.

These should be enough to keep the books for a typical small business. Facilities for summarising credit card transactions are rarely included, which may add extra complications to the lives of sole traders and other people who use the credit offered by a credit card. Currently the only way to deal with these kinds of transactions is to 'fudge' them using the existing facilities. Alternatively, a more complex package may be needed.

---

**CASE HISTORY: Julie**

Julia Simpson is a freelance press and PR consultant who works from home. She invested in some accounting software and found that her finances suddenly started to make sense.

'Well, the big problem for me is that I'm really not interested in that side of the business. I rarely kept track of my finances and I used to let invoices go unpaid for months at a time or wouldn't even bother sending them out to people. My accountant finally took me to one side and suggested politely that I ought to get myself sorted out financially, otherwise both the tax and VAT people would come down on me like a ton of breeze blocks if I were ever investigated.

'So, with a little help from him I did some shopping around, and eventually bought a software package called Sage Instant Accounting. It keeps track of invoices for me; works out VAT returns (which meant it paid for itself right away as I had been paying my accountant £150 a quarter for VAT); and keeps everything reconciled with where the bank tells me I should be. It took me a while to work out what I was supposed to do with it. I've never done proper book-keeping, so I had no idea what a 'nominal ledger' was or what you're supposed to do with one. But the penny eventually dropped. There is even a 'to do' list, which reminds me when I'm supposed to chase people for payment.

'One thing I haven't worked out how to do is incorporate my credit card payments into the system. I have two cards, and they're both quite battered financially. I pay for things with them because it's much more convenient, a lot of places won't take a company cheque, and company charge cards are expensive. As yet I haven't found a way to keep track of them neatly. Instead I treat them as another creditor, and make the interest payments in that way.

'But other than that, the accounting package has made a big difference to my finances. I'm happier because I get paid more quickly now, which has made more of a difference than you might think.'

## More complex accounting tools

The money-management basics outlined above are suitable for a company that consists of a single person, whether trading as a sole trader or as a limited company. Once other people are employed, or the company starts dealing with more complex transactions, extra features become essential. These include:

**Payroll facilities** These should be able to produce various employment-related forms (such as P45s), deal with overtime, holiday pay, sickness benefit and maternity leave, handle all tax and National Insurance calculations for PAYE, deal with Attachment of Earnings for community charge and maintenance payments, and be able to cope with special situations such as payment in stock options and company car allowances for directors and employees. There should also be no problem handling a regular payroll schedule, including fortnightly, four-weekly, monthly and occasional payments for contractors, as well as irregular payments for occasional staff. If your company has multiple departments, a useful feature is the ability to summarise the salary bills for each department. At the very least you should be able to produce a year-end PAYE summary, which can be sent to the Inland Revenue and copied to the final profit-and-loss account, as well as the actual payment slips.

**More complex invoicing** Simple packages offer a 'one size fits all' invoicing facility, which is used – with minor variations – for goods sold as well as services provided. A more useful and complex package can provide different kinds of invoices, including pro forma invoices, quotations, and so on. Customers can be assigned discounts on specific sales (perhaps over a certain amount, or over a certain number of products), for every purchase they make from you, and perhaps also for very prompt payment. Similarly, late payments can be charged interest automatically. On occasions it can also be helpful to personalise invoices, perhaps by department or by sales representative.

**Fixed assets** These list your assets at the time, and are part of the balance-sheet facility included in simpler packages. A more complex tool may include the ability to depreciate these assets automatically, to add or delete items when needed, and to deal with the consequences (including the VAT implications) of selling or writing off fixed assets.

**Order processing** Sales and purchase orders can be integrated with the nominal ledger, and suitable paperwork (including delivery notes and stock-picking lists) can be printed automatically.

**Credit control** This becomes useful once payments need to be chased, or the company starts dealing with a large number of customers. Credit reports can be produced on a per-customer or a per-period basis. Customers can have individual credit limits, which can be changed to suit their circumstances. Warnings are produced when customers go over their limit. Consistent failure to pay can be noted, with the bad debt written off and the customer marked as an unreliable business risk. Suitable letters can be produced automatically. In contrast, top customers can be noted and perhaps rewarded with an extra discount or some other favour. Full or partial refunds can be handled easily and marked as such in the books. Credit notes can be produced and handled efficiently.

**More advanced reports** Reports are essential for keeping track of how well the business is doing overall. Summaries can be produced for year-end and month-end automatically. Ideally, reports can also be integrated with other office tools – for example, a word processor – to produce attractive documents with the minimum of fuss and effort.

**'Undo facilities'** Remarkably, some of the early versions of popular accounting software packages lacked the facility to correct mistakes. Once an entry was made it was almost impossible to change it. The ability to remove the effects of the previous action is known as an 'undo' feature in the computer world, and is essential to any financial-management package.

## Managing time, stock levels and sales contacts

Very advanced financial software packages offer features that go beyond traditional accounting and book-keeping. These are designed to make a range of other essential business tasks easier. These extras are sometimes known as commercials – just as basic accounting tools are sometimes known as financials. Commercials include stock control and other kinds of asset management. A related facility offered by some software is the ability to deal with time-sheets and job costings.

### Stock-control tools

Keeping track of stock can be a major headache, even for a small business. Maintaining a list of items in stock is the smallest and simplest part of the problem. For effective stock management, it is also essential to know how much current levels of stock are worth, when to re-order specific items, how to deal with stock that changes in value, which items are most profitable, and so on. Useful features to look for in a stock-control package include:

- price-list generation and maintenance
- stock explosion (the ability to deal with composite items made of smaller stock items)
- shortage warnings, and automatic reordering
- stock-value analysis in terms of actual value, profit and turnover, both monthly and annually, with optional depreciation
- discounts by both value and quantity
- stock revaluing and repricing
- reports on best-selling and most profitable items and products
- stock shortfalls between the computer records and the items on the shelves
- product profitability and a bill of materials for products
- integration with invoicing tools and order generation.

Apart from the financial aspects of stock management, it is also essential to introduce a consistent physical management scheme so that products can easily be found in a warehouse. In the same way that a library uses the Dewey system to arrange books, stock has to be arranged according to some other consistent layout scheme. Taking the time to design a scheme that links stock codes with the location of products in the warehouse in a simple and obvious way makes a huge difference to efficiency and profitability. It should be done at the planning stage before the operation becomes too unwieldy and complex to streamline.

## Sales-management tools

Apart from keeping financial records, a sales department can also benefit from maintaining a list of prospective customers and the current status of any sales negotiations. This can be as simple as keeping a list of people who have been cold-called and their reactions. For example, potential customers who are obviously hostile to cold calls can be removed from further sales efforts. This saves a company money in terms of phone bills, causes sales staff less stress, and also creates less annoyance for people who are genuinely uninterested in a company's products.

A more advanced system can perhaps include personal information about customers, so that sales staff can use it to build up a rapport with customers. This kind of approach has to be used carefully, as, if it seems too forced and lacking in sincerity, the results can be counterproductive. However, it does allow skilled sales staff to consider personal information when talking to customers without being unsubtle or manipulative, and they will find that access to this kind of information can be a very good way of improving customer relations. Features in sales-management tools to watch for include:

- activity lists that keep track of all meetings, faxes, phone calls, emails, etc., with a note of any results
- sales records by region and salesperson
- sales analysis by region, product, season, etc.
- mail-merge and letter-creation facilities (a word processor can be used for these, but having them integrated into a single package is more convenient)
- links to other features in the software, so that, for example, sales are automatically logged in the order-processing tools
- network facilities, which are essential for a sales team with more than one member.

## Time-management tools

Some companies and individuals sell their time instead of selling products. Again, it is useful to be able to automate this process to some extent. For an individual, keeping track of the time spent with a small number of clients is a relatively simple task and special software may not be needed. However, once more than one person becomes involved, or the number of regular clients starts to grow, it can be useful to use a computer to keep track of all the relevant records. Time-management tools should be able to:

- keep track of a large number of clients
- distinguish between hours for which you can and cannot bill a client
- calculate the total number of hours for which each client can be billed

- deal with different hourly rates for different staff and different clients
- work effectively with intervals of time that are less than an hour
- produce totals for each staff member and each client
- handle expenses
- provide search facilities to make it easier to find staff and clients (codes and even names can be hard to remember, especially if there are a lot of them).

## Advanced extras

Other useful advanced extras to consider for money management include:

**Support for other currencies** This may appear an unnecessary luxury, but the arrival of the Euro at the start of 1999 means that EU members face the possibility of payment in Euros instead of pounds. Any company trading in Europe will have to include facilities for Euros. Foreign-currency support is also sometimes of interest if an offshore holding company is used to keep tax bills down.

**Support for direct-banking access** Some software can work with PC-based banking or more old-fashioned technologies, such as CHAPS and BACS (both of which offer direct-transfer facilities), either by using a modem link, or by preparing a floppy disk containing information that can be sent to a bank. Your bank manager will be able to offer you advice about the different direct-payment systems that are available. Normally one-off bank transfer payments are very expensive – perhaps £25 for a single transaction. But once a large number of payments, such as a payroll run, is made regularly, this option becomes more economically viable for both your business and also the bank. (Electronic transfers are both cheaper and more convenient for banks than paper-cheque payments. The latter still have to be sent from branch to branch by letter post.)

**Support for multiple companies** Summarising the accounts of a holding company with a number of subsidiaries can be a fairly complex process. Allowing a single package to deal with the accounts for multiple companies makes the job much simpler.

**Preprinted or customisable stationery** Many companies that supply accounts software also offer suitable stationery, which includes blanks in places that the software prints to automatically. Sometimes this stationery is supplied in layered form, so that multiple copies for internal use and for the benefit of outsiders can be produced simultaneously when it is printed on a dot matrix printer (see page 281). For companies that use a lot of stationery, it can be worth considering using this preprinted stationery as a template and asking a number of commercial printers to personalise it with different graphics while keeping the spaces in the same places. You may find that this beats the price that the software companies charge. Invoices and payments are not 'image critical' on the whole, so only the last criterion is important. But using customised stationery can add an extra touch of professionalism to a company's image, which may matter in some situations.

**Upgradeability** How big will your business be five years from now? If you plan to take on staff, open other offices, and expand as much as possible, then it is essential to consider getting accounting software that expands with your needs. If you buy a simple package now and find that you grow out of it later, you – or your staff – may find that you have to move old records from one package to another. This can be time-consuming at best, and very inefficient at worst, as errors may creep in.

Apart from making it possible to add new features, such as payroll support once you take on new employees, a good package will be scaleable. This means that it will be able to handle as many or as few transactions as necessary without grinding to a halt. It also allows you to move the software and your information to a network with the minimum of fuss, and that employees will be able to work with the information held in the package using network facilities. For example, you may find that you are selling so many items that you need to employ two or more sales staff, instead of just the one person you had originally. Once two or more people start contributing to the same job, a product that can work over a network becomes essential.

**'Just in time' ordering options** The Just In Time (JIT) business model was developed in Japan as a way of minimising the working capital tied up in warehousing and stock. Normally a business keeps a certain working level of stock on its premises. With JIT, the relationship between products being produced and sold and stock levels is much more tightly controlled, so that the production process is run as efficiently as possible. Ideally stock is only bought in just before it is needed. Some stock-control software offers this kind of tight integration with ordering information.

**Compatibility with other software** As a simple example of software compatibility, it is useful to be able to copy information from a book-keeping package into a word processor to create an attractive end-of-year report. A more complex task might involve copying information about a complete set of stock items into a different package (for example, a spreadsheet or database) to make use of the analysis tools that these more complex packages provide.

**Y2K issues** All new financial software should be fully able to cope with dates before and after 1 January 2000. While the Y2K issue is complex (see Chapter 13), the simple fact is that anyone who buys a financial package that is not ready for dates in the next century is wasting their money. Reputable software manufacturers are able to offer plenty of support and information about this issue, as well as being able to provide guarantees that their products will work properly when used on computer hardware that is also Y2K ready.

## The Euro question

At the time of writing, the UK has not yet made a definite commitment to using the Euro instead of the pound, although the signs strongly suggest that this will happen before 2005. However, since the introduction of the Euro on 1 January 1999 businesses throughout Europe have to be ready to deal with it. The principle of the single market means that there are no trade barriers of any sort between the UK and other European countries. With the arrival of the Internet and e-commerce facilities (see Chapter 12), this means that even small businesses may find themselves having to deal with both pounds and Euros at the same time.

Although trade barriers may not exist, differences in VAT rates most certainly do. Anyone buying something from Germany, for example, will currently pay VAT at 16 per cent. This can be reclaimed if someone is VAT registered, but it does not fall neatly under any of the standard VAT-rating codes used by both HM Customs and Excise and various accounting packages.

For all of these reasons, true multi-currency support in general, and support for the Euro in particular, are likely to be essential for any larger small business. However, adding support for the Euro may be a bigger job than it appears to be. For example, none of the computers advertised in late 1998 included a Euro symbol on its keyboard, and only one company – Cherry, a popular keyboard manufacturer – is offering a keyboard with a Euro symbol. This means that, at the very least, a new set of keyboards may be required to provide easy support for the currency. Software will also have to be updated. This includes operating-system software such as Windows 98 (see page 310) as well as software tools and applications themselves. While it may be possible to limp along using a Euro substitute such as a capital 'E' for a short period (in much the same way that 'UKP' has become a standard abbreviation for the pound sterling sign on the Internet), eventually proper support for the Euro will be required.

When considering financial software in the medium term, it is useful to ask searching questions about how all of these issues are going to be handled. If a supplier claims that Euro-ready software updates are to be made available at a later date, it is important to know in advance when these are likely to appear, and whether or not they will cost anything.

## The future of electronic finance

Currently it is not possible to send in tax and VAT information, or make tax and VAT payments, over the Internet. This is partly for security reasons and partly because it will be a while yet before the government bodies in question adopt the kind of technology that will make this possible.

However, a sign of things to come in the UK is the Barclay's Endorse card, a plastic card with an embedded identification chip, which was being tested in late 1998. The card is used to 'digitally sign' electronic versions of the documents that new businesses need to send to the Inland Revenue when they start trading. Swiping the card through a reader and then emailing off the details is as legally binding as signing the forms with a pen. By the end of 2010, systems that use related technologies will be commonplace, and electronic form-filling and payment schemes will have taken the place of paper-based transactions for many businesses.

## Spreadsheets and speculations

All of the products outlined above are designed to work in a fixed and pre-programmed way. When you buy an accounting package the facilities you get are designed to be used for book-keeping and other tasks that are related to keeping track of your money. Even if you have hundreds of employees, customers and suppliers, their basic function remains unchanged.

Spreadsheets (see page 22) are the other kind of financial management tool that you may need to use. Spreadsheets offer a totally open-ended environment for almost any kind of automatic calculation. They are most often used for finance, but they can just as easily be used for science and engineering. While good for most applications, spreadsheets are unable to deal with very advanced calculations that require either simple calculus or more complex differential equations. For work of that complexity more specialised tools are required. However, spreadsheets do offer facilities for calculations that involve manipulating matrices, and can solve certain kinds of standard algebraic equations.

A typical use for a spreadsheet is the preparation of a business plan. Various sources of expenditure, both one-off and regular, can be included in the calculations, in addition to estimates of income. Taken together, these can provide an estimate of the financial results for a period of trading. If these estimates are accurate – something that relies as much on intuition and guesswork as sound business practice – the results can be used to help find finance when starting up. Bank managers, venture capitalists and other sources of start-up income will scrutinise a business plan very carefully, and it can be helpful to show the different results caused by different trading situations – for example, changes in sales, changes in interest charges, and so on.

Apart from creating business plans, spreadsheets can also be used for:

# Managing money

- estimating the financial effects of a move to new premises
- working out the cost-effectiveness of investing in new machinery and plant
- calculating the effects of taking on or laying off staff
- investigating various finance options, such as the results of consolidating different loans
- working out budget projections for a large project
- looking at the results of boosting sales with advertising.

Overall, a spreadsheet is the financial equivalent of a Swiss Army knife, with the difference that it can be used for almost any calculation at all, instead of supplying you with a fixed collection of tools.

Another powerful facility of spreadsheets is their ability to create tables and graphs. Displaying information in graphical form often makes it easier to assimilate. The range of different graphing options offered by a modern spreadsheet, such as Microsoft's Excel, is dazzling, and provides examples of the many ways that information can be usefully presented.

Another extremely useful feature of spreadsheets is the ability to copy whole groups of calculations from one part of the sheet to another. For example, if the formulae used to calculate monthly income and outgoings are the same for each month's trading, it is possible to duplicate them for subsequent months with a few mouse clicks. Additional one-off payments or receipts can be added to the calculations very easily.

Many useful financial formulae are already built into most spreadsheets and can be readily added to calculations. Calculating the compound interest on a loan, for example, can be a moderately involved task with pen and paper, or even calculator. However, all but the very cheapest spreadsheets include facilities for this kind of calculation 'straight out of the box', as well as for related calculations, such as the repayment period on a loan, given the starting capital and the interest rate. Because of these built-in facilities, spreadsheets can be used to answer common business questions with a minimum of effort.

Advanced spreadsheets include the ability to work with multiple sheets simultaneously. This feature, sometimes known as a '3D spreadsheet' makes it possible to calculate sub-totals on separate sheets and then summarise the results on a master spreadsheet. **Pivot tables** are a useful feature that makes it easy to re-arrange and summarise data on a spreadsheet according to the kind of summary you would like to see. For example, monthly trading results can be displayed in quarterly form using a table.

All of these features can be extremely useful in the planning stages of a business, although getting the very most from a spreadsheet takes time and practice. Setting up a spreadsheet to add columns of figures is very easy, but using it to produce a realistic business plan is rather harder. It is, unfortunately, unrealistic to assume that it will be possible to do this without a period of possibly quite intensive study or training.

### CASE HISTORY: Tina

Tina Martin runs a company that offers cleaning and other maintenance services for companies in central London. She has made herself familiar with spreadsheets and used them to plan her next business expansion.

'We started back in 1984, but things really took off after the recession at the start of the 1990s, and I now manage the company myself and employ 17 other people.

'I've had to learn about computers from scratch and spreadsheets have been one of the hardest things to understand. The accounts were easy. Once you learn all the words that accountants use it makes sense, but spreadsheets are something else. I understood the basics quite quickly, but it took me a good few months before I really understood the more advanced things like graphs and the built-in financial formulae, and the like.

'Once I'd got that, it really sank in just how useful these things are. Recently, we were looking at an advertising campaign to drum up new business, trying to decide whether direct mail, or hand-delivered mail shots, or posters, or even a bit of radio would be the way forward. Some of it was guesswork, but if you do some research the take-up rates for different kinds of advertising are easy to estimate. So I ran some of those numbers through the spreadsheet, to get some idea of what would happen with different kinds of advertising spend. It turned out that paying people to deliver thousands of leaflets by hand in the area that we work in was the best way to get results. It seems that even though most go in the bin, secretaries and door staff do pass them on to the people who make decisions often enough to make it worth our while. So we did that, and our turnover increased by 12 per cent as a result.'

# Chapter 5
# Working with information

For many companies, information is just as important as working capital. Without readily accessible information it becomes impossible to keep in touch with old customers, find new ones, maintain comprehensive business records or get an overview of how well a business is doing.

There are three ways in which software can help with these tasks. Contact managers and personal information managers can deal with the everyday chores of keeping an address book, maintaining a list of important tasks to do, tracking details of conversations and meetings with customers, and managing appointments and schedules. Variants on this idea are packages designed to do a specific task, such as keeping personnel records. Ready-made information in the form of maps, mailing lists and telephone directories can help replace paper records and make it easy to find customers, both for telephone contact and for physical meetings. Finally, databases offer the ultimate business tool for keeping track of information in a completely free-form way, which can range from the electronic equivalent of a card index to a sophisticated tool for analysing and summarising financial and other records.

## Keeping track of people and appointments

Personal Information Managers (PIMs) are the most popular way to manage everyday information, and are electronic versions of the once-ubiquitous paper organisers. Typical PIM features include:

- an address book
- an appointment diary

- a 'to do' list
- a year planner
- space for general notes
- alarms for regular or occasional reminders
- a list of anniversaries and other noteworthy regular occurrences.

The best PIMs use a simple display, which looks very much like a paper organiser, making them very easy to understand and use. Some PIMs also include telephone support, incorporating an auto-dialler facility, which will dial out a selected phone number when connected to a modem. This can be a real time-saver for anyone who makes lots of calls. Support for prefixes such as '9' for an outside switchboard or '132' to access the Cable and Wireless network for cheaper long-distance calls may also be available. A related feature is a phone log, which keeps track of calls after they have been dialled. This can be useful for people who charge for telephone time. Other useful features to look for include:

**Flexibility** The least useful PIMs supply a fixed template for name and address records. It is far more convenient to be able to create your own templates to order. It is also useful to be able to create different templates for different types of contact, such as templates for business contacts, personal contacts, useful names and addresses such as shops and restaurants, and so on. For example, business contacts may include a company name and perhaps address, while personal contacts may include a work telephone number as well as one for home. Many PIMs use the same template throughout, and simply include a 'category' item to distinguish between different types – a somewhat less satisfactory approach.

**Links between sections** If you enter an anniversary such as a birthday, it should appear automatically on the relevant pages that show daily or weekly appointments. Similarly, it is very useful to be able to link an appointment for a meeting with someone with his or her contact details.

**Links to email and fax facilities** If your email software does not already have an address book, it can be practical for your PIM to take on the task instead. Some PIMs, such as Microsoft's Outlook, include very strong links with related email facilities.

**Different displays** At the very least you should be able to show daily, weekly, and perhaps monthly summaries of appointments. The ease with which you can switch between different dates is also important. For example, you may find you want to check a date a couple of years ago. Some PIMs force you to step through each month in turn until you get there. With others, you can select the right month much more quickly and conveniently.

**'Floating' tasks** While some tasks need to be completed at a set time, others can be done at any time during a day. There should be no problem with the latter, given a good 'to do' list facility. It is most useful if unfinished tasks are carried over to the next day indefinitely until they are completed.

**Prioritised tasks** It can also be very helpful to group tasks according to priority, so that the most important tasks appear at the top of the list.

**Regular occurrences** Apart from annual anniversaries, it can be useful to have regular reminders for anything that needs attention at other time intervals – for example, monthly, weekly, fortnightly, four-weekly, and so on. Ideally, it should also be possible to set up reminders for events that happen on a certain day each month.

**Alarms** It should be possible to set up audible and visual alarms and reminders so that they appear some time *before* a planned event or anniversary.

**Search facilities** These become essential if you have very many records, and are useful even if you do not. It should be possible to list information chronologically, by name, by category, and so on. More complex and useful search facilities should make it possible to find all your contacts in London, or in a certain county, for example.

**Security** You will probably not want strangers to see your personal information, and the ability to protect some or all of your records with a password can be essential.

**Network facilities** With these facilities team members can schedule appointments with their colleagues automatically, or use the network to find a time when everyone is free for a meeting. Some PIMs offer network facilities as standard.

## Contact managers

The difference between a PIM and a Contact Manager (CM) is that the latter is geared more towards keeping track of both existing and potential customers. A major feature of CM software is the ability to keep a list of all contact made with each customer. This includes emails, fax messages, phone calls, meetings, and so on. The best CMs will also produce automatic reminders, so that if you contact customers regularly, or if a customer says that they would like you to get back in touch after some period, the CM will remind you that this needs to be done.

CMs are often used on a network. Customer queries are collected in a central information store, to which anyone in the company (or at least anyone authorised) can refer. A good CM system will keep track of every customer record, and not just sales queries. If a customer has problems or needs support, the information will be noted, so that future sales efforts can refer to it if necessary. Advanced CM systems can be linked to automated order-processing and accounting tools, offering a complete sales- and customer-contact package. They may also include links with other office tools, such as word processors, so that letters can be created using a mail-merge facility that uses the CM's own customer list directly. Very advanced systems can be linked with a telephone caller identification service, so that whenever a customer calls a salesperson their records appear on-screen automatically (a connected modem passes the caller's number to the software, which looks up the relevant records and displays them). Other options to look out for include:

**Built-in fax support** Fax communications should be integrated seamlessly.

**Network facilities** Single-user CMs are available, but CMs become much more powerful and useful when information can be shared between staff on a network.

**History logging** The more comprehensive the tools available for keeping track of contact with customers, the more useful the product.

**Document preparation tools and mail merge** These make it possible to prepare personalised standard letters. Unlike a word-processor-based mail-merge tool, a CM should be able to perform

81

extra functions, such as quoting the amount a customer has spent, and perhaps offering discounts or special offers for the most enthusiastic customers automatically.

**Reports** It should be possible to produce summaries for different customers, by geographical area, by salesperson, and so on.

## Taking it on the road

Both PIMs and CMs should include data-integration facilities for use with mobile computers. If you take a laptop or PIM/CM-equipped palmtop on your business travels and make changes, it should be easy to merge the updated information with the records held on your desktop machine once you return home or to the office.

However, the current state of portable technology means that PIMs and CMs can be oddly unwieldy away from a desk. Palmtop machines that include these features do very much better than laptops in practice, because they are lighter, cheaper, more convenient to run, have a much longer battery life, and can be ready and working very quickly. Laptops, on the other hand, can take a few minutes to 'warm up', and are also much bulkier and less convenient in other ways.

A compromise used by some people is to print out PIM and CM records on paper and use a traditional ring-binder organiser away from the home or office. This will only work in certain situations, but it does have benefits from a practical point of view. Records will need to be updated by hand back at base, which invariably means extra work, but for sheer ease of note-taking and even access to information, a well-managed paper organiser can be hard to beat.

## Pre-packaged commercial information

While customer records and useful addresses are likely to be unique to an individual or business, it is also possible to buy in information that is generically useful. Examples of information products include post code summaries, which can convert a post code to a partial address, electronic telephone directories, maps, and route planners. Other options include pre-packaged company documents, such as handbooks and boilerplate legal contracts, prewritten business letters, business-plan templates, and even health and safety information.

## Electronic texts and summaries

Templates, summaries, and sample letters are essentially cut-and-paste information that helps with a very specific problem and can easily be used with other products, such as word processors. Most of the value of the information comes from the text itself, rather than the way it is presented, and often it could be sold almost as effectively in paper form. The main advantage of software over equivalent paper products is that they sometimes include report generators, or forms that can be used in a formal or legal setting. For example, a Health and Safety package may be able to produce the F2508 and 2508A forms required to report accidents and injuries.

The main disadvantage is that information may not necessarily be completely accurate or up-to-date. This particularly applies to pre-written legal documents and other situations where the printed output of this software has to be taken in the context of the law, or of government regulations. While the output *may* be appropriate for a given task, there will sometimes be loopholes and other problems which legal beginners will miss. Similarly, buying a package like this does not guarantee that it will remain current indefinitely. If regulations change, the output produced by the package should change too, but in all likelihood the software will continue to be used regardless, and this could cause legal or official problems for a business at a later date. A sensible approach when considering these packages is to ask for advice from a relevant professional before buying – for example, a Health and Safety officer.

## Information-searching facilities

The other kind of information is that which can be searched. Here the main attraction is the way that you can search through it quickly to find something specific. While you could also supply this information on paper, the fact that it is available electronically means that you can use it in ways that the paper form would render impossible. The most obvious examples of this are address-finders and telephone-number collections. The former are now very widely used by both large and small businesses in the UK. Based on the Post Office Address File (PAF), these products include more than 1.6 million UK postcodes. Typing in a postcode and a house number produces a full postal address that can then be copied and pasted into other software, or, in more advanced systems, integrated seamlessly into sales and invoicing software. This saves time for sales staff when they are taking telephone orders, and also helps create a better impression with customers. Originally PAF software cost thousands of pounds, but now packages that offer a full set of PAF information start from about £100. Quick Address Lite is a typical example. This puts the facility in reach of almost any business.

Telephone-number collections are rather more controversial. These are essentially a CD-based version of the directory inquiry service from British Telecommunications (BT). The official BT-authorised package again costs a four-figure sum, which is generally beyond the reach of a small business. Some companies, such as PlanIt Software, offer an alternative source of the same information. While free trial copies of such software are often given away with magazines, these versions are really almost useless, and lack any of the facilities that a business might need to use the product effectively. The full version of the software costs around £250, and offers true name- or location-based searching, as well as the controversial ability to convert a telephone number into a name and address – something that BT's public service refuses to do. It is also possible to search for numbers based according to location, which has obvious uses for telesales.

Whatever the legal and ethical ins and outs of using this software, it is worth noting that the software does not list ex-directory numbers. While this may not be a major drawback for many kinds of work, prospective buyers should be aware of this shortcoming.

## Maps and route planners

A very useful subset of the 'searchable' product category is the electronic map and route planner. The Ordnance Survey, for example, is available in electronic form, with its series of 1:250,000 scale maps covering the whole of the UK. The advanced version of the product, known as Personal Navigator, adds geographical postcode information, so that you can plan journeys by typing in postcodes rather than having to find specific locations on the map itself. It also includes a gazetteer of interesting places, *The Good Food Guide*, as well as *The Which? Guide to Hotels*, and *The Which? Guide to Country Pubs*. An advanced feature is the ability to connect the software to a GPS (global positioning system) receiver. This is a kind of electronic navigator that uses information from a network of satellites to pinpoint any location on the Earth's surface to within 100 metres or so. With a GPS receiver and this software on a laptop computer, it is almost impossible to be lost in the UK.

Other related products concentrate on route-planning facilities. These can be very useful for road-haulage and courier companies, and for anyone who needs to travel moderate to long distances regularly. At their simplest, route planners calculate the best route between two locations, based on considerations of travel time, distance and/or cost. A car can be assigned various fuel consumption estimates based on its speed, and different kinds of road are assigned realistic driving speeds – for example, 70mph on motorways, 55mph on good A roads, 40mph on less good A roads, and so on. The software uses this information to calculate the best overall route. Advanced packages can include any number of 'vias' or 'way points' along the route. Planners can weigh up the pros and cons of different routes far more effectively than human guesstimates can, and anyone who regularly travels long distances by car will find that these packages pay for themselves very quickly.

The most important thing that distinguishes route-planning products from each other is the size of the maps that are included. Some products limit themselves to roads in the UK and perhaps Ireland. Others include all of Europe and/or the USA. The most complex packages include road maps for tens of countries. 'Professional' products can link with other software packages to transfer information between them in both directions. For example, customer addresses can be copied to the route planner to make journey planning easier, while route information can be copied to word processors and spreadsheets to produce quotations or reports. Another useful option is the ability to find the customers within a given travel time or geographical radius.

## Databases

All the products mentioned so far have been designed to work with information that has a well-defined structure. Databases, dispense with this necessity. With a database, you can define any structure you like. Once the information is available in the database, it can be manipulated and summarised in useful ways. You can filter the information in different ways by presenting the database with a **query**. This produces a broad picture, known as a **report**, which conveniently summarises the facts and can help spot trends, anomalies and other patterns.

For example, a business can easily produce a list of customers who live in East Cheam and spend more than £350 a year. For many larger businesses, databases are absolutely central to their operation. Apart from keeping track of trading records, the ability to examine huge amounts of information and create a useful cross-section of facts, figures and trading contacts makes them a uniquely useful business tool.

### Databases versus accounts packages

In practice, databases are often used to do the same kind of work that accounting software does – keeping track of finances and stock, managing customer details, and so on. The advantage of using a database is that it can easily be made to include almost any feature that is required. For example, a traditional accounts, payroll and stock-control package is very unlikely to be able to include photographs or illustrations, while adding this kind of information should present no problem to a database.

The major disadvantage of databases is that they can be difficult to set up. The set-up process defines what kind of information is held in the database both by label (for example, 'product ID') and by type (such as number, text, date, image, and so on). It also defines the way that different items are related to each other – for example, a supplier code may be linked to a supplier's contact details, and perhaps also to the amount of business that has been put their way. Queries and reports and forms define the way that information is summarised by the database, and also how it is typed into it. These are the parts of the system with which users spend most of their time.

Setting up a database can be a very complex job. Some database products attempt to automate the process by providing automated set-up tools, which guide users through the process by asking them questions and offering ready-made templates for common kinds of work. But even these can be daunting for beginners if they do not already have some idea of how databases work in both theory and practice. Mastering database design, even using the built-in set-up tools, is something that will take most people quite a while. Designing a completely original database without using these tools is likely to be a job for an expert. Using a database is rather more straightforward, but even here it can take beginners a while to master all the options. As with spreadsheets, databases require a period of study before they can be used most effectively.

For businesses with simple needs, there is a lot to be said for buying an off-the-shelf accounting package that will deal with all their work in one go. Apart from typing in customer and stock information, no further setting up will be required. A database, on the other hand, may be cheaper to buy initially, but the setting-up costs may be significant. A good rule of thumb here is to always check the off-the-shelf accounting products first to see if they do what is required, before considering a database.

Whether you hire an outside contractor to set up the database for you, or attempt to do it yourself, the setting-up process is likely to be more expensive in both time and money than you expect. If something does not work as expected, you may find that support is a problem, as you are effectively undertaking a computer-programming task. On the other hand, the flexibility of databases means that they can be used for almost anything, and in some situations this makes them the ideal and perhaps even the only choice.

## Database types

The simplest kind of database is known as a **flatfile**, and is very much like an electronic card index. Flatfile systems work well with relatively few records that are fairly simple. A personal address book is a good example.

However, flatfile databases are not suitable for more complex work. Imagine a system that has to keep track of orders, each of which contains customer details. It would certainly be possible to copy the name and address of a customer in full for each order they make, but it is far neater and less complicated to give each customer a code, which in turn links to their contact and delivery information. This uses storage space inside a computer more efficiently – there is only one record of a customer's details – and sales staff can always call up customer details immediately. This kind of system is known as a **relational database** and is a staple information-management tool for many businesses, both large and small.

## Networks and scalability

An important feature of database systems is their ability to work well under pressure. The best systems are **scalable**, which means they are just as happy working with 2 users as with 200, or even 2,000. Many of the same comments about scalability, expanding and networked systems that apply to accounting packages (see page 63) also apply here. When choosing a database system you should make sure that if you need to expand, the database will expand with you. You do not want to transfer your information to a different product or system unless absolutely necessary. Ideally, you should be able to add better and faster computer hardware and more networked users almost indefinitely. When considering a database, consider your future needs as well as your current ones.

## Anatomy of a database

At the heart of any database is the software that maintains its internal records. This is known as the **database engine.** The engine is like a librarian – it makes sure that new information is filed away consistently and that requests for information are handled efficiently.

Users enter information into the database using **forms.** These are very much like paper 'fill-in-the-blanks' forms, and designing these forms is an important part of the setting-up process for a database. Forms make it possible to add, change and delete individual records in the database. Some commercial database products include design options for forms that make them look more interesting. These are purely cosmetic, but they can make the results easy on the eye for the people who have to work with the database every day.

## Working with information

Information in the database is summarised with queries, reports and tables. Again, these can usually be made more appealing with a range of different text and graphic options. More importantly, they make it possible to extract useful information from the database. Part of the power of databases comes from the way in which this can be done in all kinds of ways – for example, sales figures can be summarised by month, by salesperson, by region, by product, by profit per product, and so on. Once the information has been stored in the database, it is possible to design new ways of looking at it. This can be done at any time – queries, reports and tables are not fixed by the set-up process but can be modified or added at a later date.

A system known as **Structured Query Language** (SQL, sometimes pronounced 'sequel') is often used to extract information from a database. It is a text-based system that offers various criteria for searching a database. SQL looks a little like English, and is fairly easy to master (at least compared to the other aspects of setting up and using databases). For example:

SELECT * FROM SALES
ORDER BY SALE_DATE DESC, SALESPERSON ASC ;

is an SQL query that will search and print a list of sales records in descending order by date, and ascending (i.e. alphabetical) order by salesperson. Many commercial databases hide the details of SQL queries away behind a simplified, perhaps graphical, query-creation system. SQL is such a widely used system that for medium to large database projects it is very hard for businesses to avoid it. Products such as Microsoft's SQL Server offer a networked database system that uses SQL as its foundation.

**Programming facilities** are the final component of a database. These make it possible to change some or all the information in a database according to a set of rules. Programming facilities can also be used to create more complex forms and queries, which respond to information in more complex ways. They also add a gloss to the design and presentation of a database by making it possible to incorporate company logos or other images into the screens that people see when they use the database.

This level of sophistication is strictly for experienced users only, but it indicates just how powerful database products can be. For example, if the UK ever starts using the Euro as its currency, any company information that refers to pounds will have to be modified to refer to Euros, taking into account the exchange rate. Most accounting packages will have serious problems with this, and it is likely that most often the job will have to be done either by hand or via some kind of complex work-around that extracts information from the package, changes it, and then sends it back to the package. Doing the same with a database should not take a competent user more than a day's work, even with a very complex database.

## Office-suite integration

Some commercial products offer a programming environment that extends to other products, such as word processors and spreadsheets, as well as databases. These kinds of tools can be very useful, but also very hard to use. For example, a professional writer might create a tool that worked out word counts in his word processor, passed those numbers to a spreadsheet that calculated an amount in pounds based on a word rate, and then passed that amount back to the word processor, which created an invoice automatically. The invoice in turn could be noted in a database, which could be used to calculate end-of-year turnover or to summarise the amount of work done for different clients.

This is just one example of what is possible. Almost any tool can be built from scratch, and companies use tools like these every day to simplify their work. In practice, however, creating tools like these is a job for the expert. For example, Visual Basic, the framework used to build the tools that Microsoft supplies with its Office suite, is a fully fledged software development system. Even professional computer programmers need time and sometimes training to master it. It is unlikely that this kind of work will appeal to beginners, as producing tools such as these can be very time-consuming. However, consultants or bespoke system developers will sometimes suggest creating a specialised tool using an office suite instead of a different software system. For them, office-suite programming is quicker and more productive than having to develop a complete software product from scratch using a more open-ended development system.

Working with information

**CASE HISTORY: Paul**

Paul Merson is a computer consultant and database developer who supplies and installs database and other systems for small businesses.

'The first thing I do is listen to the clients and work out what they want from the database, and then summarise it back to them so we're clear that we're talking about the same things.

'Then, if it's what I think they need, I'll steer them towards an accounting system, such as Sage, Pegasus, or whatever. Most people don't need a database, and cowboys out there have been known to charge thousands to build something when a cheaper, ready-made system would have done the job better. Passing business to other companies is no problem because I still get a consultancy fee, and I'm saving money for people in the long run.

'Having said that, if it's obvious that a client really does need a database, we'll sit down again and work out what's required in more detail. One project I did recently was an archive for a photographer, who was just starting out by offering a picture library. He wanted a quick way to find scans of his work, and to do billing for re-use, photo credits, and so on. That was one thing that an accounts package would never have done – a database was really the only way.

'When I'm developing I start with a generic, all-purpose database and change that to suit what is required, rather than starting from scratch each time. I'll build in any extras around that. That way I can lose a few days off the development time, which makes things cheaper for customers and is less stressful and boring for me. In terms of costs, though, having a database developed is not cheap. If you want full-scale development work I charge between £1,000 and £2,000 a week, depending on the project, how busy I am, and who's paying.'

# The Data Protection Act

If you maintain any kind of information about living people on your computer, you may be liable to register with the Data Protection Registrar. This is a relatively painless process, which costs a standard fee of £75 for three years. The penalties for not registering are much stiffer – up to £5,000 plus costs in a Magistrates Court, or an unlimited sum in the Higher Courts.

There are a small number of exemptions. If you use your computer for writing letters, and the information you keep is used solely for that purpose, then you will not need to register. But if you start to include personal details – and these can include a name and basic contact details – you become liable for registration. Even if you do not need to register, according to the Act you should ask the people whose information you hold if they have any objections.

The other main exemption is the information used for payroll calculations. If you keep this, and use it for no other purposes, then you are exempt. However, if you start to maintain credit histories and other details, such as payments to the Child Support Agency, then you will need to register.

You should register even if the information is kept on a computer that you do not own. If you contract out the maintenance of a list of details to a computer bureau, then you are still the person 'in control' of the records and should register accordingly.

Once you are registered, you must follow the code of good information-handling practice set down in the Act in the eight Data Protection 'Principles'. Broadly, these state that personal data must be:

1. obtained and processed fairly and lawfully
2. held only for the lawful purposes described in the data user's register entry
3. used only for those purposes, and disclosed only to those people, described in the register entry
4. adequate, relevant and not excessive in relation to the purpose for which they are held
5. accurate and, where necessary, kept up-to-date
6. held no longer than necessary for the registered purpose
7. accessible to the individuals concerned, who, where appropriate, have the right to have information about themselves corrected or erased
8. surrounded by proper security.

If you are registered you will have to convince the Registrar that you are not collecting information unnecessarily. This can sometimes have surprising implications. In one case the Registrar was called in to deal with a video hire shop that was collecting the passport and driving licence numbers of its customers as a security measure. The Registrar advised the shop to stop this practice, as collecting this information was inappropriate in the circumstances. Registration will require you to look at the records you keep and to ensure that you have good reasons why you need to continue keeping them.

For a free information pack about the Data Protection Act and details of how to register contact The Data Protection Registrar (see Address section at the back of the book).

Chapter 6

# Advertising and promotion

Computers can help with three kinds of promotion. Print promotions use traditional media such as posters, flyers, mail shots, catalogues, magazine advertising, and magazine inserts (essentially anything that can be printed on paper). Live promotions use computer technology to enhance lectures, presentations and perhaps stand space at exhibitions. Electronic promotions use the Internet, and, in very specialised cases, home-made CD-ROMs. As a very specialised option, businesses can now use computers to create their own CDs, videos, and even radio and TV advertising.

## Print promotions

For many companies, printed publicity is the main way of finding new business. In addition to everyday printed promotions (posters, flyers, etc.), businesses may need to produce proposals for tender, business plans to support loan applications, or less formal proposals, such as suggestions for creative projects in the arts and media. In an ideal world the contents of a proposal would be more important than presentation, but in practice this is never the case. The presentation quality of both publicity materials and more complex proposals has a big influence on whether or not potential customers and clients take notice.

### Using word processors

Simple print promotions are now very easy to do in-house. For very simple work, such as a mailshot printed on headed notepaper, a good word processor, including those found in the popular office suites, will be up to the job. With the help of a high-quality laser printer it is easy to produce a letter with a computer-generated letterhead that is indistinguishable from a professionally printed one. This can save on letterhead costs because there is no waste, and no need to pay for hundreds of pre-printed letterheads when only tens of letters are being produced. A suitable letterhead design can be scanned or created by hand, using special fonts. The result can be saved as a style sheet to form the basis of subsequent letters. For mailshots, this process can also be automated with mail merge. Good laser printers can even cope with the kind of heavy, high-quality, watermarked paper that is often used to create an impression of quality.

This approach does have limitations, but they are relatively minor. You cannot create special effects, such as multi-coloured letterheads (inkjet printers are too slow and too crude to do this well) or embossed/raised lettering. However, these extra touches are unnecessary for many small businesses, and the simpler approach outlined above will be enough for their needs.

For more complex effects it is possible to buy preprinted coloured paper and use this as a foundation for business stationery. A company called Paper Direct supplies a range of suitable papers in various sizes, including A4 (letter), compliments slips and business cards. It also supplies software which can help with the design process. The software makes it possible to create lettering layouts on-screen, and ensures that designs are always aligned correctly with the paper when printed. The results can be quite impressive. However, there may be situations when a more sophisticated approach is required.

All word processors now include facilities for pasting (the technical term is 'importing') graphics and photographs into a document, and editing its position on the page. Some also include special text effects, including 3D lettering (perhaps with coloured shading) and the ability to run text along a curve to make it more eye-catching. These effects are useful for simple posters, and for certain kinds of electronic publishing (see below). In general, word processors have the capability to create far more than just letters. When planning a promotion it may be worth taking some time to investigate the options to see if a word processor has features that can help with a job and make it unnecessary to buy other software.

A good way to create a visual image for a company is to look for logos and design styles that are appealing, and then copy them with minor but distinctive variations.

## Desktop publishing

Flyers, newsletters and complicated posters need more versatile tools. Many flyers, for example, consist of an A4 sheet folded, vertically, in three, with a block of related text running down each of the three column sections. Word processors are too unwieldy to cope well with this (in fact, some do not cope at all), and so work of this kind needs a desktop publishing (DTP) package. These are available from £50 upwards, although professional packages, such as those used in magazine publishing, cost around £1,000. In approximately ascending order of price and complexity, products to watch for include Serif's PagePlus range, Microsoft Publisher, Adobe's PageMaker and Quark XPress.

DTP software is designed to help with complex page layouts. All DTP packages can divide a up page into rows, columns or other subdivisions; lay out text and images within those subdivisions; 'flow' text around images and across boundaries (for example, spread text across a three-column flyer); and work with different fonts and letter sizes. The more advanced systems are capable of special effects, including flowing text around jagged or irregular shapes, printing text or images at an arbitrary angle on the page, or specifying the location of items on a page to the nearest decimal of a millimetre. Some products, notably Quark XPress, can be expanded with 'plug-ins', which add useful optional extra facilities. These range from simple utilities, such as summaries of how much computer filing space a project is using, to more advanced all-in-one tools that are tailored for specific work, such as producing magazine layouts.

Printing hundreds of copies or more of a colour image is something that is best left to a professional printer because today's desktop colour printing technology is still too slow and expensive to do the job efficiently. When designing a project it can be useful to call various print shops to get quotes, and also to discuss the best way to send them all the computer information necessary to produce the run from their own machines. Small flyers and posters should fit on a single floppy disk. Larger projects may need to be 'burned' on to a

# Advertising and promotion

home-made CD-ROM (see page 107) or sent on a tape cartridge (see page 288). Some print shops offer an ISDN facility for copying information directly from computer to computer over a phone line. This usually requires special software and, ideally, an ISDN connection of one's own. A good print shop will be able to advise on the best way to link its computer to yours. It is worth noting that computer-friendly print shops often advertise at the back of the various Apple Macintosh magazines. Some of these will turn around a large print run very quickly, sometimes overnight.

Anyone who plans to send page designs from a DTP package to a professional printer needs to buy a package with professional features. The first of these is colour separation. Professional colour printing usually combines four separate inks – cyan, magenta, yellow and black (without the latter it is hard to create the deep black needed for sharp text). This system is known as CMYK printing, and printers usually expect to have information presented to them in a CMYK-compatible format. For each printed page, four separate pages of information are required, each of which specifies the intensity of each of the ink colours, hence the name colour separation. Cheaper DTP products lack this feature, making it hard or even impossible for print shops to make sense of the information these packages produce.

A related feature is Postscript support. Postscript is the print industry's standard way of squeezing all the information required to print a document, including letter sizes, image details, layout information and page sizes, into a single file of information. A DTP package with Postscript is better suited for professional printing work than one without it because there is no guarantee that the latter will produce information comprehensible to the printer.

DTP packages that lack these features are still useful, but are perhaps best thought of as 'home' printing systems, designed to work with a cheap colour printer. These are only suitable for small runs, or for producing 'proofs', which can be photocopied in colour with the loss of sharpness and clarity.

## CASE HISTORY: Jan

Jan Templeman makes silver jewellery in her studio in the West Country. Although not much of a computer fan, she has experimented successfully with creating her own flyers and leaflets using various DTP tools.

'I'll admit I have a love/hate relationship with computers, but I've been oddly fascinated by what you can do with them creatively. I suppose it's because I do design anyway, and they're just a means to an end. So, with DTP I first started experimenting with my own PR back in 1993. I tried out a free DTP offer that was in a magazine. It came with some examples, which is just as well as I don't think I'd have worked it out from scratch. I had some photos of my work scanned by another friend who works for a magazine and I eventually managed to lay out something that looked like it might do. But, to be blunt, it wasn't anything to write home about. I was using a laser printer and the photos looked blotchy and rough. Of course there was no colour, so I used coloured paper instead, which wasn't wonderful. Even so, I used those flyers for a couple of years, going around craft fairs and selling direct to the public from the studio.

'Then business started to pick up, and I also inherited quite a bit of money. I bought a rather more expensive PC, added some nice design and art packages and a graphics pad, a scanner, and one of the newer colour printers. As well as using it to sketch out and file away design ideas, I realised that I could make a much better brochure to sell the jewellery. Another friend, who is a professional photographer, took some excellent shots of my best pieces of jewellery, which I then scanned. When you use professionals you not only get their eye for an angle, but you also get their lighting equipment and their ability to use it.

'Next I used a proper DTP package, Quark XPress, to do page layout and colour separation. I created some textures in the art packages and used those as borders and decorations on the pages. I also found some interesting typefaces from a catalogue. I then took the files to the printer and got a few hundred copies printed up.

'I can't say it's brought in hundreds of pounds' worth of new business, although I did send copies out to certain magazines, and got a fair amount of interest from that.'

---

A general rule of thumb, you will get better results from DTP work if page design is done thoughtfully and with care. There are a number of good books that can suggest simple but very effective improvements in design. For anyone who plans to do a lot of DTP, or who wants to produce work that needs to stand out, these can be well worth investigating.

## Working with images

DTP's strongest asset is its ability to combine text with images in interesting and eye-catching ways. While text is obviously home-made, various sources for images are available, which can make a DTP project look more appealing and professional.

With the exception of clip art, all of these can make quite heavy demands on a computer. If you plan to do any of the following kinds of work on a regular basis you need to buy a machine that is faster and has more memory than average. (For more information about how speed and power are specified, see Appendix I.)

### Clip art

Clip art is simple ready-made computer artwork that can be placed in a project very quickly. Typical examples include faces and poses, flags, symbols (such as arrows and traffic signs), the shapes of countries, financial images (such as coins and bank notes), vehicles, animals, and serious and humorous cartoons. Cheaper DTP packages often include large quantities of ready-made clip art. Sometimes there is a printed catalogue to show what images are available, but most often the catalogue is electronic and rather more unwieldy. Images are divided up into lists and categories and it can take a while to find a suitable image from the list. Clip art also comes in 'bumper packs' of DTP add-ons, which contain thousands (sometimes tens of thousands) of clip-art images, and perhaps a few hundred distinctive fonts.

Clip art is suitable for business reports and simple advertising, but can look rather cheap and is unsuitable for more prestigious projects. Even the best art has the feel of a cartoon, and this limits its potential for projects that need to appear glossy and expensive. However, it is very useful for simple posters and flyers, and offers a relatively cheap way to add extra interest to a page layout.

### Illustrations and artwork

The easiest way to get hold of high-quality artwork, including company logos, is to hire a graphic designer. Many print shops have their own in-house designers who can produce artwork to order. Often this is sold as part of a package that includes printing costs. As a rough rule of thumb, a few hundred letterheads, compliments slips and business cards with custom-designed artwork will cost around £200.

The designers that are employed by print shops tend to produce functional and rather unremarkable work. This suits many businesses admirably, but it can be useful to know how to find work that has more character. Design companies specialising in corporate-identity work can charge hundreds of thousands of pounds for a new logo, which is clearly ridiculous for a small business. Freelance designers who charge more realistic rates can be found in the *Yellow Pages* and also in some of the Apple Macintosh-friendly computer magazines. A small business that wants a more distinctive design will have to pay somewhere between £100 and £200, depending on the complexity of the design and whether or not colour is required. All designers tend to have a particular style that shows through in their work, and it is essential to look through a portfolio of past work to see if their style fits your company's needs.

Designs are usually delivered on paper, although some designers can also provide a floppy disk that can be used with a word processor or DTP package. The latter is preferable, as safety copies can be made more easily, no scanning is required, and the work can be used immediately.

### DIY design

For those who feel they have the artistic skills to produce their own designs, three different kinds of package are available. **Art packages** provide a 'virtual art studio' with a range of creative tools. These are best used with a **graphics tablet** instead of a mouse. This is a large flat pad that comes with a plastic 'pen' that can be moved over the surface. The best tablets are sensitive to how hard the pen is pressed down and also to the angle at which it is tilted. With suitable software, the pen can simulate a number of drawing tools, including pencils, watercolours, oils and airbrush. The range of colours is infinite, and it is even possible to paint with textures, such as scales or bricks, to fill areas of the screen with different colours, and to create special effects, including mosaics and glassy finishes. Certain software can even remember a set number of pen strokes, so that the designer can backtrack and correct a mistake. Many image-editing packages (including those mentioned below) contain simple painting and drawing facilities. However, for more serious work a professional package, such as MetaCreations Painter, is recommended. This has a dizzying array of features that can simulate almost any kind of artistic environment.

**Drawing packages**, such as Corel Draw, offer a simpler version of the same idea. With Corel Draw it is possible to sketch all the parts of a large illustration separately, and combine them only when the image is finished. Some people find this easier to work with. Drawing packages offer a halfway house between software optimised for no-compromise artistic creativity, and the kind of illustrations that are used in business advertising.

**Illustration packages** work with shapes instead of images and lack the complex textures found in art and drawing packages. They are used for logos, advertising graphics, and other work where images tend to be two-dimensional. The most popular professional packages are Macromedia Freehand and Adobe Illustrator. An example of the kind of work for which these packages are ideal is the British Telecommunications' 'piper' logo, which is made up of broad areas of colour combined in an interesting shape. To produce an image like the piper, curves are manipulated and combined with the mouse to create the various different shapes that define the image. These are then 'filled' with single colours to create the final result. An illustration package makes it easy to change these shapes, try out different colours, and perhaps stretch or squash the entire result.

Technically, the main difference between this approach and an art package is that the software works with mathematical definitions of the curves, rather than with the actual image. This makes it easy to scale an image to poster size with no loss of quality: the curves stay smooth and accurate whether the image is half a centimetre or 500 metres high. This approach is known as **vector drawing**. Most art packages use **bitmap editing**, where an image is treated as a flat grid of coloured dots. If the grid is scaled up, each cell is made correspondingly bigger, and the result can look blocky and rough.

## Using 3D design

For those with even more artistic ambition, 3D-design tools make it possible to create virtual worlds. While popular with hobbyists, these can have serious business applications that are especially useful for creating eye-catching electronic publicity.

The 3D-design tools combine simple objects (spheres, squares, cones, planes, etc.) in a virtual space, giving them character by adding textures (for example, bricks, metals, stone, or even fire, planetary surfaces, waves or weather effects), defining light sources, and then 'rendering' the final arrangement to create a surprisingly realistic result.

Advanced packages include animation effects. Each single image is treated as a 'frame' (like a single still from a film) and the software renders a series of frames in sequence to create a complex film-like effect. Objects can appear to move, textures can change between frames (for example, a ball can be made to pulse different colours), and the viewpoint can be moved to make it feel as if the viewer is flying through the scene. It is even possible to move lighting sources to simulate different times of day.

Professional 3D-design tools are expensive and are used to create animation sequences for film and TV. For example, SoftImage, which is used in many film and TV projects, costs £7,000. Fortunately, much cheaper alternatives are available. MetaTools' Bryce 2 offers animation facilities, which include some very dramatic and striking ready-made textures, and costs £200. With tools such as Bryce it becomes possible to create the kind of animated logos that companies sometimes use in promotional videos. However, this kind of work demands a very fast computer indeed.

## Using photographs

High-quality photographs can make a big difference to a brochure. The three possible sources of photographs are home-made pictures, pictures taken by a professional photographer, and image libraries.

Home-made images can be taken with an ordinary film camera and 'fed in' to the computer using an extra called a scanner. This typically looks like a flattened photocopier and connects directly to the back of the computer. Scanners are now very cheap indeed. Prices for budget models start at around £75, and very high-quality results are possible for £300. Professional scanners costing thousands are also available, but the difference in quality is only really noticeable in specialised work. Even the cheapest scanners can handle transparencies and negatives.

Digital cameras will eventually replace scanners. They work by taking photographs electronically, producing images that can be copied straight into a computer. No film is involved at all. Pictures are stored in the camera's own memory. When the memory is full the camera is connected to the computer with a cable, or sometimes a wire-less infra-red link, and the images are transferred directly to the computer. Some cameras take the slightly more convenient approach of storing information on a floppy disk, which a computer can read in the usual way.

While digital cameras are fast, they are also quite expensive, and image quality on the cheaper (under £1,000) models is still relatively poor. Where speed is not essential, the combination of a good film camera and a mid-priced scanner is capable of much better results and is better all-round value. However, for certain kinds of work – for example, sending photographs from a remote location to the office over the Internet – they are the only practical choice.

For the best possible results it can be worth considering a professional photographer. They can be rather expensive with rates starting at around £250 a day, and the best charging rather more, but a professional will usually produce much better results than an amateur. Some professionals use very expensive digital cameras, which provide the same image quality as a top film camera but produce computer-ready images. Professionals will also be able to perform photographic tricks such as superimposition, although, as mentioned below, these kinds of effects can now be produced quite easily with suitable software.

Image libraries offer an alternative to custom photography. These provide an almost infinite range of 'stock' images, which can be bought-in for a project. Image quality, both artistic and technical, is usually excellent, and images from the libraries are often grouped in themes to make suitable images easier to find. Examples of themes include business situations (people meeting, shaking hands, debating, etc.); visual metaphors (staircases, whirlpools, fire and lightning); ordinary activities (shopping, eating out and reading); people of different ages (babies to old people); household objects; and business objects. With such variety, they can be a fertile source of novel promotional ideas. They also create a strong professional approach by association, because designers in advertising agencies often use them.

Low-quality trial images and catalogues, available on paper, on CD-ROM, or from the Internet, are available either for the asking or for a nominal cost. Images are then bought and paid for individually, or in groups (the latter being equivalent to buying in bulk). Note that images are *licensed* rather than bought, and there may be restrictions on how they are used. Jobs that require a very large number of copies of the image – for example, music-CD artwork – may be charged on a royalty basis instead of a flat fee. However, this is unlikely to apply for most business applications.

### Working with photographs

Both stock and custom photographs often need to be edited before they can be used. This can mean cropping, re-sizing and adjusting colour balance, contrast and brightness. Alternatively, it can mean more creative effects, such as motion blur, which makes all or part of an image look as if it is moving; superimposition, where part of an image appears on top of another (a process originally known as 'photomontage'); posterisation and solarisation, which create psychedelic effects; artificial colouring; and other kinds of retouching.

All of these are now very easy to do with a computer. In fact, the range of possible effects is vast, and mastering this kind of work can take years. However, even beginners can pick up the basics very quickly. The most popular packages are the professional Adobe Photoshop for Mac and PC, and the simpler, but still fairly comprehensive, PaintShop Pro (for PC) and Graphic Converter (for the Mac).

Simple editing, which usually means cropping or resizing images ready for DTP use, or correcting exposure problems, is a straightforward task, and should cause no one with basic computer experience any problems. More advanced creative design is rather different, and requires a certain amount of flair and practice to do well. As with DTP, some effects have become clichés and are probably best avoided. Again, the best way to learn the tricks of the trade is from books or the many courses that now offer help with Photoshop, combined with plenty of experimentation.

## Live promotion

The most common sort of live promotion is the presentation, and the most widely used tool in presentations is the overhead projector slide, or view graph. A presentation is made of a series of slides, each of which includes a relatively small amount of information on an attractive background. The full set of slides can be printed out as a handout, printed on to a set of view graphs, which are changed by hand, or displayed electronically, using special presentation hardware. This comes in two forms: projectors, which create an image on a screen, and presentation displays, which fit on an overhead projector and act as a kind of 'intelligent slide', displaying information under computer control. Projectors are stand-alone items that look rather like transparency projectors, but are much more expensive (prices start at around £2,500). Presentation displays are see-through flat-panel LCDs (Liquid Crystal Displays). Sometimes these are attached to a computer via a cable, or they may form part of a specially modified laptop computer, which is placed on top of the projector (this kind of display has a sliding back cover, which can be removed). Some laptop computers also provide a standard TV output, which can be connected to a television monitor. An ordinary television may not be suitable because the image is produced using a direct electronic connection (known as S-Video), which is incompatible with the kind of information a television receives from an aerial. Some ordinary televisions do have S-Video facilities, and these will be up to the task.

**Presentation software** is used to prepare suitable slides. Examples are often included with office suites. For example, Microsoft Office contains PowerPoint. Slides are very easy to create. Most software includes a range of ready-made designs, each of which is suitable for presenting a different kind of information. For example, one or more lines of text, a table, an organisation chart, a graph, and so on. Text is usually typed in by hand, but the other kinds of information can be copied from a different application. A spreadsheet could be used to prepare some figures in graphical form, and the resulting graph could be pasted straight on to a slide. Slides can also be made more interesting with clip art.

A 'live' presentation consists of a series of slides that are displayed in order. Moving to the next slide usually involves a single key press or mouse click. Remote-control mice are available that can control the presentation from the back of a room with no attached wires.

The presentation can be made more interesting with animated transitions between slides. These are rather like the special effects used on television, in which one picture fades into another in various creative ways. For example, one slide can appear to push another off the screen and slide into its place. Background music and sound effects may also be added. These are supplied as 'clip music', the musical equivalent of clip art, examples of which are sometimes included with presentation software. While it is possible to use any music, such as commercial recordings, clip music is legally safer for copyright reasons. Anyone planning to use a commercial recording at a large public presentation will need copyright clearance, which is available for a fee from the Performing Rights Society.

Using music complicates a presentation because suitable amplification and loudspeakers have to be used. Some venues include these as a matter of course, and in these cases it is simply a case of connecting the computer to them with an appropriate cable. However, for smaller meetings a small pair of computer speakers may have to be used (the speakers built into laptops are usually too small and sound too tinny to do a good job).

## Computers at exhibitions

It is not usually a good idea to take a computer to an exhibition for display and presentation work, especially if it is going to be accessible to the general public. Accidental damage is common at exhibitions, and security is also a major worry (exhibition organisers very rarely guarantee that a venue is secure out-of-hours).

However, for those that have to use a computer, a number of special hardware accessories are available. **Monitor splitters** make it possible for one computer to drive several screens. The screens are connected to the splitter box, which in turn is connected to the computer. All the screens will then show the same information. **Switches** (sometimes known as KVM switches) can connect a single keyboard and monitor to different computers. These are useful for networks, where a server usually sits in a corner of the office unattended but sometimes needs input from a user. As their name suggests, **extenders** extend the range of a keyboard and monitor, so that the main computer unit can be hidden somewhere out of sight. At exhibitions these make it possible to hide most of a system away from the public. They are also useful when the noise from a computer's fan is a distraction, or the computer needs to be placed close to machinery or other electronic equipment that cannot be moved.

Computers at exhibitions should be used with the password facility turned on. This makes it impossible for anyone to change information inside the machine. If possible, the system should be run without a keyboard altogether, or with certain keys (such as CTRL and ALT) blanked out or physically removed.

## Electronic promotion

Electronic promotions use the Internet, or new media such as floppy disks, digital video disks or digital versatile disks (DVDs), and CD-ROMs. While slightly harder to master, these make it possible to bring in completely new customers, and to advertise existing products in more effective ways.

The biggest drawback to electronic promotion is that very few people have the equipment needed to view them. However, this is changing very quickly indeed, and by about 2005 electronic advertising, particularly on the Internet, will be as ubiquitous as today's print promotions. Internet promotions are covered in Chapter 11, but the other three main ways of creating electronic promotional materials, such as electronic catalogues and brochures, are discussed below.

### Hypertext markup language

Hypertext markup language, more commonly known as HTML, is the system used to create pages of information for the World Wide Web. When web pages are accessed (viewed), a web browser normally copies these pages to a user's computer and then displays them. The copying process is one reason why the web can appear to be so slow.

However, HTML pages can also be supplied on a floppy disk, CD-ROM or DVD and still be viewed with a browser in the usual way. In fact, if you already have a web site, the whole site can be copied and distributed on disk, making it possible for potential customers who do not have an Internet connection to see what you have to offer. This saves design time because the same advertising materials can be re-used in two different settings.

In practice, a web site may need to be modified slightly before it will work from a disk, although this is a relatively straightforward process, and of course special features, such as on-line ordering, will no longer work and should be removed. Nevertheless, in general most of a site can be copied 'as is' and will appear exactly the same as it does on-line. (For more information about web design and HTML see page 227.)

Distributing a site on disk makes it much easier for customers to explore it. Information appears much more quickly because it does not need to be copied from the Internet first. Apart from saving time, this has the additional benefit of making it possible to add complex effects, such as sound and video, which would otherwise be impractical with today's Internet connections. It is also possible to create a much larger and more complex site with more detailed photographs and graphics than would be possible on-line. A CD-ROM, for example, actually has enough storage space for around 65 fairly simple sites, or perhaps half that number of more complex commercial sites. Because HTML is fairly easy to master, and plenty of good HTML-design software is available at reasonable prices, this can be a very good way to produce electronic publicity. HTML is also **platform independent**, which is the industry's way of saying that it will work on any computer. There is no need to produce different designs for Macs and PCs.

An example of using HTML is available on Which? Online's own CD-ROM, which is available with this book.

## Portable Document Format

A different approach to creating electronic catalogues and brochures is portable document format (PDF). Invented by Adobe, one of the pioneers of desktop publishing, PDF is typically used to create electronic documents that look more like traditional books or magazines. Unlike web pages, which have no numbers and can be viewed in any order, PDF pages are strictly sequential. Web-like 'links' can still be built in, but overall the structure of the information is more conventional.

One of the advantages of PDF is that it can work with scanned paper documents. These are stored as an electronic photograph of a document, which can be magnified or made smaller to fit a user's screen or to change the amount of detail available. PDF can also include non-text information, such as sounds and video clips. To view a PDF document, users need a PDF reader. Adobe gives away its Acrobat reader for free, and so this can be included when a PDF project is distributed on disk.

PDF's main drawback is that it can be very slow. Even on a very fast computer, complex multi-layered illustrations can take a long time to finish appearing on the screen, and even text can appear sluggish. On a much older and slower computer, such as one from around 1994, complex PDF documents can be almost unusably slow, although simple pages of text are usually readable.

PDF is a popular choice for software manuals as it saves on printing costs. It is also a good choice for business documents, because its text formatting and styling features are more advanced than those of HTML. However, it may be a little cumbersome for promotional materials. On the other hand, at around £140 for the Acrobat design software, it is no more expensive than HTML. PDF is, like HTML, platform independent (can be used on Macs as well as PCs).

## Director and other multimedia tools

A product called Director, made by Macromedia, is often used to create educational and entertainment CD-ROMs. Director costs nearly £900 and is also quite difficult to master (some universities run multimedia degree courses, based on Director, which take a year full-time). Using Director is very much like writing a computer program, and, while it is capable of very complex design and animation effects, the cost and complexity involved put it out of the reach of most promotional projects.

However, there are similar, but rather simpler and cheaper, tools that are worth considering as an alternative for certain kinds of work. For example, Digital Workshop's Illuminatus can be used to create animated photo slide shows and complex Director-like interactive multimedia projects, but costs £149. The advantage of using a multimedia design tool like Illuminatus is that animations and other special effects can be produced much more easily than by HTML or PDF. A browser or a special reader is not required. However, a project produced with Illuminatus can be viewed only on a PC.

## Audio and video

The availability of cheap camcorders, music synthesisers and high-quality sound- and video-editing equipment makes it possible for businesses to consider promoting themselves in creative new ways. While at the moment this is likely to be a fairly specialised interest, in future these kinds of promotional trimmings will become more important as Internet use grows, and static catalogues made up of words and pictures start to look relatively dull and unexciting.

**CASE HISTORY: Martin**

Martin Lewis works as a semi-professional musician and composer, and recently used new technology to put together a promotional package himself.

'In this business you get work by putting together what's called a showreel, which is basically a summary of your greatest hits with images and music. The problem used to be that creating a showreel cost an arm and a leg. Time in a professional video-editing suite can cost up to £1,000 a day.

'But what's happened over the last few years is that video hardware and software have absolutely crashed in price, and for that thousand pounds you can put together your own editing suite at home. It won't be quite as slick as the real thing, but it's good enough for even quite advanced editing. And when I say editing I don't just mean chopping sequences together, but taking advantage of very professional special effects, such as fades (when one image 'turns the page' into another), the application of three different sequences to different faces of a cube that spins across a moving background, or the superimposition of one image on another.

'You can use these video effects to capture the attention of whomever you're trying to impress. So that's what I did with my showreel. I used the PC to create an animated logo at the start, which made this look like a business rather than just some guy in a back bedroom with a couple of keyboards. Then I edited together a selection of video clips in different styles – period drama, news/documentary, sport and the like – with quite short sections and rapid cuts between them. Then I wrote a score that chopped and changed to suit the mood of what was happening on the screen, and added a few sound effects to give it more impact. Finally, I ended with the logo again, and a "theme" that goes with it.

'Did it work? Well, I sent out around 100 copies, and while no one's given me a Hollywood Oscar nomination yet, I have had enough new work to recoup the original outlay and I'm getting spin-off work from those projects, which is growing all the time.'

---

The details of setting up a simple music or video studio for promotional use are beyond the scope of this book. However, a full studio may not be necessary. In the same way that clip art is widely available and high-quality photographs can be sourced from photo libraries, video clips and music can be bought in bulk.

Music is rather more widely available. Music libraries offer collections of music to suit different themes and situations, or to set a specific mood. Some are available on a royalty-free basis and can be used without restrictions once a CD has been paid for. Others require royalty payments, which have to be made to the Performing Rights Society. For small production runs of less than 2,000 CDs, the payments are quite reasonable, perhaps £200. Sample CDs are advertised in music technology magazines and include sound effects and sections of music that can be layered together to create a more complex piece with minimal music effort. Video clips are less widely available, although some sample CD companies offer them.

Chapter 7

# Buying for business

Before embarking on a computer project it can be useful to take a step back to look at its impact from a strategic point of view. Buying a system, especially one that involves a network, is never as simple as ordering some boxes and installing whatever they contain. Your company will be changed irrevocably by the new technology, and it can be valuable to look at what this means, for better or worse, before going ahead. Some suggestions for managing the project from a business rather than a technical perspective include:

**Get your house in order first** Computers are not a panacea, and a company that is having problems before a computer system is introduced will very likely have problems afterwards. In fact, the problems may be made worse. It is worth looking at operating procedures and management structures in general to see if they can be streamlined before considering a large computer project. The changes do not necessarily have to be made immediately. In an ideal world they can be made while the new systems are being installed, to prevent two sets of disruption. But overall it is important to remember that a computer is just a tool and not a magic business solution, and it will only contribute to general efficiency if its introduction is planned and managed carefully.

**Buy tools, not technology** For business, you should always buy a system rather than a collection of grey boxes. You are buying a tool that does a specific job for you. Ultimately the fact that computers and information technology are involved is irrelevant. From this point of view a computer system is like any other item of plant or machinery, and it needs to be bought as a whole package, including maintenance, training, installation, etc. Unlike a home PC, an office system does not need to be general purpose. As long as it does one particular job well enough to save time and money and perhaps create some new business opportunities, it can be considered a success.

**Don't be a guinea pig** When your business relies on technology, you need to be sure that the technology works reliably. This means you need to be ruthlessly objective about the merits, or otherwise, of whatever systems you are considering. There have been a number of cases where large organisations have spent a fortune on technology, only to be left with systems that do not work and have to be sold off at a loss. In general, do not buy anything before it has been available for at least six months. This applies most obviously to software, although there have been many cases where hardware has caused problems as well. Within the six-month period after a product becomes available most of the problems that should have been sorted out before the product was shipped *are* finally sorted out.

**Consider people as well as computers** Apart from the training that staff need, you should look at the ways that technology can change the culture of a company. This is most obvious with systems where employees can communicate with each other, with managers, and even with the world at large. Technology can be time-wasting as well as time-saving, and in some cases employees can use it for ethically dubious and perhaps even illegal activities without anyone finding out (for more information see Chapter 10).

**Look realistically at the total cost and the presumed benefits** Apart from the cost of the technology itself, staff will need to be trained, new furniture may be needed, and buildings may even need to be modified. There will probably be lost work days due to disruption while the system is being installed. All of these need to be assessed and perhaps quantified to see if they are likely to have a sizeable impact on profits. If possible, try also to quantify the benefits. What is the project going to do for your business in terms of extra turnover and profit? Be ruthlessly realistic about the possibilities here. You may discover that the actual benefits may not be as great as anticipated.

**Learn from example** If you know of anyone in the same position as you who has tried to benefit from computer technology, it may be useful to arrange a conversation with them so you can learn from their mistakes. The same applies if you know someone who has created a completely successful outcome for themselves.

All of these factors matter hugely to the success of a project. When they are not considered properly, a project can go horribly wrong.

## Buying in practice

The main practical issue involved in buying a computer system is deciding whether to go for a 'DIY' approach (where you or someone else in the company does all the research and buying), or whether to use outside assistance ('out sourcing') from consultants, manufacturers and suppliers. Each of these offers different strengths and weaknesses.

### DIY buying

Doing all the research and buying yourself has the advantage that you are in full control throughout. The disadvantage is that it takes more of your time, perhaps much more of it. In spite of this, DIY buying is likely to be the approach most smaller businesses choose.

Apart from making sure that you buy a system that does what you really want, you also have to consider other issues such as:

- places to find product information
- warranties and maintenance
- user support
- training
- running costs
- furniture and office space (see Chapter 2)
- installation costs (especially for networks)
- finance options, including leasing.

### Finding product information

As a first step, you need to find out what kind of software is available. The packages listed in this book offer a good starting point, but to find the full range of what is available you should also read the listings in computer magazines and trade journals, visit trade fairs and investigate products advertised on the Internet (if you have a connection). The free products or trial offers mentioned in Chapter 2 are also invaluable resources.

It may be that there is no single 'right' product for you, and there are two or three options, each of which are acceptable. But you do need to reach a shortlist stage before you go any further. This is because software determines which hardware you should buy. Even if you do not understand technical specifications and have no wish to, all software comes with a list of hardware specifications that you can copy down and quote to hardware suppliers. This can make the buying process much simpler if you are not interested in learning much about computer jargon. With that in mind, places to look include:

**Newspaper advertising** While there is no reason not to buy from a newspaper, you will not, by any means, get a complete idea of the full range of choice that is available to DIY buyers if you just look at newspaper advertising. Some companies that advertise widely regularly score badly in customer satisfaction surveys, and it makes sense to look further afield to see if you can find a bigger range of products and more competitive prices elsewhere.

**High-street and trading-estate stores** The same drawbacks for newspaper advertising apply to these stores. Staff training can be very patchy, and some staff get far more training in sales than they do in computer technology, which in practice means that you will be steered towards machines that are in the store and on offer and which may not truly be appropriate for your needs. On the other hand you will be able to get first-hand experience of important features such as keyboard and screen quality. Some stores will also be able to demonstrate printers.

**Computer magazines** These provide mostly advertising, and so provide a good source of information about popular products, as well as manufacturers' contact details so that you can send off for further information. Prices in magazines can sometimes be significantly lower than those in high-street stores.

**The Internet** An excellent way to find out more about specific products and manufacturers is to look at their web sites. Some companies even offer an on-line buying service, so you can put together a system to suit your needs, pay for it electronically and have it delivered in the usual way.

## Making sense of warranties

On buying a computer, you will, as a matter of course, be given a 12-months parts and labour warranty with your system. This is the bare minimum needed by law, but unless you only use your computer system occasionally and can live without it for long periods, you will need better protection than this. Warranties come in three main types: return-to-base, collect-and-return, and on-site. In addition, you can also consider buying a service contract, which will support your hardware once the warranty period is finished.

**Return-to-base warranty** This is the same as a standard parts-and-labour warranty. If something goes wrong your machine will be repaired eventually, but there will be no guarantee given about how long this will take. You will also be responsible for getting the computer back to the supplier, which will mean paying shipping costs or delivering it yourself.

Turn-around times of a fortnight are quite typical (some suppliers do simple work at their offices, but ship more serious problems to a repair company with more advanced facilities, which adds to the repair time.) You may be able to hire in a replacement for this time (short-term rental companies advertise in the computer press), but this adds further to the cost. More importantly, your information will be with your computer. Copying it to a rental machine may be impossible, impractically complicated or expensive. While there are ways to deal with these problems – for example, you may be able to pay an engineer to do a 'hard disk transplant' to your rental machine – they will cost you even more time and money. The rental company may also not be happy about a third party taking apart one of its machines.

For these reasons a return-to-base warranty is only suitable for businesses that can afford to be without a computer for a significant period. If you hardly ever write letters, do not use the Internet, and can put off dealing with cheque stubs and receipts for a couple of weeks without problems, then a return-to-base warranty will be all you need. However, most businesses require a more comprehensive service.

If you buy a computer from a larger computer store, it may have its own workshops on-site, and you may be able to have machines repaired with a quicker turn-around time. It can be well worth finding out what the typical turn-around time is, preferably by talking to the engineering and repairs department itself, rather than taking the word of a salesperson.

**Collect-and-return warranty** This is similar to a return-to-base warranty, but shipping costs are paid. You simply hand over the hardware to a courier company, and then receive the repaired products back some time later. While offering a slight improvement over return-to-base warranties, turn-around times are likely to be similar, which means that you will still need to work around the loss of your computer system for anywhere from a week or two to, possibly, much longer.

**On-site warranty** An on-site warranty means that an engineer comes to your premises and attempts to repair the problem on the spot. For many businesses this is the only warranty option worth considering.

The main question to consider with on-site warranties is call-out time, that is the time it takes an engineer to arrive after you report a fault. Some companies now include an on-site warranty with their products as a selling point, but it is important to find out what the standard call-out time is. Companies based at locations at the outer limits of the UK should find out whether or not this call-out time applies to them. A company in the Outer Hebrides, for example, may find it needs to add at least a day to any quoted times.

It is also important to find out whether or not the call-out time is guaranteed in any way. Some companies quote an achievement percentage for call-out times, for example 'within 4 hours on 95 per cent of all calls'. Others make vaguer promises, such as 'We do our best to be there within . . .'

Even given a guaranteed call-out time, there may not be a guaranteed repair time. If parts are not available and need to be ordered specially, this can add a day or two to the repair. However, in general you should find your hardware working again within a couple of days with an on-site warranty, and perhaps very much more quickly than that.

## Service contracts

A service contract is a way of buying an on-site warranty if one is not offered at purchase. Contract costs can be expensive, ranging from £75 per year to thousands of pounds, depending on the amount of equipment covered and the contract details. This can present a business with an interesting dilemma: is it cheaper to call out an engineer as and when something goes wrong, or to pay for a contract?

One problem with calling in an outsider is that this may void the warranty on the machine. In many cases this is not a problem, as often there is no way to tell that a machine has been opened or even that parts have been replaced. However, you should check with the supplier before allowing a third party access to your machine. Of course, if you plan to use the same third party for future servicing the original warranty becomes less important.

The big problem with service contracts is that if you have an office full of equipment they can become very expensive indeed. You will need to pay for a contract for each item at a cost typically calculated as some percentage of its cost price. Companies that have more than 25 computers can start to negotiate 'bulk' service deals with a supplier. And longer-term contracts are usually much cheaper than short-term ones. However, you can easily find yourself spending thousands of pounds a year on service contracts, while your equipment hardly ever breaks down.

To work out if this is necessary, it is worth noting that usually all a contract gives you is a guaranteed call-out time, usually either within four or eight hours, depending on how much you are paying. If your business can survive for a day or two if one or two computers have problems, then it can be very much cheaper and simpler to call in an engineer when problems occur. It can also be helpful to prioritise equipment and only buy contracts for equipment that needs a very fast response, for example, your main office server.

Another option is simply to keep one or more spare items that can be plugged into place at short notice. This can even include a complete computer. You have the option of paying a large three-figure amount for the spare computer, or a much larger four-figure amount for an office-wide service contract. You may also need to budget for a hard-disk transplant (see below), but even with the time and expense involved in that, keeping a spare computer often remains a cheaper option.

The final option is simply to decide to buy new hardware if a machine fails. Again, the costs of a full service contract can make even this a financially viable possibility, although buying a more up-to-date machine to replace an older one makes a hard-disk transplant more complex than it would be otherwise.

### 'Hard-disk transplants'

You can 'clone' a computer very easily by simply transferring the hard disks from one machine to another. If successful, this will create a machine that has all the same software, all the same settings, and all the same information. This is a simple and quick job if the two machines are identical; an experienced engineer should be able to do it in less than two hours. It takes slightly longer if extra hardware, such as a network connection or a modem, needs to be transferred at the same time. However, if the two machines have significant hardware differences it can become a more complex job. Even so, at worst it should not take more than three or four hours.

### Training and other help

Training is about understanding what computers can do, and how to make them do it. Technical support is about answering specific 'How do I?' questions when dealing with a specific piece of software. Sources of training include:

- expert friends and colleagues
- college courses and classes
- books (and to a lesser extent magazines)
- software manuals
- multimedia training (CD-ROMs and videos)
- commercially run training courses.

Training is pre-emptive because good training makes further technical support unnecessary. Well-trained users not only know how to perform common tasks, they also know where they can find immediate answers to questions if they have a problem. Training should always be practical. You are unlikely to learn anything useful unless you can practice your knowledge. Whichever form of training you choose, it will need to be enhanced with time spent working through practical exercises and projects.

You should expect two things from training. The first is to gain enough working knowledge of your computer to be able to find your way around it, understand the basics of how software should be used and perhaps installed, and know enough to perform simple operations like printing or saving information. This really amounts to basic computer literacy. The second goal is a detailed understanding of how to use a specific software package. This need not be exhaustive as very few people need to know how to use a word processor to track changes by different authors to a document. However, you should be able to do whatever your work demands without needing to panic in frustration, or stop and refer to manuals every few minutes.

## Sources of training

Friends and colleagues may, perhaps, be able to provide training, but this is likely to be sketchy and informal and may leave you with more questions than answers. They can, however, be extremely good at informal technical support, and may be able to offer help with specific problems.

College courses and classes can be an excellent source of training. Many local education centres offer classes both in the evenings and during the day, and IT-related subjects are almost always widely available. Some colleges offer free computer literacy courses, which can help computer phobes through their anxieties when they are just starting out. College lecturers can also be a good source of informal technical support. One drawback to these courses is that many classes are limited to a specific subject or product. If, for example, your business uses or plans to use Sage Accounting, you may find that a suitable course is not available. In general, only the most popular and widely used software is covered. For other products you will need to look further afield.

Books are now very widely available, covering almost any computer topic under the sun, at almost any level, from complete beginner to expert. Prices range from around £25 to £100, although those at the lower end of the range are more common. Books can be an excellent training resource, and can also offer very good value for money when compared with the cost of a commercial training course. You will not, of course, be able to ask a book questions, but the best books attempt to anticipate what your questions will be.

Complete beginners' guides, such as the 'For Dummies' and 'For Idiots' ranges, are extremely popular, but some series seem to vary significantly in quality from title to title. Another problem with some books is that they are simply rewrites of the original software manual. There seems little point in buying these if you already have the manual. In general, about £50 worth of books will provide you with enough information to work out the basics of using a computer for yourself, and £100 should be enough to help you master the most widely used software.

Multimedia training is available on videos and CD-ROMs. These can be surprisingly cheap compared to books, and offer the advantage of making it obvious with animations and video clips just what is supposed to be happening. However, these are still experimental sources of training and help, and the quality is patchy. A good approach is to try out one or two possible examples, if you have the money to spare, and see how well you can work with them.

Software manuals are a frequently overlooked source of training. In fact, computer manuals are traditionally ignored, which is a shame as many are an excellent source of information to help you get started, and some now include tutorials that will take you through the ins and outs of a piece of software step by step. Manuals should always be your first choice for any training. You have paid for them already, and paying again to get the same information elsewhere is expensive and wasteful. Some manuals are now only available in electronic form, and to read them you have to use special software, typically Adobe's Acrobat Reader. Although less convenient in some ways than a paper manual, electronic manuals do take up less space on your desk, and because they have electronic search facilities it may sometimes be easier to find information in them.

Commercial training is advertised in the computer press. Some software companies either run their own training courses or buy in relevant training from an outside training source and offer it to business customers. Another source of commercial training is available from freelance training companies and individuals. Some training companies like to maintain a 'blue chip' image and so can be very expensive. Courses start at around £100 a day, but can cost more than £300 a day for specialised help. Courses are usually held in big cities rather than on your premises, so you will need to add travel expenses to the costs. For longer courses you will also have to budget for overnight stays.

However, local commercial training may also be available more cheaply from computer shops, private freelance trainers who specialise in training for small businesses, and from consultants. Computer shops in your area, local newspapers, Enterprise Agencies, the *Yellow Pages* and even your local Chamber of Commerce are all good sources of information about local training.

Microsoft and Novell run a certification system for people who work with certain products, or train others to do so. This is, in effect, a set of formal exams and qualifications that are intended to demonstrate expertise. Certification is expensive and really intended for computer experts, but if you have the resources it can be worth putting yourself or one of your staff through the process so that you have the best possible formal background knowledge of your computer system. This is not recommended for very small businesses, as the certification can cost thousands of pounds in course fees and examinations. But for larger businesses it can be a useful option to consider. Similarly, when looking for training, certified trainers are likely to have a more in-depth knowledge of the relevant products (for more information see page 129).

## Technical support

Technical support is about getting help in using your computer when you become stuck and do not know what to do next. Examples range from questions about how to print, use different fonts, insert images in a word-processor document, transfer information from one spreadsheet to another to odd or inexplicable behaviour (a real-life example was a moving mouse pointer that created a very subtle ripple-like effect on the screen).

The first port of call for technical support is always the manufacturer's original documentation in the form of printed manuals and 'on-line help' (electronic information that appears on the screen). Although manuals and on-line help can both be sketchy and less than completely clear, they can still answer many questions immediately, and familiarising yourself with them is a good first step.

The next option is support from software and perhaps hardware manufacturers. Most problems are caused by software, and most software companies offer a period of free telephone support, which can last anywhere from 90 days to a year. The period starts from either the registration of the product (i.e. when you send in a postcard that says that you now own the software) or from the first call you make to the support line. Software companies typically log all calls and keep a database of common problems and solutions, so response times can be quick. If your problem is specifically with one particular package, there is an excellent chance that you will be able to get help in this way. Some companies continue to offer this service indefinitely, so if you have problems you will be able to call them for expert help at any time.

However, the free-support period is really meant to help with the initial learning process. The theory is that you will ask most of your questions at the start when you are finding your way around the software. In practice, of course, you may still have questions once the free period has finished. You then have two choices.

Support contracts taken out with software companies provide product support on an on-going basis. Payment schemes can be complicated, with some companies charging a flat fee, while others charge per 'incident' or specific query. You may have to pay different sums for access to support for different products. In any event, this kind of support is not usually good value for money unless you use these products in an unusually complex way, or you are dealing with the detailed intricacies of very complex products (for example, the Windows 2000 operating system). Another problem is that support is specific to one manufacturer. Where you have problems caused by a combination of different products tripping over each other, you may get caught in a support loop where company A suggests you call company B, which in turn denies all knowledge of the problem and says you should call company A for help.

Support lines offer a similar service, but are designed for more general use and can offer help with a range of products. Many retailers offer support lines, although in some cases calls are charged at premium rates, which can make persistent calling expensive. Other support lines are advertised in computer magazines, and often run in association with them. Although some of these lines also offer premium-rate telephone line support, they may also offer a support contract for you or your company, under which you will be able to call them with any number of problems on an ordinary line after paying a flat fee.

A final source of support is the Internet. This can be an informal but still occasionally very useful way to get help with specific questions. Completely new and unique questions are very rare, so the chances are good that if you look through various Internet archives (see page 193) your question will already have been discussed. Alternatively you can ask your question 'live' and see what response you get. If you have an Internet connection, familiarising yourself with how to get help can be a very worthwhile investment.

### Running costs

In terms of electricity, computers are relatively cheap to run. Monitors (screens) use by far the most power, but even a large screen uses only as much power as around six 100W light bulbs. Even so the cost of running many computers in a large office is likely to be almost negligible compared to heat, light and rent.

Other running costs include consumables: floppy disks, tape cassettes, paper for printing, and printer ink or toner. The most costly consumables are backup systems (see page 166) and printer supplies. If you plan to do a lot of printing, it can be an extremely good idea to check the costs of consumables for different printers before you make a choice (see page 283). For example, some printers need to have a large and expensive part (known as the drum) replaced every few thousand copies. Others will only print a small number of colour pages before the ink runs out.

With those exceptions, computers are relatively low-maintenance items. They do not need a regular service like a car, and, serious failures aside, they should keep working almost indefinitely.

### Installation costs

In general, with a do-it-yourself purchase of a computer, you receive a set of boxes and are expected to do the rest yourself. For a single computer this can be simpler than it sounds, and most dealers include instruction sheets that explain how everything is connected together. However, some dealers offer a set-up and installation service, carried out by an engineer, for a relativey small fee (perhaps £50). If this service is available, you should ensure that it includes everything that is needed to get your computer up and running properly, including installation of all software and the setting up of printers and other accessories.

If you want to set up a network, installation costs can be considerable. Again, you can do the job yourself, but bear in mind that network cabling needs to be installed with some forethought in order to avoid electrical interference from other sources, such as fluorescent light fittings, and also to allow for the arrangement of office furniture. If a company is offering a 'network in a box' system, with which you buy everything that you need as part of a package deal, check whether the price includes installation. If it does not, and you are unhappy about doing the job yourself, ask whether this is available as an extra, either from the dealer or from someone they can recommend for the job.

## Finance options

You have three choices when buying your system: you can buy it outright, using your working capital; you can take out a loan or buy using a credit card; or, if your company qualifies, you can use a business leasing scheme.

Buying outright qualifies your purchase for capital allowances, but the value of the purchase depreciates rapidly. In practice the value of computer equipment depreciates far more rapidly than the 'writing-down allowances' that are offset against tax, and a computer more than four years old is almost worthless on the second-hand market.

Loans and credit cards can be a better option from the point of view of short-term cash flow. Credit cards are almost invariably an extremely expensive way to borrow money, but they do offer the advantage of security. If something goes wrong with your purchase, or the seller has problems and your goods never arrive, the credit-card company is obliged to compensate you. Credit cards also offer an instant purchase facility, either by phone or email. In addition, they offer a fixed period of interest-free credit, up to 60 days in some cases. One disadvantage is that some suppliers pass on the credit-card company surcharges to their customers, so you may find yourself paying an extra 1.5 per cent or so on top of the total bill. However, overall credit cards are a very convenient way to buy.

In contrast, loans provide an excellent source of long-term funding, which can, of course, be transferred to a credit-card account to make a purchase. Interest payments are tax-deductible, which lowers the effective interest rate significantly.

Leasing options are popular with many companies. These offer a way to 'buy' systems without tying up any capital whatsoever, and they also have no effect on your overall credit rating. Leasing payments are also fully tax-deductible, and some companies offer combined schemes that include leasing and on-site support. The disadvantage of leasing is that you have to sign a contract to make payments of a set amount for a set piece of equipment for a set period. If technology changes, you may find yourself stuck with something you no longer need. Some companies offer 'upgrade' schemes, in which your leased hardware is regularly replaced with the latest model.

## Buying with consultants

Consultants can do everything from advising you on your choice of system to providing a full installation. Their main advantage is that they make sure you have far less work to do. You simply specify what you want, and, to the extent that you choose, the consultant helps you acquire it. Typical consultancy skills include:

- analysing your requirements, and turning a paper specification into a workable technical design
- installing all the required hardware, software and (where necessary) network cabling
- knowing where to find the most cost-effective solutions
- arranging, or perhaps providing, training and on-going support.

The big disadvantage of consultancy is the cost. Fees vary from around £25 to £250 per hour, depending on the skills involved, although most consultants will be happy to quote on a per-project fixed-fee basis. Both fixed-fee and hourly-rate work should be carefully defined in a mutually agreed contract so that your legal and professional positions with respect to each other are clearly defined.

However, even with the extra outlay, consultancy can still be cost-effective. When chosen wisely, a consultant will save you money and time overall, and will also side-step all the most common pitfalls involved in creating a working system.

If you are buying one or two computers for an office and are reasonably practical, then you will probably be able to get by without a consultant. But if you are trying to connect up 50 PCs in a building and install a new accounting system at the same time you will almost certainly need to call in an experienced third party.

## Finding consultants

Larger companies will be able to ask the Computer Services and Software Association (CSSA) for consultancy referrals. CSSA is a trade organisation for companies in the IT field that agree to work within a code of conduct. The CSSA web site at *http://www.cssa.co.uk* includes a search facility that lists consultants by their different skills and locations. Note that the CSSA offers three different levels of membership, and only full members offer a minimum of two years' sound trading and financial histories, good management experience and references from bankers, customers and suppliers. Associate and affiliate members lack some or all of these.

Finding consultants willing to work with a very small business can be problematic. The list of sources for finding a consultant is similar to that required for finding local sources of training (see page 122). If you have an Internet connection, it may also be worth searching for the word 'consultants' and the name of your county.

A cheaper way to get consultancy-like services is offered by some larger dealers. These have 'account managers' who are, in theory at least, specially trained to help companies that are interested in making volume purchases ('volume' here usually means 'more than 25 users'). The best account managers have back-up from sales and support staff who can recommend a suitable, cost-effective solution when presented with a set of requirements.

The problem with this system is that account managers are still first and foremost sales staff. So it can be very useful to contact a number of different companies on a formal tender basis to see who offers the most prompt, efficient and professional service. It is also extremely useful to have some simple technical questions on hand to test the knowledge and professionalism of a supplier's support staff.

## Choosing consultants

Ideally you should be able to shortlist two or three consultants who will be able to work with you on a project. To help choose between these, consider the following:

**References** Good consultants will be happy to provide details of work completed successfully in the past. You should always take these up and contact the people in question for a frank discussion about how well the consultant did the job and if there were any areas of the work with which they were unhappy.

**Listening skills** Some consultants are technical wizards with minimal people skills. While good for a very narrow range of work, they may not be able to see your needs in anything other than technological terms, and are more likely to assume that you should change the way you work to suit their technological preferences, rather than the other way round. Good consultants will be able to listen to your needs, mirror them back to you, and explain how they are going to proceed in plain English. They will also be able to suggest workable alternatives if your specification for a project is unrealistic. You should feel that you are communicating clearly with them at all times.

**Contractual skills** Good consultants are familiar with industry-standard contracts, and will be willing to help you draft a suitable one, although you should still have it looked at by an independent third party before signing.

**Financial management** Good consultants will keep detailed records of all their spending, so you know exactly what you are paying for. Similarly, they will be able to cost and time a project accurately, so that the work is finished on time and within budget.

**Good follow-through** A good consultant will offer some level of support once a project is completed, or will arrange for support from an outside source.

**Formal qualifications** These may be relevant for certain kinds of projects, although note that to date all qualifications are offered by single manufacturers exclusively for their own products, and choosing a consultant with a given manufacturer's certification means that they are likely to push that manufacturer's product. Unfortunately there is no equivalent general-purpose qualification for someone who is familiar with all the available products and can recommend any of them in an unbiased way. The table opposite lists the current qualifications that you may come across.

### Formal certifications

**MCPS (Microsoft Certified Product Specialist)** Certificate holders must pass one exam covering a Microsoft operating system, which means, essentially, someone who knows the ins and outs of MS Windows.

**MCSE (Microsoft Certified Systems Engineer)** Certificate holders must pass six exams, qualifying them to manage an entire networking project.

**MCSD (Microsoft Certified Solution Developer)** Certificate holders must pass four exams, qualifying them to design custom software.

**MCT (Microsoft Certified Trainer)** Certificate holders must pass one exam, which qualifies them to train others in Microsoft products.

**CNS (Certified Novell Salesperson)** Certificate holders must pass one relatively easy test, which makes this an insignificant qualification.

**CNA (Certified Novell Administrator)** Certificate holders must pass one test about Novell's networking products, which qualifies them to install or manage these products.

**CNE (Certified Novell Engineer)** Certificate holders must pass seven tests, giving them expert-level understanding of Novell products.

**MCNE (Master Certified Novell Engineer)** Certificate holders must pass 15 tests, giving them a master-level understanding of Novell products.

**CNI (Certified Novell Instructor)** Certificate holders must pass two or three tests, gain teaching experience, and pass a training evaluation to become a qualified trainer.

### Working with consultants

Whoever you choose to run your project, you need to be in control from the start. Even small projects can go disastrously wrong. No project is a totally guaranteed success, but it is possible to avoid the most obvious pitfalls by following a formal project-management process.

**Formal specification** This is a detailed description of what you would like your computer system to do. In effect, this is your shopping list of features. The clearer you can be about this part of the process, the more likely your project is to succeed. Consultants know that many projects fail because specifications are either not clear enough, or subject to apparently random and irrational changes. So you should liaise with everyone on the project about this stage of the process to make the specification as clear as possible. Moreover, when creating a specification, always consider future needs as well as present requirements. If your system is too limited you may find yourself with little room to expand.

**Design and review** This is a technical description of how the system will work, including details of all the hardware and software, the sequence of operations for different tasks carried out at the computer, and what appears on the screen in specific situations. If you are using outside help, it is essential that you review the outline design before going any further. *Any review should include comments and queries from one or more representatives of the people who will actually use the system.* They will be able to provide essential feedback about how they work in practice (this may be very different from how the designers think they work, or, worse still, how they think staff should work to suit the technology that has been chosen). The users' needs should always come first. A review should also include detailed plans for scheduling the project, including milestones and 'deliverables' (points at which specific parts of the system should be shown to work properly).

**Installation and testing** Hardware has to be installed and tested first. Only when it has been shown to work correctly should software be installed and tested.

**Beta testing** This is where the prototype system is tested under real working conditions. This is an essential part of the process, and should be considered a review point. Changes to the specification and design may become necessary at this point. Always beta test a product with real users, and listen to their feedback. Ease of use and simplicity can make a huge difference to the efficiency of a system, and any problems with these should be considered strictly the fault of the designers of the system rather than blamed on the ignorance of the users. Never, under any circumstances, allow or expect the designers to do their own beta testing without consulting anyone else. This simply fails to provide a useful test, because computer-savvy designers and users frequently have very different mindsets, and approach problems completely differently.

**Rollout** This is where the system is 'delivered' and is considered fully installed.

**Project review** This final stage gives you the opportunity to clarify any remaining issues.

## Dealing with contracts

Any project lasting more than a day or two, and which involves an outside contractor, needs to be defined under a legal contract. This is to prevent misunderstanding as much as deliberate fraud or shady behaviour. A good contract will not harm a project, but the lack of a contract very possibly will. In fact the process of creating the contract can be just as important as the contract itself, as it is a useful focusing process that helps with the specification of the work. As part of a contract, you should include the following:

**Working schedule** This includes all milestones and deliverables.

**Payments and payment schedule** It is usual to split payments so that specific amounts are paid initially and at various stages up to final acceptance.

**Delivery of working documentation on completion** You should have access to all notes, schedules, internal memos, diagrams, and other relevant communications. These can be helpful evidence if something goes wrong and you need to take legal action, but are also useful from a practical point of view, because they provide extra information about your system that may be helpful at a later date.

**Delivery of system (or 'internal') documentation** These are formal specifications that explain how the system works technically, and how the different parts connect together.

**Delivery of user documentation** This is information for you and your staff about how to use the system.

**Penalties** Specific penalties for non-delivery or late delivery of certain features.

**Bonuses** Financial incentives for early delivery. Bonuses need to be balanced with penalties carefully. Generous bonuses are more likely to give the result you want than stiff penalties. If the latter are too draconian, you may find it hard to find anyone who wants to take on the project.

**Contingency** Plans often change in mid-course, so there should be a clause allowing you to change the system specification in writing, and the contractor to change estimates of the timing of milestones and deliverables as a result, with respect to the overall schedule, and to penalties and bonuses in general.

**Conflict-of-interest and non-disclosure clauses** These make it clear that you agree to make sensitive information available to a contractor where necessary, and they agree to handle it professionally.

**Other conflicts** An agreement to take conflicts to independent third-party arbitration can save a fortune in legal bills and court costs if something goes wrong.

**Technical support** This makes it clear who is responsible for offering support for the system if problems arise once it has been installed, or if corrections become necessary.

**'Bug fixes'** Software and hardware systems often suffer from subtle problems, known as bugs, which slip through beta testing because they only occur in very rare and specific circumstances. These problems can still be crippling, and so-called 'showstopper' bugs will bring a system crashing to a standstill. The contract should specify a further period during which the contractor will agree to repair any problems, preferably for free.

## Consumer issues: buying safely and wisely

As with the purchase of any major consumer item, it is wise to be aware of some of the pitfalls of buying. While some computer companies do have a genuine interest in the needs of the customer, others concentrate on aggressive marketing and not much else. Creating reliable software appears to be rather lower on the list of priorities of some companies, as is offering useful and affordable customer support.

Hardware retailing suffers from similar problems. Here the culprits are not the manufacturers, but some of the larger retailers. Certain companies do very well selling inferior products at a sizeable price premium, while again offering relatively poor service and support. Fortunately, excellent retailers do exist, but their products may have to be searched out deliberately as their advertising is sometimes confined to the computer press.

Software pitfalls are very hard to avoid. Inferior products, even from major names, have been and continue to be sold, causing users hours or even days of wasted time as a result. Legal action can be difficult to consider because software is sold under license, rather than as a specific working product such as a fridge or washing machine. This makes it possible to 'sell' software under entirely unreasonable terms and to limit the liability of manufacturers under law.

Suppliers also make it difficult to return faulty software. Clearly they have no way of knowing if you have truly removed a product from your machine, as there is nothing to stop you keeping a copy, even if you return the original package. Getting a supplier to consider a return on a faulty software product is an uphill struggle, and it can be worth asking potential suppliers about their policy on returns of software.

For consumers, even business consumers, prevention is better than cure. The harsh reality seems to be that at the moment business users have a choice between entangling themselves in legal action that is unlikely to be successful, and simply putting up with the shoddy products that are widely sold and working around their shortcomings. If you protect all your information and keep it safe (see page 166), you will be better placed to deal with occasional disasters. And the reality is that disasters do happen, much more regularly than they should.

Problems are easier to prove with hardware, but even here the issue is not as clear-cut as with other technological products. Sometimes hardware simply fails, and there is no question that something has gone wrong. But at the other times it exhibits very sporadic problems, which may be temperature-related, or may be simply due to a single faulty solder joint on a component that contains thousands of such joints.

One ploy to watch for is the infamous recovery disk, which is offered by many manufacturers as a support option. This simply wipes all the information on your computer and forces you to reinstall all your software from scratch. The theory seems to be that this will somehow magically cause both hardware and software problems to evaporate. The reality is that a recovery disk cannot, under any circumstances, fix a hardware problem. Hardware problems, especially regular outbreaks of erratic behaviour, are most likely to be caused by either memory issues (i.e. an inadequate kind of memory chip has been used) or simply bad design. In both these situations it is the manufacturer's responsibility to make good the defects as long as they are noticed and commented on immediately. To determine if a problem is caused by the hardware or the software, you could try to borrow a computer from somewhere else, install exactly the same software and information on it (software license permitting), and then use it exactly in parallel with the original machine. If the original machine stops working at any point while the spare computer continues to function, that offers almost complete certainty that there is a hardware problem, and that the machine either needs to be repaired or replaced immediately. Naturally not every one will be in a position to do this, but for those who are convinced there is a problem, this will provide strong supportive evidence.

While hardware problems can never be completely avoided, it can be extremely helpful to look out for the regular user satisfaction and reliability surveys that are published in computer magazines, and also in *Which?* magazine. These at least give an indication of the makes and models that are more prone to problems, and which manufacturers deal with problems most professionally.

---

**CASE HISTORY: Buying a problem, not a solution**

Rachel Maurice and Deborah Reynolds are owners of the Mustard Seed, a small Christian bookshop and teashop in Marlborough, in Wiltshire. They decided to buy a business-specific package, but feel there may have been better choices.

'Originally we had an old 80286 computer, but we felt we needed to upgrade when we moved to our new premises in 1997. So we bought a computer from a major supplier and found a stock-control package at a book fair. It was really an add-on to an accounts package, but it was specifically designed for bookshops and it came with an Electronic Point of Sale (EPOS) keyboard and barcode wand, which meant that information about stock and sales went straight into the computer from the till. It cost about £3,000, including the computer and printer.

'We ended up buying an accounts package that's very unwieldy, and which we never use. Rachel does the accounts at home now on her computer, using a much cheaper package called Money Manager. It can handle VAT, and it does everything we want, and I think it cost around £100.

'The computer has been an issue too. I am in deep dialogue with the computer company about it, because there are clearly some problems with it. For example, sometimes it appears to freeze for no reason at all. I've spent more time than I want to backing up all our records to floppy disk, wiping out everything on the machine, and reinstalling everything. It's been a real bind and I've had to learn more about computers than I would like. It is all so annoying because when the computer works it's a wonderful tool and we probably wouldn't be able to run the business without it.'

# Chapter 8
# Choosing the right hardware

A good rule of thumb when choosing a system is to choose the software first, and then choose the hardware to match it. Most software comes with typical hardware specifications, which define the kind of computer needed to use it. You can quote these specifications at a dealer even if you have no idea what they mean, and the dealer will be able to suggest hardware to match.

While this approach is ideal for smaller businesses, larger businesses may need to be more specific. The most important question to consider is the lifetime of the system, and whether it will need to be expanded. Technologically, the working life of a modern computer system is between one and three years, depending on the application. From a business point of view this may be irrelevant, as a system bought for a specific purpose may continue to do the work expected of it for a decade or more. But for certain kinds of work, such as running a database with many users on a large network, it is impossible to have too much speed or power. For these situations hardware may need to be updated regularly, especially if staff levels increase. Networked systems can run out of power very suddenly and without warning so that adding even one more person to a network can suddenly slow it to a crawl. There are a number of ways to deal with this problem. It is also worth looking at the ways in which non-networked hardware can be updated.

## Hardware types

Computers are available in a number of standard types, regardless of manufacturer. It can be helpful to understand what the pros and cons of these are, and how they differ in practice.

## Desktop computers

Desktop models are the type of computer with which most people are familiar. They are large and relatively heavy, and vary hugely in speed and power depending on the make and model. Desktop models are completely general-purpose and can be used for any kind of work. Updating a desktop computer is straightforward (see Appendix II), but can be very expensive. Prices of desktop machines have fallen so quickly that the cheapest models (at about £300) are now significantly cheaper than some of the software that are supposed to be used with them. This means that it is often cheaper to buy a new machine than to try to update it, except perhaps in very limited and simple ways. In any case, there is no business need to update a desktop machine until it starts to 'feel' slow, and you seem to spend most of your time waiting for something to happen.

## Network servers

Network servers are fast and powerful computers that cover a range of specifications and prices. They are not advertised as widely as desktop models, and tend to be more expensive because they use more specialised components. In general, servers are designed for a corporate market and are sold at corporate prices.

At the low end of the price and performance scale these machines use the same technology as the more powerful desktop models, perhaps with some enhancements, such as more memory or a fault-tolerant filing system (see page 163). Cheaper models that do not offer fault-tolerance or extra reliability are usually overpriced – they are simply desktop machines built into a more impressive case, fitted with a network connector and given the 'server' label quite arbitrarily. For low-performance applications, for which reliability need not be guaranteed, it is often perfectly practical to save a few thousand pounds by using an ordinary desktop machine instead.

At the higher end of the server market, advanced machines that can cost anywhere from £5,000 to £20,000 use a number of extra features to improve speed, power and reliability. Fault tolerance is a major feature on these machines. Faulty hardware can often be replaced without needing to turn the server off. They also offer more memory, more filing space, and so on. Memory can be particularly important on a server, and it is not unusual to see systems that can have more than four times as much memory as a typical desktop model.

Some servers use a multi-chip system, which makes it possible to upgrade performance by adding one or more extra processor chips. These share the workload between them. This process suffers from diminishing returns, so that even with four chips the computer may still be slightly less than twice as fast as a single-chip machine.

### 'Workstations'

'Workstation' is simply marketing-speak for a completely ordinary desktop computer. The only exception to this rule are complex and expensive scientific high-performance computers that use very specialised parts and are between 2 and 20 times faster than the kinds of computers that are widely advertised in the computer press. Computers for graphic design and animation are sometimes also sold as workstations. These machines may again be ordinary desktop models, but some have been fitted with extra, expensive hardware that helps speed up the computer when it is producing images and drawings on the screen.

## Makes and models

The world of computer hardware is a strange one, and brand names are less important than they are elsewhere. This is perhaps because there are only two main kinds of computer to choose from (the others are bought to special order for very specialised work, and are typically much more expensive than the machines mentioned below).

**PCs** are based on a standard originally developed by computer giant IBM (International Business Machines), but subsequently hijacked by other companies. The letters 'PC' stand for 'personal computer', but this has more to do with history than with the fact that PCs necessarily have to be used personally by individuals. In practice a PC is simply any computer that can use software or hardware designed to work with the PC standard.

PCs are available from hundreds of manufacturers, ranging from multinational companies with billion-dollar turnovers to fledgling businesses working from someone's back bedroom or garage.

Although a handful of manufacturers design their own parts from scratch, most simply assemble their computers from a range of parts that are shipped from the Far East. This means that there is often very little to distinguish one PC from another, and brand names are far less important than specifications. As a result PCs are often distinguished by the name of the main computer chip inside them (for example, a 'Pentium II') rather than the manufacturer.

While PCs are now relatively cheap – prices for the cheapest new models start at about £300 – they are not particularly reliable. Problems are perhaps more common than they should be, and in typical use it is possible that something will go wrong at least once a week. Most problems are not very serious and can be solved by the clumsy expedient of turning the machine off and on again, but sometimes work is lost. In extreme cases all the information inside a PC disappears completely, although this is relatively rare. These problems and drawbacks mean that it is important to be careful and thorough about making safety copies of important information with PCs. It can also be quite hard to add new hardware to a PC, although for typical small-business use this is unlikely to be a major problem. In general, while PC prices are low, the cost of owning a PC – in terms of maintenance problems, poor software reliability and general time wasted in everyday use – can be higher than many business buyers expect.

However, PCs are based on the most widely used computer standard on the market today. There is more software available for PCs than for any other kind of computer, and spare parts and extras are cheap and widely available. Most PCs use the Windows system developed by American software company Microsoft. Windows provides a framework within which other software can be used, and because of Microsoft's strong marketing practices it has become one of the best-selling software products in the world. Many popular business software packages are only available for PCs that use Windows.

**Macs** (short for Macintosh) are made by the Apple computer company, which is the only company still trading today that makes small computers not to the IBM standard. Macs have always offered much more in the way of consumer satisfaction than PCs. They appear to be 'friendlier' and easier to use, and people seem to take to them relatively quickly. (As an example, anyone who wants to connect two Macs together so that they can share information can do the job simply by connecting them with a suitable cable. Connecting two PCs together is a very much more challenging process.) Reliability, however, is variable. At worst it is comparable to PCs, at best it is significantly better.

Apple seemed to lose its sense of direction during the 1990s, but regained credibility in 1998 with the launch of the iMac – a small, distinctively styled, moderately powerful but easy-to-use computer. Sole traders can benefit from the simplicity of a computer like the iMac to help keep running costs down and make it easy to get started with as little familiarisation as possible. More powerful Apple computers are popular in magazine publishing, Internet design, music composition and video production. They are less widely used in small businesses because the range of business software available is relatively limited.

---

**PCs versus Macs**

**PCs**
- often used by businesses
- available with a much larger range of software than Macs
- very cheap
- not very reliable
- harder to upgrade (requiring more technical knowledge from users) than Macs
- not quite as fast as Macs
- technically and visually rather clumsy
- usually built from standard parts imported from the Far East.

**Apple Macs**
- often more reliable than PCs, but with major exceptions
- easier to upgrade than PCs
- popular with users
- technically and visually appealing
- limited range of software available, especially for advanced business use
- often used for creative applications such as page layout, graphic design, etc.
- significantly more expensive than PCs.

For very small businesses, either a cheap PC or a cheap Mac will do the job just as well, especially if a limited selection of simple business software is to be used. Both will handle accounts, word processing, and the Internet with equal ease.

For larger businesses the wider range of software available for PCs makes them more appealing, although the higher cost of maintenance and ownership in general should be taken into account.

For creative applications such as music, artwork, and so on, Macs are still by far the most popular choice, and offer significant advantages in terms of ease of use, speed and reliability.

## Obscure and advanced hardware

If your business expands significantly, you may find yourself in a position where you need more expensive and complex hardware. Buying such an advanced computer is a very different experience from buying a cheaper machine. Manufacturers of these products always produce their own hardware, including their own proprietary computer chips, rather than buying in parts from outside. Dealerships are strictly controlled, and you will either have to talk to the manufacturer directly or deal with one of a restricted number of suppliers. When buying such a machine a service and support contract will often be included in the price. These more expensive machines – some of which cost six figures, although the cheapest models are comparable to a mid-priced server – are aimed very much at advanced users, and both the machines themselves and the way they are sold are rather more professional as a result. Full details of these advanced products are outside the scope of this book, but some names to be aware of are listed below.

**Silicon Graphics Inc (SGI)** are makers of very powerful and variably expensive computers that range from desktop models, often used for computer graphics and animation, to advanced scientific machines. SGI now owns Cray Research, which once produced the fastest and most expensive scientific computers in the world.

**Sun computers** are also used for scientific and technical applications, but they are also popular with ISPs who frequently use Sun equipment to manage their Internet connections.

**Hewlett Packard, Compaq** and **IBM (International Business Machines)** all produce their own high-performance equipment for both scientific and business use. These manufacturers also produce standard PC-like products across a range of markets.

**Alpha** was created by the Digital Equipment Corporation (DEC), but is now owned by Compaq. The Alpha was a very fast and powerful computer chip and is still available from a small number of sources. Machines that use the Alpha cost perhaps twice as much as standard Pentium-based desktop computers, but are between two and four times faster using software specially developed for the Alpha chip. They can also pretend to be a Pentium computer and work with standard PC software, albeit at speeds which are comparable to, or slower than, a true PC.

## Portable computers

Portable machines come in a range of types including:

**Luggables** These are the size of a pilot's briefcase, but may be rather heavier. Luggables are now almost obsolete and are only available for very specialised applications.

**Portables** Large, heavy and relatively unwieldy machines, these are smaller than luggables, but larger than today's more lightweight machines. Again, they are no longer being produced.

**Laptops** Sometimes known as notebook computers, these are around the size of a large computer magazine or phone directory, and weigh a few pounds.

**Palmtops** These are truly pocket-sized, although the larger models require very large, robust and possibly reinforced pockets. They are 'slimmed down' computers that offer basic facilities without the sophistication and complexity of larger models. Palmtops are discussed in more detail in Chapter 2.

### Laptops

Laptops are the most popular choice of the portable computers, and the main aspects to consider when buying one are:

**Battery life** This can be abysmally disappointing with some models – often less than two hours. Three hours is good, and any more than this is quite exceptional. It is sometimes possible to use two batteries simultaneously to double battery life, although this usually has to be done by removing some other part of the laptop, such as the floppy-disk or CD-ROM drive, to make space for the battery. It may also be possible to 'hot swap' these extra batteries without turning off the laptop. If you plan to use a laptop on long journeys, you will need to carry spare charged-up batteries with you. Be warned that these are heavy and, at around £100 or so, rather expensive. (Some airlines now offer laptop power points in their business seating areas, but this practice is by no means widespread and is not yet available in economy seats.)

**Battery working life** Some batteries stop working after a while. Older NiCad (Nickel Cadmium) types have to be completely discharged before recharging, otherwise they will no longer work at their full capacity. NiCad batteries are best avoided as a result. This is not a problem with more modern NiMH (Nickel Metal Hydride) and LiOn (Lithium Ion) designs. It is important to ask how many charge/discharge cycles are available from a battery before it needs to be replaced.

**Voltage compatibility** The best laptops will work with any mains supply in the world between 100V and 240V, although, of course, special adaptor plugs will be needed outside the UK.

**Display quality and size** TFT (Thin Film Transistor) displays are very bright and clear and usually worth paying the extra for. A display size of 13.3in is comfortable, and will provide a display resolution (see page 272) of 1024 × 768, which is better than the capability of a cheap desktop system. The larger the display, the shorter the battery life, so if you plan to spend a lot of time away from home – and away from a convenient power source – it can be worth getting a smaller display.

**Pointing device** The 'trackpad' is now becoming a standard on many machines. This small pad tracks the position of your finger electronically. Some machines still use buttons to move the mouse pointer, and these are rather less easy to use. The alternative 'trackpoint' system uses a tiny plastic stub on the keyboard to move the mouse pointer; again, for most people this is a less appealing option than a trackpad.

**Processor chips and speed** It is possible to buy a laptop that uses the latest and faster computer chips, but these tend to shorten battery life and are often unnecessarily fast and expensive for ordinary use. 'Portable' versions of computer chips help cut down on battery consumption. A standard £1,500-laptop will use technology that is perhaps a generation or so behind that found in the newest desktop machines, but this should still be adequate for most kinds of work.

**Memory** Laptop memory is more expensive than conventional memory, but manufacturers have started including large amounts of memory – such as 64Mb or even 128Mb – to help sell their portable machines, and you are unlikely to ever need more than this.

**Dimensions and weight** Dimensions are becoming standardised. Most laptops are now slightly bigger than a magazine, and anywhere between 2cm and 5cm deep. Weight can be surprisingly important. Struggling through an airport check-in weighed down by a bag containing a laptop, two spare batteries, and various accessories, is likely to be awkward for most people. If you do a lot of travelling and can afford the extra expense, a super-light machine is worth the extra outlay. It can also be useful to take out specific extras when they are not being used. You may not need a floppy-disk drive or CD-ROM drive on a long journey, for example, and to save weight you could leave them with your luggage instead.

**Options and extras** Some laptops can be fitted internally with a range of extras, including DVD drives, LS-120 or Zip drives (see page 288), which provide further storage space for information. Perhaps the most useful extra is a modem. Standard external modems can be connected directly, although these can easily result in a rat's nest of cables around the laptop. Internal modems use the PCMCIA system, which is used to provide credit card-sized extras for laptops. Apart from standard telephone modems, which simply plug into a PCMCIA slot at one end and a phone socket at the other, it is also possible to use cellular modems and network cards. Cellular modems either connect to a portable phone or use a built-in aerial to tune in to the cellular network. In the former case it is essential to make sure that the modem matches both the phone and the network, as there is a confusing array of options to consider. If in doubt, your mobile phone supplier or manufacturer should be able to advise you. It is also possible to buy PCMCIA network cards, which make it possible to connect a laptop to a company network while at the office. Some companies now sell combined cards that include network, standard modem and portable-modem facilities all in one.

## Shopping by price

Although it helps to understand the underlying technology, computers can be bought on price to some extent. The following list offers an indication of the capabilities of machines in different price ranges.

### Price ranges for desktop models

- **£300–£750** Good for basic office work. Possibly a little slow compared to more expensive models (especially if used to connect to the Internet), but this is unlikely to be noticeable in everyday use.
- **£750–£1,250** A good solid machine. Suitable for use on the Internet and every kind of office work. Models around the £750 mark often offer the best overall value for money.
- **£1,250–£2,000** Too expensive and too fast for everyday business use and most of the speed and power will be wasted. Usable, if perhaps a little slow, for more demanding applications such as very complex spreadsheets, video- and audio-editing, architectural visualisation, 3D design and animation.
- **£2,000 upwards** Over specified and unnecessary for everyday use, models in this price range would, however, be fast enough for very demanding work.

### Price ranges for servers

- **£3,000–£5,000** Basic servers that will not necessarily have much in the way of special technology. It can be worth checking to see if a similar specification on a machine that lacks the 'server' label is available at a much lower price.
- **£5,000–£10,000** Good solid server models that will almost certainly have special features to enhance speed and reliability.

They are suitable for all but the most demanding department or small business.
- **£10,000 upwards** Very powerful machines for more complex applications, but probably excessive for a small business.

## Price ranges for laptops

- **£500–£750** Old, obsolete-technology models, these are adequate for word processing and note-taking, maintaining an address book, simple accounting and perhaps spreadsheet work. They are a good choice for someone who wants a convenient, portable computer that can be used anywhere and does not take up much space. Slightly more expensive models offer better all-round value for money. But anyone who wants a laptop, and is not planning to do anything complicated or demanding with it, is likely to be happy with a machine from this range.
- **£750–£1,500** Recent-technology laptops, these are equivalent to slow desktop machines, and offer enough power for all kinds of everyday business work. Overall they offer the best value for money, with enough power to get work done but with no extra frills, features or gimmicks.
- **£1,500–£3,000** Advanced laptops, these will either be much smaller and lighter than cheaper models, or will work much faster, or both. For most kinds of work the extra power is simply unnecessary. However, the smaller size and weight can be well worth having, especially for anyone who travels a lot. In general, however, these models are not good value, and can only be recommended for those who are not overly put out by the extra expense.
- **£3,000 upwards** As much a status symbol as a computer, these are very fast, often very stylish and thin, lightweight designs. There are very few applications available which would demand this kind of power in a laptop. While they are suitable for creating computer graphics, editing video clips and perhaps designing web sites while travelling, the poor battery life of all laptops (even expensive ones) makes this kind of work problematic away from a desktop machine. In general, these designs are only for those with money to burn.

## Customising a computer

While changing the hardware inside a computer's case can be moderately complex and expensive, changing the items outside of the case, including the mouse, keyboard and monitor can be much easier. These can make a very big difference to productivity and are well worth considering as an option. Anyone who types all day will make far fewer mistakes and feel more relaxed with a high-quality keyboard. And even the choice of mouse can make a difference. See Appendix I for further details.

# Chapter 9
# Buying and using software

Businesses are not limited to widely available commercial products. Other options can be a better choice in certain situations, especially where the software needs of a company are quite specialised or trade-specific, or commercial products simply fail to offer the required features, even when using the 'programming' facilities offered by database, spreadsheet and other office-suite products. Businesses then have two options. They can look for a trade-specific package that is designed specifically for the kind of work they do, or they can have software developed to order.

## Trade-specific packages

The big advantage of trade-specific packages is that they speak the same language as your business, and are – in theory at least – written by people who understand how that kind of business should be run. Nonetheless, with this kind of software, it is best to check that it really does do what you want it to. No software should ever be bought on the spur of the moment after a short demonstration, and with a trade-specific package, which may be quite complex, you should spend anywhere from half a day to a day having the software demonstrated to you. If you plan to hand it over to your staff rather than using it directly, then at least one of them should come with you. After the demonstration it is very useful to go away and allow some time to consider how the software may be able to help your business, and specifically to try to find problems or tasks with which it will not be able to help. It may be worth producing a formal (or at least written) specification for the kinds of work for which you would like to use the software in order to see if any essential features are missing. At this stage, queries and misgivings should become obvious, and the software is only worth considering seriously if the supplier can set your mind at rest about them. Apart from the basic features, it is also useful to ask the following questions:

- **Expandability** Will the software work on a network? How many people can work with it at once, given suitable hardware? What are its limitations?
- **Support** What support is available? And at what times?
- **Cost** Is there an outright purchase price, or does the cost depend on the number of users? Is there any penalty for adding extra users or extra options at a later date? What happens if there are problems? How long will it take to fix them?
- **References** Will existing customers vouch for the software?
- **Confidence** How long has the supplier been trading? Are they likely to be trading in the short to medium term? (Buying a specialised package from a supplier who then goes bust can be a nightmare.)
- **Competitiveness** Will it really be less expensive to use this software than to use a competing commercial package, if the trade-specific software requires setting up first?
- **Compatibility** How easy is it to get information into and out of the software, if you would like to work with it in other ways, using other tools?

### CASE HISTORY: Totally Brilliant Software

Andy Hilton runs Totally Brilliant Software, a company that has developed a package for the equipment rental market.

'Firstly it's a true all-in-one package, and it will run all of the business if that's what you need. It started life as a package for audio rental equipment for recording studios, but now it's more general purpose, and you can use it for tool hire, or car hire or anything like that. We find people don't like using different things for different kinds of work. It's inconvenient to copy information between them, so our package includes all you need: an address book, accounting facilities, and of course the rental database itself. You can do things like create a mail shot, using addresses from the address book, that targets people who've generated a certain amount of turnover. We also include support for different languages, different offices (you can link them 'live' so information is updated automatically), and barcode scanning. It's written using a database system called Omnis 7 and works just as happily on Macs as PCs, so mixed networks are no problem.

'The rental business is quite complicated because you never quite know when things are going to be coming back and be available for hire again. Also, no two companies are the same, so you have to make the system extremely flexible and make it capable of working in millions of different ways. So, for example, any output produced for customers is customisable. And on the accounting side we have a system for sending out reminder statements – the letters get angrier and angrier the later the payments get.

'We charge £1,000 per user, which is obviously a lot more than buying something like MS Office and then customising it. But our package does what you want straight away, while getting something like Office or BackOffice set up to do the same takes an enormous amount of time.

'And the bottom line for any kind of system is, does it do what the people who use it want? We've had enough feedback to know that our system does. And it works reliably too, which is always a big help. As for support, well, because it's an expensive product we try to offer support to match. Someone is here 24 hours a day, 7 days a week.'

## Finding trade-specific tools

The best places to look for trade-specific software are trade journals and shows. Trade journals often include advertising for a small selection of suitable packages. At trade shows it is possible to have a limited amount of 'hands-on' time trying out the software, although it is never a good idea to buy such a product on the basis of a five-minute introduction. A full demonstration should always be a prerequisite, except for products that are designed for specialist work rather than running a business. For example, packages such as Matlab and Mathematica are the science and engineering world's equivalent of a spreadsheet or word processor.

Other sources to consider are word-of-mouth recommendations from competitors or others doing similar work to you, and the Internet. The latter can often throw up a surprising amount of information about possible software choices, which will occasionally offer a much cheaper approach than buying a fully-fledged package.

It is worth noting that although many trade-specific products have a slightly less reliable or commercial image than the most widely used off-the-shelf packages, this image problem may not reflect the quality of these products at all. Many trade-specific tools are just as reliable – if not more reliable – than the 'big-name' commercial tools that are sold in the computer press. The fact that the former are constantly being developed by relatively small companies who keep in close contact with their customers can be more of an advantage than a problem in many cases.

## Bespoke software

Bespoke software is tailor-made software, written to order completely from scratch. While very large companies with very large computer systems regularly take the bespoke approach, smaller business should only ever consider the bespoke option as a last resort. It is simply too risky and very probably too expensive to be considered in any other way.

For most financial work that involves book-keeping or stock control, a bespoke option is definitely the wrong way to go. Commercial products, including those that need setting up first, will be able to handle the needs of most companies, and any consultant who suggests otherwise should be treated with suspicion. But there are a small number of situations where the bespoke option is the only way forward. These include:

- software that needs to work with specialised machinery – for example, large security systems that rely on cameras and other sensors, or applications that use heavy machinery or robots
- very complex Internet applications
- specialised software that works in unusually complex ways – for example, software that makes speculative share-price predictions in a unique way

- very specialised trade-specific tools – for example, dosage calculators for drugs that take into account various aspects of a patient's medical record.

There is a difference between paying someone to customise existing software (such as a database, spreadsheet, or office suite) for a specific end and creating completely unique software 'out of thin air', but from a business point of view both these projects fall into the 'bespoke' category and should be handled with great care to prevent an expensive disaster. The project-management steps that are described on pages 129–32 also apply here, but before embarking on a project like this it is well worth spending extra time collecting and checking the references of prospective programmers and looking closely at their previous work and professional relationships. The same list of questions that applies to trade-specific software should be asked here too.

The worst-case scenario when organising the development of a bespoke system is to be left with a partly finished project that has cost thousands, does nothing useful, and is unlikely to be finished. Once a project has started, an unscrupulous programmer can hold you over a barrel by threatening to pull out before the project is finished unless you do whatever they demand. The existence of a contract may count for very little as you will not be in a practical position to exercise your legal rights if your business depends on the completion of the project. Security is another issue to consider. Programmers have been known to include 'bombs' or 'trapdoors' in the software they write, which give them the chance to read or destroy your records at will after the project is over.

In practice these situations happen extremely rarely, and a programmer or consultant with an excellent work record will be very unlikely to confront you with them. But the reality is that many, many software projects go over time and over budget simply because project management is a very complex task. There is a limit to what penalty clauses can do to prevent this, so a bespoke project should always be run with contingency plans in mind. Developing all but the simplest software is a high-risk proposition, and it is always essential to look at the pros and cons before taking this approach.

## Software legalities, and how to survive them

When buying commercial software it is important to remember that you do not actually buy the software itself, but a licence to use it. This becomes particularly important when you have more than one computer for your own personal use, or a number of computers connected together on a network. Legally, you may be limited to the use of a fixed number of copies of the software. Sometimes this depends on the total number of copies you have installed. Sometimes it is what is known as a per-user licence, which means that the number of people who can use the software at the same time is limited. Strictly speaking, if you pay for a single licence and use the software on two or more different computers, even for your own use, you are still pirating the software, and could be liable for damages or fines if you are caught.

The fact that software is licensed rather than bought gives software companies an interesting legal get-out from the usual consumer-protection schemes that apply to goods and services. All software comes with a complicated legal document that defines the terms of the licence. This usually includes a damage-limitation clause, which states that the manufacturer is in no way liable for damages should the software not work as advertised. Often this document appears while the software is being installed, and you will be asked if you accept the terms. This is, in effect, like signing a contract with the manufacturer over which you have had no control and have not negotiated. Your only options are to use the software, or not to use it. Attempts to challenge this practice, or to claim damages for obviously faulty software have so far been settled quietly out of court. Certainly the issue of software quality is not as clear-cut as many software licences might have you believe, and if faulty software genuinely causes you problems in a way that can be proved conclusively, it can be worth considering legal action in spite of what the licence may say.

With bespoke software the situation is more complex, and you should always allow a trial period towards the end of a project during which you can test the software thoroughly under realistic working conditions to help eliminate problems – preferably before you have paid for it in full. Realistically, all software has something wrong with it, and producing a perfect product is almost impossible once a certain

153

level of complexity is exceeded. But problems should never be so serious that they cause you to lose work or information or otherwise impact on your business in a negative way.

## Other products to consider

Apart from the main software you use for your business, there are other optional products that can help make your life easier, or that claim to make your computer easier to use and more reliable. Collectively these are often known as **utilities**. Examples of utilities are listed below.

**Crash-recovery systems** attempt to save your current information when your computer stops working, for either software or hardware reasons. However, most software has an 'autosave' feature, which files away a safety copy of the information you are working on regularly – perhaps every five minutes or so. The autosave features that are probably available to you already are much more useful than most crash-recovery systems. Even without them you should save your work regularly by hand.

**Tune-up tools** attempt to make your computer work faster or more efficiently. Mostly these do very little of any value, although if you are using Windows 95 the modem tune-up tools for Internet use can speed up your connection.

**System-analysis tools** tell you about the hardware inside your computer and check how well it is working. The best tools run detailed diagnostic tests that check all your hardware thoroughly. You can use these to pinpoint problems which you can then complain to your supplier about. However, many of these tools simply check what kind of hardware is inside your computer and produce a report – something which you could just as well find out about by asking your supplier.

**Compression tools** pack the information in your computer into a smaller space. Software and other information on the Internet is often supplied in a compressed form, and you will need to decompress it before you can use it. This is one kind of utility that is almost essential, especially for Internet users. A system called Zip is the most popular compression tool for PCs. Information can be 'zipped' and 'unzipped' using a range of tools – for example, NicoMac's WinZip. The equivalent system for the Mac is called StuffIt, and is available from Aladdin Systems. 'Zipped' and 'Stuffed' (compressed) information takes much less time, and so costs less, when sent over the Internet. These systems also make it possible to squeeze more information into your computer's filing space, especially when archiving old information.

**Disk-management tools** help you manage the information filed inside your computer. For example, if you delete some information by accident you may sometimes be able to retrieve it. **Disk-copying** tools simply copy all the information from one hard disk to another, en masse. These can be useful for backup purposes (see page 166).

**Information-management tools** make it easier to move, copy or archive information. Many of them are a waste of money. You will find it easier and cheaper to use the tools that your computer already has built into it for these very purposes. However, people do occasionally find that they prefer the working methods offered by these alternatives.

**Backup and archiving tools** and **virus checkers** are discussed in Chapter 10.

**Uninstallers and clean-up tools** remove information you no longer use or need. Software for Windows 95/98 is often extremely bad at removing itself completely if you use the built-in tools for uninstalling it. But again, it is often possible to tidy up after it by hand. In any case you do not need these tools unless you are running out of filing space, or in the unlikely event that you find yourself installing and uninstalling software regularly.

**Voice recognition** is a currently popular extra that allows your computer to understand spoken English.

**Translation software** attempts to translate from one language to another.

Voice recognition and translation are advanced products that are suited for a relatively narrow range of work (see case history: Janet).

## CASE HISTORY: Janet

Janet Sullivan works from home as a technical translator. She was pleasantly surprised, with some reservations, with voice dictation software.

'I started with a package called Dragon Naturally Speaking, which can follow continuous speech. The package includes a headset with a microphone. It works, after a fashion, straight out of the box, but you really need to train it to recognise your own way of speaking, which takes about an hour of reading from a set text. After that it learns as you go along, providing you keep correcting it. To start with, you make a lot of mistakes, and Dragon lets you correct mistakes with your voice, which is a good idea even though it slows you down. At the beginning it was taking me much longer to speak words than to type them because of all the corrections. Also, the software can, on occasions, get it spectacularly wrong. 'Esoteric' came out as 'He said Derek' once. Thankfully it does get better after practice. You need a fastish computer to deal with the software, but I understand that any new PC is fast enough.

'Eventually I was getting up to about 80 words a minute – much faster than I can type – with maybe 95 per cent accuracy. I gave up making corrections by voice and went back to old-fashioned editing, which was rather quicker. The proof-reading takes more time than it used to because I have to watch for howlers, but it's still quicker overall.

'The other thing is that your voice goes after a while. I really wouldn't want to use this for a full eight hours a day.

'Would I use it for ordinary dictation? Probably not. It works well for the kind of work I do, because I'm really just copy-typing in a different language. I had a few attempts at using it for email, but typing is much more convenient. You get time to think and make corrections. Voice dictation assumes that your thoughts are arranged in perfect sentences, which they often aren't. If you're used to dictating letters all day you wouldn't have that problem.

'I eventually decided to give IBM's ViaVoice a go, to see if it was any better. There's not much between them really, although I use ViaVoice now as the recognition accuracy is slightly better. ViaVoice also lets you dictate directly into Word, whereas Dragon uses its own notepad from which you have to copy and paste.

'As for the translation tools that are out there, well, I don't have any uses for them. I suppose they might be good for rough and ready transcriptions as long as you don't expect too much. A lot of the work I do relies on a specialised vocabulary, so these tools wouldn't be suitable anyway. I can see that they might be useful for businesses that trade abroad and don't have any multilingual employees, but the quality of their output is not up to professional standards as yet.'

Chapter 10

# Safeguarding your investment

Once you have a working computer system, you need to make sure that it continues working reliably as it is more than likely that your whole business will come to depend on it. Your computer will be able to keep track of letters, accounts, invoice and payment details, names and addresses, and a variety of other information much more conveniently than a bulky paper-filing system. Sooner rather than later paper filing will start to take second place to electronic data. Losing all of this information can be fatal to a business. Apart from the practicalities, such as losing customers' phone numbers, UK businesses may also be liable to action from the Inland Revenue and H.M. Customs and Excise, both of whom require that proper records are kept for a number of years. It is sometimes possible to reconstruct certain kinds of information from paper records, but this is time-consuming and distracting. In general, it is much more reassuring to know that your information is safe, and that you can rebuild all your records from scratch, inside a different computer if need be.

Computer technology leads to extra risks for businesses above and beyond those involved in day-to-day trading. For one, computers are simply not very reliable. The information inside them may disappear or become garbled without warning, and they are prone to virus infections or other kinds of malicious electronic attacks.

While there is little you can do to avoid bad design and hardware failure (apart from choosing products and suppliers wisely, as discussed in Chapter 7), you can do a lot to make sure that your systems and information are protected from other possible sources of trouble, which include those caused by technology, people, floods, storms, fires, and other acts of God.

## Dealing with computer theft

In major UK cities and 'high tech' areas, such as the Thames Valley, computer theft is now epidemic. Computers offer a guaranteed sale for thieves, especially systems that are Y2K ready (free of the Millennium bug), which are more or less stolen to order. Sometimes thieves strip down computers instead of taking them box and all, because processor chips are just as valuable as complete systems and are harder to trace. Not protecting your company from theft is not only foolhardy, it may also lead to much higher insurance premiums.

The main issues involved in dealing with theft are preventing access, making sure that even if access is gained, hardware is hard to strip down or remove, and marking property so that in the extremely unlikely event that it is found after a theft, it can be returned.

Preventing access depends very much on installing standard burglar-proofing fixtures: solid locks on all doors and windows, screens and bars across windows in unusually crime-prone areas, and perhaps even lockable metal door-covering plates to prevent violent access through any entrance. Local crime-prevention police officers will be able to advise here, and make suggestions based on their knowledge of crime patterns in the area. An alarm should be installed and linked to the local police station, and there should be a designated 'key holder' near the premises who can let the police in if the alarm goes off. Otherwise the police may have to wait outside while thieves have time to finish the job and get away. Professional thieves can make short work of many alarms – so, again, check with a crime prevention officer about the best make and model to buy.

Even if access is gained, it is possible to make it very hard for thieves to take away anything of value. **Cable systems**, **lock-down plates** and **cages** can be used to lock a computer to a desk or other immovable object. Professional thieves will find cable systems no deterrent whatsoever, although they will deter opportunist thieves. Cables can easily be cut, even with readily available equipment, and so this option is only really suitable for low-risk areas. Lock-down plates and cages offer a higher degree of protection, with the disadvantage that they also make it harder to get inside a computer for maintenance purposes, or move it from one location to another. Lock-down plates attach to the base of the computer and are screwed firmly into a desk. Cages go one stage further by covering some or all of a computer in a solid metal box, which again is screwed to a desk. Cages make it almost impossible to either get inside a computer or to take it away, but note that many cages are protected by combination locks, which again are a relatively minor problem for very experienced thieves. However, all these measures are as much about deterrence as absolute security, and any solution that makes it harder and more time-consuming for a thief is an advantage over nothing at all.

Property marking is another possible deterrent, but is unlikely to put off thieves who are after parts rather than systems. It is also fairly easy to strip the insides out of a PC and put them into a different case. This does not apply to Macs, because it is almost impossible to get hold of spare Mac cases, and so prominent marking is a good idea if you have a Mac. The simplest and cheapest marker system is the UV (ultraviolet) ink pen, which can be used to write post-codes or other information invisibly or outside a computer's case. When exposed to UV light the ink fluoresces and the information appears. Experienced thieves anticipate UV marking and have ways to get around it, but it can still be a useful and relatively cheap extra safeguard that will trap less professional criminals. More complex systems, such as the Kodit range of labelling products, offer custom labels with a UV backing, as well as a register of all marked products, so that if a product with a Kodit label appears it can be easily traced. In general, labelling is very much a last resort, and something of a gamble. However, the relatively low cost of labelling means that it can be worth the time and trouble, even if the chances of having any equipment returned to you after it has been stolen are extremely slim.

## Computer insurance

If you work from home, it would be unwise to assume that your domestic contents policy will cover any computer and other office equipment. Contents insurance policies vary in this respect. Some will include office equipment, others will include computer equipment provided it is not used for business purposes, while others set an upper limit on payments for single items, which is too low to cover the replacement of a computer system. The first step is to check your insurance policy to see where you stand.

If further cover is required, a number of insurers offer special 'home worker' or 'home business policies'. These include all of the standard business-insurance requirements and will typically cover non-specific office equipment, including computers, fax machines, photocopiers, etc., up to almost any amount against accidental damage and theft. You will be asked about security measures with these policies, or given the option of paying a sizeable excess, perhaps as much as £500, if your existing security measures are not adequate and you would prefer not to update them. Brokers with a commercial insurance division should be able to advise on these policies, although a selection of popular insurers is also listed in Appendix V.

Both home workers and larger businesses can also buy insurance cover for computer breakdowns and for consequential losses (money lost as a direct result of the failure or theft of your computer system). This kind of cover can be quite expensive, and premiums are usually calculated as a percentage of likely losses. It can be helpful to consider computer contingency plans, such as renting machines temporarily if there is a disaster, and making sure that safety copies of all information are kept off-site, as an alternative to these high premiums. In some cases contingency planning is simply impossible, but in others a little forethought can throw up surprisingly cost-effective alternatives. Policies are available from insurance brokers that have a commercial division, and may sometimes be offered as an option on existing commercial insurance that covers buildings and equipment.

# Avoiding hardware failure

Hardware sometimes fails, and there is little that can be done to avoid this. While computers may not be particularly reliable overall, failures and problems are usually irritating rather than fatal, and catastrophic loss of information is relatively rare. While it is impossible to guard against random equipment failure, computer hardware is prone to other sources of interference, the effects of which can easily be minimised.

## Power problems and solutions

One source of problems is power-line fluctuations. Even in cities, the mains supply is subject to power surges from lightning strikes or industrial machinery, and to sudden changes in voltage. Apart from affecting long-term reliability, power surges and 'spikes' can also be the cause of apparently random erratic behaviour. The power in rural areas is even less reliable, and power cuts or momentary disconnections are not uncommon in some parts of the country. The latter can be particularly damaging to computer equipment, especially if the power pulses on and off rapidly before failing. Apart from stressing hardware, it can also corrupt the information stored inside a computer. Lightning strikes can also affect telephone lines and modems. Even when introduced via a modem cable, lightning can thoroughly fry a computer's insides. It can also destroy the insides of any equipment attached to it. On a network this can be disastrous.

A cheap but only moderately effective way to address these problems is to buy two 'surge suppressors': one for the mains, and another for the telephone line. The surge suppressors make sure that spikes and power surges dissipate harmlessly before they reach the computer. They will prevent major disasters and the apparently random misbehaviour caused by spikes. However, they still leave the computer open to the problems caused by power failure.

Power failures can be avoided with the help of an Uninterruptible Power Supply (UPS). A UPS stops spikes and surges and smooths out supply fluctuations. It also contains rechargeable batteries that switch on automatically if the power fails. A very expensive UPS (costing £1,000 or more) can keep a large computer running for around an hour. More affordable models cost between £100 and £200 and provide a few minutes of power, which is enough time to shut down the computer properly and make sure that no information is lost.

A standard UPS is not very useful for computers that are left running unattended, such as servers. More sophisticated models are available for these, which come with a card or connector that plugs into a computer and monitors the state of the UPS. Special software turns the machine off safely and automatically if the power fails. Note that the screens draw far more power than computers themselves. The larger your screen the more hefty the UPS you will need. For example, a cheap UPS can provide around six minutes of power for a 21-in screen, but nearly an hour's worth when used with a 14-in screen.

## Fault-tolerant hardware

More expensive computers can be protected to some extent against certain kinds of hardware failure. Filing systems based on hard disks pose the most cause for concern because if the disks stop working, all the information disappears. Thankfully, some systems have been developed that are tolerant of disk problems. In practice this means that information is copied across multiple disk drives. If one disk fails the computer as a whole will keep working with all the information intact. In fact on some models the offending disk can be removed and replaced without even turning off the power (for more information see page 269). While these systems cost much more than normal desktop machines, they can be a worthwhile investment for applications where computer problems mean work stops completely.

## Avoiding software failure

As with hardware, computer software is not guaranteed to be stable or reliable. The best way to avoid software problems is simply to choose software very carefully indeed, although there are other sources of difficulty that also have to be guarded against.

**Viruses** are malicious software programs that are clever enough to install themselves either in a computer's filing system, or in documents on the system. Viruses are 'caught' by exposing the computer to information from outside. Floppy disks created on another computer and software copied from the Internet are the two most common sources of viruses. (It is not unheard of for computers to be sold with a virus already present, although this is mercifully rare.)

Viruses come in two types. **Boot viruses** copy themselves from computer to computer on floppy disks or CD-ROMs. **Macro viruses** hide in documents such as letters and spreadsheets. Their effects vary from the mildly entertaining to the catastrophic. The least toxic viruses print a silly message, often on a certain day in the year, or take over a word processor so that it adds spurious words every so often. More typically, viruses remove all the information in the computer's filing system. The information will be lost completely unless safety copies are available. The most lethal virus, which affects only PCs, is called CIH, and it reprograms the chip that starts a computer when it is first turned on. It will cripple a computer and render it completely useless, making expensive repairs essential.

There are two ways to guard against viruses. The first is to introduce a strict policy of not allowing floppy disks from outside the office anywhere near the office computers. A floppy lock – an item that bolts into a floppy-disk drive and makes it impossible to insert floppy disks – is one way to do this. Computers on a network may not need floppy disk drives at all, and so an even more effective approach is to remove the floppy-disk drive altogether. This can cause problems if the computer needs to be repaired, making a floppy lock a better choice for most applications.

For situations where a floppy lock is not practical, a **virus checker** is essential. This is a piece of software that finds and removes all known viruses. Because new viruses are being written all the time, checkers are often sold with a subscription for virus updates. New virus details are sent once or twice a year. When they are installed into the virus checker, it has all the information it needs to deal with them. The very best virus checker models cost around £100, and are essential for a busy office. Some models have a feature that allows the latest virus updates to be copied from the Internet. Some popular examples of virus checkers are Dr Solomon's, which is available in versions to suit all the most popular operating systems, and Norton's Anti-virus, which is supplied free with some computers.

**Trojan horses** are programs that claim to do one thing, but do something else. Many Trojans play on people's greed and gullibility. For example, a Trojan called AOL4FREE pretended to create free user accounts on the AOL on-line service by circumventing the usual AOL-billing system. In reality the Trojan wiped all the information inside a computer.

Trojans are a particular problem on the Internet, where web browsers often have security flaws that Trojans can exploit. These kinds of Trojans are started automatically by the browser, and there is very little that can be done about them. They masquerade as legitimate software that is used to create special effects on web pages. Browsers sometimes have an option that stops potential Trojans before they can do any damage, but not all Trojans can be spotted this way.

Fortunately, Trojan Internet attacks are still extremely rare. The only way to deal with them is to watch for security announcements from browser manufacturers, and to make sure that browser software is as up to date as possible.

**Email viruses** come in two types, the most common being hoaxes. The hoax appears in the form of a warning message that includes details of a purported virus. The virus is fictitious, but the message makes people panic and they forward it to others. In effect the virus is the message itself. *Standard Internet email software is totally immune to email viruses.* There is simply no way in which a virus can be transmitted by email if an email package is used to read it.

However, this is not true of the mail-reading facilities available in web browsers, or of the proprietary email systems used by on-line services. With these, the act of copying an attachment to your computer can, in rare cases, start up a malicious Trojan-like program. The solution here is simply to ignore all attachments from strangers.

Hoax virus warnings are harder to deal with. The best option is to alert staff to their existence to prevent them from wasting time and computer resources by forwarding warning messages unnecessarily. A number of web sites are available that discuss virus hoaxes and include details of the latest examples, and staff can be referred to these (for more details see Appendix V).

## Software maintenance

Viruses aside, simple maintenance can help prevent a computer's filing system from unravelling. Cheaper machines, and Windows PCs especially, are prone to problems that cause the filing system to gradually unravel itself, making the information it holds unreadable. If left unchecked this process may cause information to disappear altogether, and software may become corrupted, erratic or unusable, leading to more problems.

This can be avoided by regularly using a program called Scandisk, which checks for problems with the filing system and fixes them automatically. Using Scandisk repeatedly, at least once a week, can make a computer more reliable than it would be otherwise. Scandisk should also be used if a computer is turned off by accident without being shut down properly first, as this too can cause problems with the way that information is stored.

Once every six to twelve months a related tool called a Disk Defragmenter should be used. This tidies up all the information that has been filed away and can make the computer appear to work more quickly, because related information is grouped together and can be found more easily.

### PC precautions for more experienced users

Windows 95 and 98 machines suffer from problems with the **registry**, which is a collection of information the computer uses to keep track of installed hardware, software and other settings. If the registry becomes corrupted, the computer will refuse to start. This will often mean that all the software and information has to be reinstalled from scratch.

The registry is kept in two files: 'User.dat' and 'System.dat', which usually live in the Windows directory. Backup copies are kept in 'User.da0' and 'System.da0'. It can be *extremely* helpful to make safety copies of these files once a week. If there is a registry problem that Windows itself cannot fix, copying these files back into the Windows directory will sometimes save hours of wasted time.

Another convenient but very effective way to keep your information safe is to install a second hard-disk drive. A piece of software called DriveCopy from PQ Software makes it easy to create an exact and faithful copy of everything on your main hard-disk drive on the spare. If your main disk drive fails, you (or an engineer) can simply unplug it, plug in the spare, and continue with the minimum of disruption. This can be a cheap, quick but extremely practical way to minimise the chances of losing all your information.

## Keeping information safe

Even when precautions are taken, hardware and software are never 100 per cent reliable. It is also essential to guard against user error or even malicious tampering or removal of vital business records. The most important tool used for this is the safety copy, or **backup**. For a business, backups are not optional. This cannot be emphasised enough, because the consequences of not having them are so damaging. Most businesses that lose all their information are no longer trading six months later.

Backup facilities are not supplied as standard with most computers. They have to be bought, ordered and installed separately. A good consultant will include backup tools as a matter of course. Those doing their own buying need to be familiar with available options.

In outline, there are three kinds of backup systems. **Tapes** use tape cassettes, which are very loosely related to ordinary music cassettes. A huge range of different systems is available, distinguished by differing capacities, speeds and physical dimensions. Tape systems are described in more detail on page 288. The cheapest systems offer high capacities of about 4Gb for £200. However, cheap tape systems are slow and cumbersome, and are not always 100 per cent reliable. A full 4Gb backup can take up to seven hours.

**CD-based systems** use CD-related technologies. The music and software CDs with which everyone is familiar are fixed, but the computer world also offers two types of recordable CD systems. Write-once CDs can only be used once, and are rather expensive and impractical for backups. Rewritable CDs can be used again and again, and are suitable for low-volume backups. They can also be used with suitable hardware; normal computer CD-ROM drives may be unable to see the information they contain. The capacity of either system is 650Mb, significantly less than that of today's hard-disk drives, but still suitable for small one-off projects. (Rewritable CD backups were used for this book, although a cheap tape system was also used to provide a backup for the backup.)

The new **DVD-RAM system** works rather like a rewritable CD, but offers much higher capacities of around 4.7Gb, more than enough for most applications. DVD-RAM technology is only slightly more expensive than CD-writing systems, and offers the added advantage of being compatible with DVD video disks (this may be of questionable value in a business setting, but may be of interest to anyone who works from home). DVD-RAM systems currently cost around £350, but the extra flexibility and reliability of DVD makes it a very interesting, if not quite fully proven, new technology that may become a standard in the near future. One worry with DVD is that the disks may be more fragile than CDs, and so backups will need to be treated carefully, protected from dust, finger marks, scratches, sunshine, and temperature extremes.

Depending on the software being used, CD or DVD backup systems can either be very easy, or very hard to use. One of the best backup tools is Adaptec's DirectCD, which makes a CD writer appear to work just like another hard disk. Information can be copied to the writer using the standard copying tools, and read from it in the usual way. At the other extreme, Elektroson's Gear software makes the task seem rather more complex than it needs to be.

**Removable backup systems** use technology similar to that used in hard-disk filing systems, with the difference that the 'disk' and writing mechanism can be removed. They are usually rather expensive for regular backups, although they can be a useful way to archive relatively small amounts of information in a portable and easily accessible form. The largest removable system, the Iomega Jaz, has a capacity of 2Gb. Smaller systems with capacities of 100Mb are also available, although this is too little to provide backup facilities for any but the smallest projects.

**Backup software** is often supplied with backup hardware, although separate packages are also available at extra cost. Usually this software simply lists all the information in a computer, and gives the user a chance to select the information that is to be backed up. To replace the information a 'restore' facility is used, which works in the opposite direction. More advanced software can 'compress' unused and archived information so it takes up less filing space.

## Working with backups

Whatever hardware system you use, you will need to create a backup scheme that keeps both your information and your software safe. You will only change your software rarely, if ever, but information will change all the time. The ideal system will make it possible for you to recover both with equal ease. It will also minimise the number of tapes, blank CDs, DVDs, or other media you are using.

If there is very little software on your computer, perhaps just an operating system, an office suite, and one or two other tools, it can be easier to backup only your information, and simply reinstall everything else from scratch after a failure. You can then copy your information back into place in order to continue as before. The disadvantage of this approach is that you will probably lose your favourite software settings, but if you have not spent much time creating these to suit your own preferences, this may not be much of a loss.

The other alternative is to create a complete backup of absolutely everything inside your computer. This has the appeal of apparently providing complete security, but you should be aware that restoring everything from a backup can be an extremely time-consuming process. The following steps are involved:

- reinstalling the operating system (e.g. Windows 98)
- reinstalling the backup hardware to make sure that the operating system knows that it is available and working correctly. Other essential hardware may also need to be reinstalled manually, such as the screen and graphics card
- reinstalling the backup software
- creating an index of information on the tape (for certain tape systems only). This involves reading through the entire tape, which can take as long as four hours
- recovering all the information from the backup (a slow system can take another four hours to do this).

In total this can take anywhere between one and three days. The bottom line is that if you choose to backup everything, you may lose time and possibly money before you can start working again after a failure. If, on the other hand, you keep the amount of software on your computer to a minimum you will be able to recover from disasters much more quickly.

## Backup schedules

The frequency with which you need to perform backups depends on how often your information changes. At the very least you should have backups that ensure that you can reconstruct your business with minimal disruption. For some kinds of work weekly backups are adequate. For other kinds, daily backups are more appropriate. The 'perfect' backup, which guarantees no loss at all, may be impractical for reasons of time or cost, so backups become an exercise in damage limitation rather than damage avoidance.

Two kinds of backup are possible. **Full backups** simply copy everything to the backup system. **Incremental backups** copy everything that has changed since the last full backup, usually a significantly smaller amount of information. While this makes restoration even more complicated than described above (both full and incremental backups need to be restored separately) the overall amount of information that has to be handled is much less.

An almost infinite variety of backup schemes is possible. For example, a scheme that uses three tapes in rotation could work like this:

| | |
|---|---|
| Friday: | full backup |
| Monday to Thursday: | incremental backups on another tape |
| Friday: | full backup on a third tape. |

The wear on the tapes is distributed evenly by swapping them between weekly full-backup duties and daily incremental ones.

## Keeping backups safe

As the whole point of backups is to make sure that they can survive almost any disaster, backups themselves need to be treated with the utmost care. Backups have to survive fire, flood and other problems as well as ordinary computer failures. One way to ensure their safety is to keep backups at a remote location, preferably one within easy walking distance, but still far enough away to be considered safely remote. A fire at the office will not then destroy the backups as well.

Another alternative is to invest in a fireproof safe. This has the advantage of offering more convenient and also more secure access to the backups if they are needed, but can actually be less safe than the off-site option. Even the best fire-proof safes are unable to cope with fires that last for many hours, and it is possible that if a building collapses the safe will be buried and inaccessible under rubble.

## Emergency Data recovery

Even if a computer's filing system fails completely and there are no backups at all, it is still sometimes possible to recover the original information. This is an expensive process. It should only be considered as a last resort, and certainly not as an alternative to a reliable backup system. It is not guaranteed, and will only work under certain circumstances. However, for those situations where this is the only way forward, a selection of companies that offer this service can be found on the Web by searching for 'data recovery' AND 'UK'.

## Internal security and people skills

To get the best from your staff as well as your technology you need to do two things. The first is to create an environment in which people do not feel tyrannised about the way they have to use their computers, but are still very unlikely to waste time with them. The second is to make sure that no one abuses the system for criminal ends, such as reading co-workers' emails, or gaining access to company records that should be confidential.

Most of these issues only become a problem once a network, and particularly an Internet connection, have been installed. Networks can be very hard to manage and it is important to understand just what can go wrong.

## Staff time-wasting

Common time-wasting activities by staff include personal correspondence and gossip inside the organisation; personal correspondence and gossip outside the organisation; and well-intentioned but ignorant virus hoax warnings (see page 165). The latter can waste a lot of time if perpetrators forward the hoax to everyone with whom they work.

With web use, it can sometimes be hard to draw the line between useful research and idle browsing. Originally, on-line porn was the most popular kind of distraction. This made it easy to spot because, for most kinds of work at least, it was obviously not related to standard office activities. But news pages have now replaced porn as the major source of distraction, and this makes it harder for managers to assess whether or not time spent on the web is being used productively.

Since networks are primarily used to communicate, and since people enjoy communicating, it is unrealistic to demand that all communications should be strictly business only. A good rule of thumb is to allow people all the distractions they want, as long as they continue working to a reasonable professional standard and their activities are not illegal. A draconian policy of only allowing serious professional use is demeaning and authoritarian and is likely to be counterproductive in terms of office morale and perhaps lost productivity in the long run. At the other extreme, a totally open policy will encourage wasted resources and may slow work to a crawl.

An important aspect of the problem to consider is the potential cost of time-wasting activities. For example, private email and web surfing will cost a company significantly more if it uses a pay-as-you-go dial-up link to the Internet. Where there is a permanent connection and all usage charges are paid in advance, the problem is less pressing.

In general, deterrence is better than confrontation. For example, it is possible on some systems to keep a list of the web pages that employees are accessing. While this may be seen as an invasion of privacy, in practical terms the company is paying employees for their time and it is reasonable to expect that they offer a professional service in return. Often the mere suggestion that this kind of tracking is possible will be enough to make sure that excessive amounts of time are not wasted.

## Internal security

Security is as much a social issue as a practical or technical one. Some security problems are a direct result of business hostilities. Information that is valuable to a business may also be valuable to competitors, or to disgruntled employees. The removal or sabotage of that information may also be valuable to a competitor. Other problems are caused by the electronic equivalent of joyriding, a random sort of malice, which is nonetheless annoying and perhaps fatal for a business. More serious security issues include:

**Spam and other kinds of unsolicited outside mail** While only an annoyance to individuals, spam can become a serious drain on resources once it starts infiltrating a business. The unwanted mail has to be forwarded along the company network where it can take up disk space and use computer power that could be put to more constructive uses.

**Use of company resources for illegal activities** Chief among these are reading or distributing Internet porn and advertising pyramid schemes. Companies with permanent Internet connections are particularly vulnerable to these kinds of activities. Without adequate security, computer-literate users may find it easy to create non-existent user accounts, which can be used to abet illegal activities with relative impunity.

**Hacking attacks from outside** Hackers may decide to 'joyride' into a commercial system just to prove they can. Less often, they will target a company or organisation if the organisation has annoyed them in some way. (For example the web site of the film *Hackers* was electronically defaced because the hacking community was indignant about the way that hackers were portrayed.) In either case, solid security is essential. More worrying, hackers can use a company's computers as a warehouse for illegal information and make it look as if the company, not the hacker, is responsible for the appearance of the information.

**Hacking attacks from inside and internal security** Computer-savvy employees may sometimes be able to intercept private email, and disgruntled ex-employees may hold a company hostage, threatening to destroy all their records if their demands are not met.

**Real virus problems** If a server becomes infected with a virus, it can spread the virus across a network very quickly. A particularly aggressive virus (such as the CIH strain) can then destroy all of a company's PCs at a stroke on the date that it activates itself.

**Abuse of personal data** Where a computer system holds records of private individuals, some employees may find it tempting to view those records out of curiosity, or perhaps with a more serious ulterior motive.

Internet security is a subject that requires an expert. The issues are too complex to cover here, although security is discussed in slightly more detail on pages 179 and 238.

Network security in general requires formal security-oriented policies. These include making sure that:

- all passwords are secure and intelligently chosen. The most effective passwords combine two random words with a random number – for example, 'apple6742guido'. Passwords should *never* be the names of friends, spouses, hobbies, interests, children, or anything else of personal significance, which can be guessed by an outsider

- passwords are never written down, and certainly not kept on sticky notes or written in pencil on the underside of a desk
- staff are aware of who is and is not authorised to know passwords, and some form of formal identification is required. (A common network hacking ploy is impersonation, where the hacker phones someone who knows the password and pretends to be a trusted employee.)
- all security features on the network are being used as fully as possible. A formal security assessment has taken place and users are grouped according to the level of access they are granted to the network
- spam is 'trapped' as soon as possible. Spam filtering software is widely available on the Internet, and this should be installed and used.

Chapter 11

# Business and the Internet

The Internet is a worldwide public-access network, and it can, in theory, be used for anything for which a smaller network can be used. In practice, Internet technology is still fairly crude, and this limits what is possible. However, even the simple tools that it provides today can completely transform the way a business operates.

The Internet makes it possible for a small company to trade globally. Millions of people use the Internet every day, and their numbers are growing steadily. By late 1998 there were an estimated 75 million Internet users, with the number doubling every year. Nearly half of all US households now have a computer, and around 80 per cent of those use it for Internet access. As a result, trading on-line puts a business in touch with millions of potential customers, many of whom are more affluent and have more disposable income than the rest of the population.

The Internet can also be used to provide information for existing customers. Price lists, special offers and other information can be distributed electronically much more cheaply and conveniently than an equivalent mail shot. Information can also be placed in an 'electronic shop window' where casual passers-by will see it, and perhaps respond with interest.

However, the Internet can also be used as a constantly updated library of facts and figures. Some of this information is only available for a small fee, but much of it is completely free. Many magazines now supply some or all of their back issues 'on-line' (on the Internet), often with extra stories and background details that have never appeared in print. Similarly, many companies now have their own collections of useful information, including product details, contact addresses and price lists.

Two things distinguish the Internet from traditionally published information sources. The first is that many people compile and maintain useful libraries of information purely on a voluntary basis. This means the amount of information available, and the range of subjects covered, is almost unimaginably vast. Whatever your personal or professional interests, someone on the Internet will also be interested in them, and there is an excellent chance that there is a body of relevant information that you can explore for free.

The other difference is that the Internet fosters 'communities of interest'. One example of this is the tens of thousands of discussion areas on the Internet, where people can meet and debate issues, offer each other help and support, or simply argue mercilessly and pointlessly with all comers. Questions, comments and answers can be exchanged almost immediately. Archives are frequently kept, so that answers to frequently asked questions can be found immediately. These 'communities' can be very useful in a business setting. They can provide a source of new information or ideas for business development, and they can even be used to provide technical help and support.

Many people are still put off by the fact that the Internet is associated with computers, and computers are still seen (with some reason) as difficult to use and understand. However, over the next ten years or so the Internet will become as important and widely used as the telephone, radio and television, perhaps even more so, as it is likely to absorb all of these into a 'super medium' that can be used to exchange any kind of information. Current speed restrictions will disappear, and it will become possible to send and receive live video over the Internet from literally anywhere in the world. New products and services will appear and the business world is likely to be transformed as a result. Any business that may be able to benefit from the Internet will be able to give itself a head start by looking into the possibilities immediately.

Current Internet facilities are rather more basic. Email, newsgroups, the World Wide Web and the less widely used Internet tools, such as group chat facilities (see page 183) can be used in four main ways: for communication, research, promotion and electronic trading. The latter two involve actively placing your company on to the Internet and are discussed in Chapter 12.

## Communication

The most popular Internet communication tool is electronic mail, usually known as email. Many Internet users only have access to email facilities, which means that this is the only way they can be contacted as potential customers. Less popular forms of communication include newsgroups and Internet chat. Computer Telephony Integration (CTI) is a 'next-generation' set of tools that is not yet fully developed in an affordable form, but will start to become available to small businesses within a few years.

## Email

The Internet's email facilities are very similar to those available on a computer network. The difference is that Internet email can be used to send a message to anyone with an email address – currently tens of millions of people.

In general, email facilities can speed communications between staff when they are away from the office, create more effective communications with other businesses, and make a company seem much friendlier and more approachable to the public. It is important to note that email is a more informal medium than the conventional post. Indeed, on the Internet people tend to 'tell it like it is' rather than hiding behind formality and excessive politeness. While this can be a culture shock for the more conservatively minded, it does sometimes make communications clearer and more direct.

For most messages a next-day reply is adequate. If the flow of Internet email coming into a business is large it may be worth dedicating an employee to the task of dealing with them. Note that *not answering email queries creates a very bad impression*. If a telephone call is not returned, most people simply assume someone was too busy to deal with it and will, in all likelihood, call again about something urgent. An email takes longer to create than a phone call, and demands more attention. If it is not answered promptly it can reflect badly on a company. Moreover, because of the way information moves quickly on the Internet, this can sometimes do significant damage to a company's reputation. Internet email can be used for:

- general communications with employees when they are out on the road, or away at meetings or conferences
- sending job assignments and completed work to and from the office when people are working from home, or in the field
- receiving sales orders and queries from the public, and sending back suitable replies
- receiving candid feedback and suggestions from customers
- creating automated mail-shots: for example, news about new products and services or special offers
- creating an on-line community of users who can exchange messages as a group and perhaps answer each others' questions, or simply gossip
- making contact and perhaps negotiating with new suppliers
- keeping in touch with competitors and business allies around the world.

## Email drawbacks

The Internet's email systems are more limited than those available from an internal network, which causes its main drawback: sporadic lack of reliability. Most messages are transmitted very quickly, but occasionally they can take a couple of hours to get to their destination. And sometimes, for any number of technical reasons, they simply disappear without trace. This happens very rarely, but when it does the intended recipient will not usually get an indication that something has gone wrong. As a result, it is best not to rely on email for communications that are exceptionally important or urgent.

### Email and non-text information

For practical reasons to do with the compatibility (or lack of it) between all the different kinds of computers on the Internet, email tends to use the simplest technology possible. Most messages are sent as plain text with no page layout information, no colour definitions or special letter sizes, no underlining or italics, and no images or photographs.

More complex information can only be sent as an *attachment*. With most email software, adding an attachment is a fairly simple process – you simply click on an 'Add an attachment' or 'insert' button on the screen, select the piece of information you want to send, and off it goes. Sounds, photographs and even video clips can be sent in this way. Technically, attachments are sent by converting them into long streams of gibberish letter-and-number code, because this is the only way that the Internet can transmit this kind of information. It will be converted back into a sound, photograph, etc. when it reaches the recipient.

Email attachments can cause problems at the receiving end. The first problem is that attachments create extremely large messages. As an example, someone who is reading email on a palmtop computer (which has limited capabilities) will be less than pleased if they are sent a large and detailed colour picture, or, worse still, a video clip. The palmtop will struggle to deal with it. The recipients may even be unable to read any other email until they call their Internet service company and ask for the offending message to be removed.

Another problem is that the Internet itself may not be able to cope with large attachments. Some of the behind-the-scenes computers that distribute email have limits on the amount of information they can work with in one go. Mail will either not arrive, or it may not be possible to send in the first place, or it will 'bounce', which means it will be marked as undeliverable and returned to the sender.

Finally, on older text-only computers, attachments may be useless, as there will be no facilities for converting the computer gibberish back into useful information. All that the recipient will see is the gibberish itself – and there can be many pages of it.

As a result, a rule of thumb for dealing with attachments is to *never send an attachment unless you know the recipient can read it*. This may mean checking with them before an attachment is sent.

### Email security

Internet email is not secure. It suffers from three potential problems:

**Interception** means that third parties can read the email without permission. This takes a fair amount of special equipment and computer skill, but, of course, information on how to do this is readily available on-line. For sensitive communications it is useful to assume that email *will* be read unless it is protected in some way, ideally with a secret code (see page 180).

**Deletion** is where a message is simply removed, so that the intended recipient never receives it. This is harder to do than interception, but is still technically possible.

**Forgery** is used to create emails that look like they come from someone other than the true sender. Simple forgeries, where a sender gives a false email return address are very straightforward indeed and can easily fool someone who is not an expert. Very complex and convincing forgeries are possible, but again require better equipment and more advanced skills.

The two tools used to deal with these problems are encryption and digital signatures.

## Encryption

Encryption simply means that messages are sent using a secret code. The most secure system currently available is called **PGP** (Pretty Good Privacy) and creates a code that theoretically cannot be cracked with today's computer systems. It means that the calculations required to gain access would take even the fastest of today's computers longer than the lifetime of the Universe.

To use PGP you first create two very long numbers, which are known as *keys*. One of these is the **public key**, which you can make known to anyone who wants to send you a message. The other is the **private key**, which should be known only to you.

If someone wants to send you a secure message they use your public key to convert it into gibberish, and then send it to you. The clever part of PGP is that only the private key can unlock the message. This may appear illogical, but the system works because the two keys are mathematically related in a complex way. Even if someone has your public key they cannot use it to read the message, and as long as your private key is kept safe any message sent to you will be secure.

If you want to send a secure reply, you use the other person's public key to convert it into code, and they can then use their private key, which no one else knows, not even you, to read it.

This two-key system solves the problem of how to make sure that keys are kept private. With a single-key system you could – in theory – send it to someone written out on paper, on a floppy disk, or by email, any of which could be intercepted. With PGP, as long as private keys are kept private, the system will be secure.

PGP is available here in the UK from many software dealers, and is also available as shareware (see Chapter 2) directly from software libraries on the Internet. It can be slightly cumbersome to use, but the latest versions attempt to work as seamlessly as possible with popular email software. Commercial versions of PGP include useful enhancements such as **key rings**, which make it easier to manage the PGP keys of people to which you regularly send messages. These PGPs also include **key servers**, which are computers that are permanently available on the Internet to provide you with someone's public key if you know their email address (it may not always be convenient or practical to ask for a key). In practice, people who use PGP often include their public key at the end of email messages.

## *Digital signatures*
A more complex variant of the two-key system makes it possible to check that a sender is who they really claim to be. This works as follows: person A writes a message, encodes it with their private key, and then encodes it again with public key of the intended recipient, person B. When person B receives the message, they decode it with their private key and then with person A's public key. If the result makes sense, they can be sure that A is really the sender. (Again, this curious result is possible because of the mathematics involved.) Encoding and decoding complete messages twice is wasteful, so some messages are sent with a signature − a simple message that says in effect 'Yes, I am who I say I am.' The signature may include a name and address or some other information. This simple message is encoded twice. To save time, the rest of the message can then be encoded once in the usual way.

The UK government is currently considering proposals for a **key escrow** system. This would mean that a list of all the keys would be kept by a trusted third party who would make them available, under special circumstances, to the government, and hence the police and other security services. The theory is the messages remain secure, but the government has a 'back door' through which it would be able to read private personal and business messages. While fine in theory, in practice key escrow is not foolproof. The major unanswered question is, what happens if hackers gain access to the list of all the keys?

## **Mailing lists**
Usually email goes from one person to another or perhaps from one person to a group. A mailing list makes it possible for everyone in a group to exchange email with everyone else in a group. On the

Internet, mailing lists are a popular choice for closed discussion groups, within which one person – the *moderator* – has final say over who is allowed to join the discussion, and whether or not any particular comment is appropriate to the list and can be safely sent to everyone else.

For a business, setting up a mailing list can be a good way to build a community of customers who exchange help and other information. This perhaps works best when customers are private individuals rather than other businesses, because a large part of the appeal of a list is its chattiness.

Mailing lists have been used successfully for technical support. Seagate, a company that manufactures hard disks and related products, has a very successful mailing list for customers who want to discuss its products. Other possible uses of mailing lists remain unexplored. An adventure holiday company could easily use a mailing list to create a way for customers to swap travel stories with each other, and perhaps entice in new business by allowing outsiders to read the stories. Since a mailing list uses minimal resources, it can be a cost-effective way to find new business wherever there is a community of interest among potential or actual customers.

Setting up a mailing list in practice is fairly easy. It is possible to run a list using a modem-based Internet connection and ordinary email software, but this is time-consuming, expensive and cumbersome. A better approach is to ask an ISP to set up the list for you, and many will do this if asked. If you have a permanent connection to the Internet you can create a list (in fact, any number of lists) by installing mailing list software on your server. A program called Majordomo is a popular choice, and is available for free. ListServ and ListProc are commercial equivalents that work on a wider range of computers, but are perhaps harder to set up. Setting up any of these systems requires specialist skills and is unlikely to be practical for a beginner, but it should present no problems to a network manager or other network-literate employee.

## Autoresponders

Autoresponders are computer-generated email messages that are sent out automatically when someone sends a message to a specific address. Autoresponders are frequently used to send out useful information to customer queries, such as a list of current special offers. They have to be used carefully, and making them the default reply to messages for your company is as unfriendly as leaving the answering machine on all the time. A better approach is to create special email addresses, which customers can query if they want specific information. For example the Demon ISP uses an autoresponder to send out information about frequently asked technical support questions. Some business-oriented ISPs offer an autoresponder as part of an inclusive business package (see page 210).

## Live chat

Two types of live chat appear on the Internet. **Chat rooms** allow groups of people to chat simultaneously, as if they were in the same room together. Some systems include 'operator' facilities, to remove people from a room, or 'gag' them if they become disruptive. One-to-one chat is used for private messages between two people. Live chat differs from other Internet facilities in that there are a number of different systems, none of which are compatible with each other. These include:

**AOL chat** (also known as 'instant messaging') is based on AOL's own internal live chat system, but has been modified to work on the Internet. It is supplied with the Netscape Communicator browser.

**IRC (Internet Relay Chat)** is the original Internet chat system. It is cruder than the others, and harder to use.

**ICQ** (not an acronym but 'I seek you') is a very popular Internet chat system that is easier to use than IRC. It is very similar to AOL chat, and offers many of the same features.

**NetMeeting** is a Microsoft product, and is built into Windows. It provides chat facilities for individuals or groups, a shared 'white board' that participants can draw on, and the ability to share sound and video if the participants are connected to the Internet with a sufficiently fast connection (telephone connections will not usually be fast enough). NetMeeting will also work on a company network.

**Web-based chat** uses web technology to create a chat-room, and can be added to any web site. It is usually much slower and more cumbersome than the real thing. For example, in a normal chat room, comments appear automatically. The web-chat equivalent may force users to keep clicking on an 'update' button on the screen to see the latest comments.

### Uses of Live Chat

Live chat is occasionally useful as a community-building tool, but in general its business applications are limited. Its main drawback is that most people type relatively slowly, and this makes it a very cumbersome way to communicate. AOL uses it for live technical support, and other companies have experimented with using it as a way of providing live answers to questions, for example, a visitor to a web site can ask sales staff for more information about products and services. In theory it should become easier to close a sale this way, but in practice the slowness of live chat, and the fact that it is labour-intensive, makes this a very awkward way to do business.

## Internet telephony and video

Larger companies have discovered that a permanent Internet connection can be used for telephone traffic as well as computer information. Currently, in most offices, telephone and computer information are handled separately, with different equipment, different cables, and perhaps even different departments in charge. It has recently become possible to create a company network that uses only one set of cabling for voice, fax, computer data and perhaps even video traffic. Telephone handsets plug into the network by way of special adaptors. Calls to and from the rest of the world can be made over the Internet and, if necessary, connected automatically to a telephone exchange at the other end of the call. This can lead to huge savings, as calls abroad become almost free.

Unfortunately, the cost and complexity required for this kind of super-network is prohibitive for smaller businesses. The hardware and software costs themselves are relatively modest, but consultants who have the skills and knowledge to create a reliable network are very expensive indeed. This is likely to change soon, and by around 2005 these kinds of networks, built with cheap off-the-shelf parts that can be linked together without any special computer skills, will start to become the norm for both businesses and homes.

In the meantime, Internet telephony, known as IPVoice, is still in its infancy, but experimental systems are starting to become available. Some US companies now sell products that will connect an ordinary desktop PC to a phone anywhere in the world. Connection costs are still paid by the minute, but at vastly reduced rates compared to standard charges, especially for calls abroad. One company, Net2Phone, has a number of UK agents, including Uninet (*http://www.uninet.co.uk*). Net2Phone makes it possible to call US toll-free numbers for the cost of a UK local call.

Related products allow two computer users to talk to each other through microphones and speakers or headphones over the Internet. Both people need to be able to use the same software, and there is, as yet, no incoming 'ring' signal unless they stay connected to the Internet all the time. Another problem is that sound quality is very poor. However, for non-critical conversations this system can be a good way to save money on international calls.

A related product idea is **on-line video**. This makes it possible for two people to see as well as hear each other. Small cameras are available that can sit on top of a screen and produce live video. The image is small and its quality poor. For business use there are currently few compelling reasons to use on-line video, although once connection speeds improve it may start to become popular.

Products come and go in these areas. The best way to find the latest information is to use the web to find out about 'Internet telephony' or 'Internet video'.

## Getting information from the Internet

There are three main sources of information on-line: the World Wide Web, pre-packaged 'content' from an on-line service, and newsgroups. A fourth source is the less popular and slightly more obscure service known as FTP (File Transfer Protocol).

There is, of course, no guarantee that a given piece of information will be available on the Internet. Computer-related subjects are grossly over-represented, as are other kinds of technology and science. Business-related news and commentary are plentiful, although much of it is US-centred. The arts and humanities are less well represented, although plenty of information about popular culture and various classics can be found. Company advertising and product information is easily accessible in the computer field, but less widespread elsewhere. However, most business 'household names' have collections of relevant information that can be examined, and the number of companies and other organisations that have a contact point on-line is increasing steadily.

After an initial spurt of interest in the Internet in 1994–1995, there was a backlash, which meant that information that appeared originally was not regularly updated. Since about 1998 this has changed, and now that the initial idealism has worn off, the information available on-line is becoming less gimmicky and more useful. The main sources of Internet information can be used to:

- get help and technical support from experts or other people with similar questions or problems
- find solutions to frequently asked questions about many topics
- find out details of products, services and prices
- track down hard-to-find books
- find 'how to' information that is related to various skills and trades
- check for specific information, for example share prices, company details from Companies House, consumer news
- catch the latest news and weather before they appear in the newspapers, and sometimes before TV and radio
- find background information about almost any human activity, both professional and personal
- find contact information for professional organisations
- find specialised sources of news that are not readily available elsewhere, such as news for small businesses, or science news
- explore libraries of useful facts and other records, for example collections of art or music, biographies of famous people, background information about films and television programmes
- copy new software to your computer.

### CASE HISTORY: Peter

Peter Nelson is a farmer based in Wiltshire, who found the Internet had some unexpected uses for him.

'We got it for our daughter, really, to help with school. We already had a computer, which I use for the usual business things and also to keep track of our dairy herd, using software that's been specially written for farmers. I did some research to find out what it would cost, and discovered it was only fifty quid for a modem, so that was that – she got the modem and a connection to AOL as a Christmas present in 1997. Since then she's spent a lot of time on it, too much in fact.

'Anyway, for me, I first got interested when I found out there were weather forecasts on there. You can listen to the radio, but it's not always that detailed. It's much more useful to get things that are aimed specifically at farmers. I think what really did it was discovering that *Farmers' Weekly* has a web site, with the latest market prices and some commentary about trends, proper weather forecasts, farming news, job offers, and classifieds – more information than most people want, really.

'The problem was that I soon realised that it would take too long to read the whole thing every day, and the phone bills do start to mount up. So now I ration myself to the basics during the week, and sometimes do heavier browsing at weekends when it's cheaper.

'The rest of the Internet? Well, I can't say I've explored it much. My wife has discovered some long lost friends with email and they've been sending messages back and forth. I've looked at all the web sites that get listed in the mags – like the Electronic Telegraph and the BBC news pages – and once in a while I'll buy one of the net mags to see if there's anything interesting in there. But I think it's way too slow for general browsing. I get bored waiting for things to appear, and usually there are better things I could be doing anyway. I suppose if it was faster I might be more interested.'

## The World Wide Web

The web is rather like an almost unimaginably vast number of books, brochures, magazines, and shop windows, written by millions of different authors and loosely cross-linked by subject matter.

In practice it is made up of **web sites**, which are collections of **web pages**. Each page can contain text and pictures, and perhaps optional extras like sound and music. Every single web page – and there are tens of millions of them – has a unique address called a Uniform Resource Locator (URL). Typing the URL into a web browser will display that page. Pages can also be **bookmarked** so they can be found again quickly.

What makes the web unique is that each word or image can 'link' to a different page. To 'follow' a link the user simply clicks on it with the mouse. The new page then appears, and of course this can have links of its own that lead elsewhere. When done casually, **'surfing' the web** is rather like following a train of thought. It is easy to drift from one set of information to another by following links out of curiosity to see where they lead.

There are no limits set on who can and cannot contribute to the web. This means anyone at all can create a web site, and the existence of cheap and simple site-creation software has meant that there are now countless sites available. You can, of course, advertise your own business on the web, although, as mentioned in the next chapter, doing this successfully requires an overall strategy and some extra forethought that more casual web contributors do not need to consider.

### Finding specific information on the web

Good places to start looking for specific information are special sites known as **search engines.** These index and list as many other sites as they can, and make it easier to find specific information. The two ways to search are keyword searching and index searching.

**Keyword searches** look for occurrences of a given word. For example, typing in 'Apple' will produce a partial list of every site that mentions the word 'Apple' anywhere. The full list for a popular word will contain hundreds of thousands, or perhaps even millions of matches (these are known as 'hits'). To narrow the search it helps to use specific phrases or combinations of words, for example 'apple pest control' or 'apple AND pest AND control'. 'And' and 'or' can be included to make searches either more or less specific. Hits are shown as links, with a brief introductory sentence and related information, such as the time and date that information was created.

Some keyword search facilities include attempts to understand questions written in plain English, for example 'Tell me how to do my accounts.' It is fair to say that these systems need further development. Computers are really very bad at understanding English and the results of a 'natural language search' like this are likely to be unexpected and quirky.

Related facilities are the 'natural language translations'. The Alta Vista search engine (at *http://www.altavista.com*) will attempt to translate web pages into different languages, making it possible, in theory at least, for English-speakers to make sense of pages written in German, French, Italian and so on. In practice the translations are very poor (sometimes to the point of being unintentionally entertaining), but they provide some idea of what foreign-language sites contain.

**Indexed searches** are more like looking for a book in a library. They divide sites up into categories, then sub-categories, then sub-sub-categories, and so on. For example, the 'science' category includes sub-categories about physics, chemistry, astronomy, etc. The astronomy sub-category is further divided up into optical astronomy, radio astronomy, and cosmology, while optical astronomy will include details of star catalogues, telescope designs, practical hints and tips, and telescope manufacturers. By working down through the different categorisations it is easy to find a list of sites devoted to a specific subject.

## Portals

Search engines pay for themselves by selling advertising. The more visitors they get, the more advertising revenue they attract. In reality it is very hard to make money like this, and most sites run at a significant loss. However, in defiance of conventional business logic, search engines continue to flourish.

During 1998 many search engines decided to reinvent themselves as *portals*. These are supposed to provide such a compelling jumping-off point for Internet exploration that visitors return again and again, and even set the 'default page' on their web browsers to take them to a portal automatically. To this end, portals include extra features, such as:

- free email addresses, which use a clumsy web-based email system that is very cumbersome compared to the real thing
- news and other topical information
- background information for areas of specialist interest, such as business news.

In practice, portals seem to be an advertising gimmick that does not offer much to most businesses. There are exceptions to this: for example, the Lycos portal includes a collection of web links and news for small businesses. In general, however, it is likely that portals are only a temporary feature on the Internet landscape, and will soon be replaced by yet another fad intended to produce advertising revenue.

## Using an on-line service for research

While there is a huge amount of information available on-line, even with the help of search engines it can be difficult to find it. On-line services try to solve this problem by 'predigesting' information from a number of sources, and presenting it in an accessible form.

Simple examples are the weather reports. There are countless sources of weather information on the World Wide Web, but many are designed for scientists or academics, or concentrate solely on weather in the US. For a novice British user, it can take a while to find a UK forecast.

In contrast, an on-line service such as AOL simply has a button on its main screen that says 'weather'. Clicking on it produces weather summaries for the different regions of the UK, with forecasts and a satellite image. There are also discussion areas for weather where people share their weather-related experiences or debate weather-related topics. The information is easy to find and immediately useful.

More obscure information is available 'behind the scenes'. Recently AOL and CompuServe have started to become more aggressive about this aspect of their work, and now offer information that is not available elsewhere, such as a complete searchable version of the *New Oxford Dictionary*. However, most of the information they provide is still the kind that would once have been offered by magazines: lifestyle features, popular medical questions and answers, useful background details for different professions, etc. These are arranged into themed 'areas', which often include links to the World Wide Web that have been investigated and found to be relevant. Areas can be found by using a keyword search facility, or by looking through a complete listing.

Some businesses will find that on-line services provide an invaluable resource, because they make the information they need accessible very quickly and easily. Nevertheless, it is worth pointing out that there is far more information available on the Internet itself, both in terms of subject matter and detail.

## Newsgroups

Newsgroups are a problematic source of information. At best they can provide near-miraculous help and an answer to almost any question. At worst they are a time-wasting source of pointless hostility and personal aggravation from complete strangers. The public newsgroup network is called Usenet, and has tens of thousands of discussion areas, all of which are open to everyone with an Internet connection. Most are *unmoderated*. No one reads or vets contributions or has the power to remove disruptive contributors. This means that anything goes, and in general the level of discussion in many groups is rather poor, often with more juvenile name-calling than useful information.

Because of the way that Usenet works, only very large companies, such as Microsoft, are able to set up newsgroups devoted to their own products. In general, Usenet has a strong non-commercial ethic. The advertising of goods and services is frowned upon and is usually the sole preserve of the insensitive, the desperate and the ignorant. Collectively these are known as 'spammers' because they send the same information to thousands of newsgroups irrespective of its relevance to the group. (The name 'spammers' originates from the Monty Python sketch about spam with everything.)

As a result, the newsgroup system is of limited interest to most businesses. The only exceptions to this are situations where newsgroups can provide help and support. For example, a group may be read by hundreds of telecom experts, and, if asked politely, they will provide help and advice about competing telephone companies, their pricing structures, etc. Experts contribute to these groups because they enjoy the discussions, and not because they are under any obligation to do so, and genuinely stupid questions often get a rude response. With that in mind, however, it is possible to use their knowledge to advantage by asking questions in public and reading their responses.

The two main problems with newsgroups are finding good ones, and using them correctly in a way that maximises the chances of getting useful answers.

## Finding useful newsgroups

There are currently more than 50,000 newsgroups, although for technical reasons, coverage of some groups is patchy, and not all are available to everyone. The first step to finding a worthwhile group is to understand how their names are organised (see Appendix IV for full details), but in general groups are arranged in categories, sub-categories, and an indefinite number of sub-sub-categories, each separated by dots. For example, the 'uk.category' consists of a number of UK-related groups, 'uk.business' is a sub-grouping devoted to business topics, and 'uk.business.telework' is a group for teleworkers. Similarly, 'uk.jobs.offered' is a UK-based group containing job offers.

Some group names are hopelessly obscure (such as clb.30.c) and these can be safely ignored, as can names in foreign languages. The ones that are left can be searched for a given word. For example, someone looking for information about teleworking would search for 'telework' and find the group mentioned above. Note that computers are extremely literal and lack any kind of initiative or intelligence. A search for 'teleworking' would not find anything, but a search for 'tele' would, even though it is not a proper English word. It is a good idea to be somewhat lateral when using these kinds of search facilities. Anyone looking for a group about hi-fi should also search for 'audio' and perhaps 'music', and even the names of some popular hi-fi products.

Once a likely group has been found, the next step is to see whether it contains anything of value. The Deja News service on the web archives messages that have been contributed ('posted') to a wide range of newsgroups. These can be scanned in summary and individually to see to what extent the group contains useful information or 'noise' (people arguing with each other).

If the content looks worthwhile (or the group is not carried by Deja News and the content cannot be scanned) the way to read current messages is to *subscribe* to the group. Different software does this in different ways (for more details see the documentation with your news software), but the effect will be to send a stream of the most recent messages from the group to your computer.

## Using newsgroups

Newsgroups work rather like a larger and more complex version of a mailing list. A message posted by one person will be seen by everyone who reads that group. Similarly anyone can post a reply, either to the group or directly to you via email (or both). If you find a noise-free group and ask a question, you should get an answer very quickly – perhaps within the hour, probably within a day or two, and almost certainly within the week.

However, many groups are fiercely political places, and newcomers may be treated with scorn and suspicion. This is not true of all groups, but it is a problem that seems to afflict many. To avoid being labelled a 'newbie' it can be helpful to watch for a while to see who has something useful to say, and who does not. Some groups maintain a useful document called an *FAQ* (Frequently Asked Questions). This contains a list of common questions and answers, compiled so that regulars do not have to keep repeating themselves. FAQs are posted regularly – daily, weekly or fortnightly – to groups that have them or made available on the web. They will often contain useful information.

If the FAQ does not answer your question, the archive might. If the group is carried on Deja News, it can be worth using its keyword search facilities to see if the question has been discussed already. If you draw a blank with Deja News, and the FAQ is either non-existent or does not answer the question, then it is time to post the question to the group and see what responses appear.

Newsgroup information is offered informally and not guaranteed in any way. So even if suitable replies are received, there is no guarantee they are correct. However, for many subjects the replies received can be very useful, or will at least provide a good starting point for further research.

## File Transfer Protocol (FTP)

File Transfer Protocol (FTP) is used to copy information from one computer on the Internet to the other. It works in much the same way as copying information into your computer from a floppy disk or CD-ROM, with the difference that it is very much slower. Web browsers have built-in FTP facilities, and these are by far the easiest way to work with FTP. To use them all you have to do is 'click and copy': select the information you want, select where in your machine you want it to be copied, and click on the 'OK' button. Specialised FTP software is available on the Internet itself but it is rather more complex than perhaps it needs to be. It is unlikely to be worth experimenting unless you are looking for advanced FTP facilities, such as the ability to copy information that is not available to the general public.

## Getting your business on-line

Businesses have a range of different ways they can connect to the Internet, as well as a selection of Internet-related services that can help with self-promotion (see page 107), or make an Internet connection more productive. The simplest connections are really designed for home use (see page 27), although they can be used by a business that only uses the Internet sporadically. For more serious use a permanent connection is required (see below). This is, however, a considerably more expensive option. A good compromise is the *hosted* option, where information is sent via a third party that has a permanent connection. This can make it look as if a company has an expensive full-time Internet presence when really it only has a much cheaper telephone connection.

### Simple domestic connections

Domestic connections are widely advertised, and generally affordable. They create a temporary telephone link (known as a **dial-up connection**) using an installed modem and either a standard telephone line or ISDN (Integrated Services Digital Network), which provides email, newsgroup and web-surfing facilities. Almost all domestic connections also include *web space* – the facility to create your own web site, which can be seen by anyone who uses the Internet. Domestic connections are available from On-line Services, Internet Service Providers (ISPs) and Combined Services. Each of these has different strengths and weaknesses. (See also page 27.)

### On-line services

On-line services are an excellent choice for beginners, casual Internet users, dedicated computerphobes, and anyone who wants to do a little exploring to see if the Internet might be for them. The main on-line services offer free trials – usually available for the asking, and often given away on computer magazine cover disks. They last a month and give plenty of time in which to evaluate a service. Note that when you make use of one of these offers, you are effectively signing up for the full service, but your first monthly payment is waived. *If you do not cancel the subscription at the end of the month, you will continue to be billed, even if you never use the service again.*

The disadvantages become obvious with more serious use. Spam (unwanted junk email and postings to newsgroups) is a perennial problem, because spammers can easily 'harvest' the names of people who use an on-line service from a variety of sources. Mailboxes soon fill up with rubbish, much of it advertising for pornographic web sites or on-line scams. The software provided by on-line services also lacks features that are useful in a business setting. Email may have superficially attractive extras, such as the ability to use large letters or coloured text, but lacks more productive facilities, such as the option to 'filter' messages into different mailboxes according to sender or message content. Reading your email when abroad is also either problematic or expensive. Newsgroup facilities are relatively crude, as are the web browsers supplied by some services. You can sometimes use an alternative browser instead, if you can work out how to set it up, but you are usually stuck with the built-in facilities for news and mail.

For all their disadvantages, on-line services are still a good choice for very light business use, and for anyone who is not too concerned about developing an Internet shop front for their business.

## Internet Service Providers (ISPs)

ISP companies provide a 'straight' Internet connection, which is essentially just a pipe that links your computer to the Internet for as long as you stay connected. They supply some basic software to get you started, and perhaps some useful pointers about places where you can find interesting information, but after that you are on your own.

The biggest advantages of this kind of connection is that you can use whichever software you choose, and indeed you can often find better software than an ISP provides for free on the Internet itself. In general, with this kind of service it will take longer to master the basics, and so you should allow for a moderate 'culture shock' before you become acclimatised to the service. However, once you start to become familiar with the Internet, the simpler and more direct approach will help you get work done more quickly than a connection through an on-line service.

ISP connections are also significantly cheaper. Some are available for free, but an average figure of about £100 a year is more likely. Most services offer discounts for full payment a year in advance. However, monthly payments are only slightly more expensive. The difference is likely to be around £20, at most. In comparison an on-line service can cost as much as £18 a month. And some services, notably CompuServe, charge by the minute for access to certain kinds of information. However, as with some ISPs, cheaper options are available for light use.

ISPs typically use the **POP3** (Post Office Protocol) email system. This has the advantage of making it possible to read and send email from anywhere in the world that has an Internet connection, such as a cybercafe, a library, or even from a friend's computer. The alternative – **SMTP** (Simple Mail Transfer Protocol) – can only be used if you are connected directly to your ISP. Your ISP should be able to explain how to use POP3 to read and send email when abroad.

### Combined services

Combined services are simply a combination of the different features of on-line services and ISPs. They offer some of the facilities of on-line services, usually summaries of useful information on a large web site that can only be viewed if a password is known, but give users standard Internet software instead of their own unique proprietary package. Which? Online is a good example of a combined service. It has focused on the traditional *Which?* areas of consumer interest, but has also created a community of users who read reports on-line instead of on paper, share information and comments with each other and sometimes even meet socially.

### Special cases

One oddity among the various services in the UK is BT Click, which has been set up to compete with traditional ISPs, including BT's own BTInternet service. BT Click provides web access at a fixed 1p a minute. As usual, this is billed on top of telephone charges. Assuming your ISP charges £10 a month, if you spend 17 hours a month or less on-line, BT click is the cheaper option. For serious web users 17

## Business and the Internet

**Choices for Internet connections**

| Company type | Usage | Best choice | Estimated all-inclusive cost |
|---|---|---|---|
| Very small business | Occasional email and web browsing | On-line service | £100 per qtr |
| Small business (option 1) | Regular email and web browsing, distributed via a network; simple web page | ISP via telephone or ISDN link | £400 per qtr |
| Small business (option 2) | Regular email and web browsing, distributed via a network; more complex web page; perhaps electronic trading | ISP via ISDN; hosted web and email facilities | £1,000 per qtr |
| Medium-sized business | Heavy email/web use on a large network; complex electronic trading system integrated with other software | Permanent link (leased line); own specialised Internet connection to the company network | £2,500+ per qtr |

hours a month (just over half an hour a day) is not a great deal. For those who use the web occasionally, however, the service can be cost effective.

A number of companies are now offering completely free Internet connections; you simply pay phone charges (and since connection is a standard 0845 local-rate number, these are no more expensive than any one else's). An example of a free Internet service is Dixons Freeserve. Any Dixons or PC World store will supply a CD-ROM of suitable software for the asking, which includes a copy of Microsoft's Internet Explorer, and a sign-up system. While the service itself is free, Dixons charges £1 a minute for support calls, and presumably they hope to make a profit by doing this. Even with this extra cost the service appears to be a bargain, as the average person is unlikely to need more than an hour of support time to get started. Once on-line, further informal help is available in newsgroups.

Some experts believe that free services are too good to be true and point out the possible catches: the service or the support may be particularly inept so that huge phone bills are run up rapidly; the service may sell lists of subscribers to advertisers, who will deluge users in junk mail; the service may find itself swamped and overwhelmed by more subscribers than it can cope with. So far it is too early to tell if any of these are more than speculation. In general it seems that free services are worth experimenting with, although a business may find it useful to have a 'true' ISP in reserve just in case the level of service becomes disappointing.

### Domestic services for business use

Hundreds of Internet services are now available in the UK, and it seems that almost anyone with money to burn is setting themselves up as an Internet connection service. Industry pundits have been predicting a shake-out of smaller companies for some years now, but instead the reverse seems to have happened, and there are now more small companies than ever.

With so many potential choices, it can be hard to find exactly the right package. For real-life use, there is no single best overall service. They all have strengths and weaknesses, which will appeal to different kinds of users. Some qualities to look for include:

- **Speed** How quickly web pages appear when you ask for them?
- **Reliability** Are there regular problems dialling in to a connection, or sending/collecting email?
- **Support** Can the support desk help you if you have problems? Are they open outside of office hours, in case you want to work late? Does support cost anything? Is it on a freephone, a local call or a premium-rate line?
- **Email addresses** Do you get one, or more? Do you get as many as you like?
- **Spam** How much of a problem is it?

Connection-reliability figures are listed in magazine league tables. Web speeds are not, and the best way to assess them is to experiment with the different services yourself, and, perhaps, to go by personal recommendation. Support is also hard to check, although occasionally the Internet press prints 'user-satisfaction tables', which indicate the quality of service that support teams offer.

A minority of ISPs offers free trials. Most do not, and the only practical way to check them for speed and quality is to sign up for a month and then cancel. This can be expensive, because some ISPs charge a one-off 'set-up' fee, which discourages this kind of experimentation. Unfortunately at the moment it is the only practical option for anyone who wants to find a reliable, fast service. Word of mouth can be a useful starting point, with the caveat that sometimes people who have never experienced a good service can say surprisingly complimentary things about a shoddy one.

For users who need a no-expense-spared service, a good option to consider is paying for connections to both an on-line service like AOL and an ISP for more general email and newsgroup use. This will not save money, but it can save time. On-line services are often able to offer very fast connections to US-based web sites, because they use a very high-speed connection across the Atlantic (some web pages may appear perhaps five times faster than they would via an ISP). However, ISPs offer more flexibility about the software that can be used with their service.

All domestic services now offer web space, although the amount varies from 1Mb to more than 10Mb. The average is around 5Mb, which is ample for a simple site.

## Connecting your network to the Internet

If you have a business network, then you will probably want to connect it to the Internet in such a way that any computer on the network can read email and connect to the World Wide Web. An important point to note about the more business-oriented products that can provide this service is that prices can vary by as much as 500 per cent. This is one area that repays very careful research. Unfortunately the most useful products are not widely advertised, even in the Internet press. It may well be worth trying to find a good consultant to help with the search.

Sharing a web connection is fairly straightforward on a simple network. **Modem-sharing software** makes it possible for more than one person on a network to use a modem at the same time. It is quite rare that the full speed of a link is being used, and there is always some spare capacity (known as bandwidth), which is available for someone else. A related but more complex product is an **ISDN router**. This connects a network to the Internet using an ISDN link, and typically adds extra features, such as the ability to double ISDN lines to get twice the speed. The better routers include firewall features, which can prevent hacking attacks while your network is on-line.

Sharing out email is rather more complex, and usually requires *mail server* software. This provides a local 'post office', which queues email from the network, sends it out in bulk, receives replies and sends them to the correct staff. The first version of Windows 95 (available from 1995 to early 1997) included a simple post-office facility, which could do this job, and also deal with internal business email at the same time. More recent versions of Windows lack this, and you will need to install some other package. Microsoft's Back Office software includes a mail server, although cheaper options, including Eudora's WorldMail and Electric Mail's InterMail Post.Office, also exist. This kind of software usually requires a computer all to itself, and will only work with an advanced, and more expensive, operating system, such as Windows 2000.

All-in-one solutions to both these problems are also available. **Internet Servers**, also known as 'black boxes', plug in between an Internet connection either over a phone or ISDN line, but more usually over a permanent link, and the rest of a network. They provide a mail server and web-sharing facilities for a small office. They may also provide fax and other features. Usefully, web pages can be *cached*, which means that copies of frequently accessed pages are kept on the server. If someone wants to view one of these pages, they see the local copy instead of the one on the Internet. This feature can save on phone bills for dial-up links, and on bandwidth for permanent connections. Internet servers are often leased rather than sold outright. The best internet servers include free on-site service call-outs, and free setting up. All you have to do is work out where to put the box in the office, and to sign a cheque. Prices range from about £2,000 to £5,000 a year. While it is possible to create a home-made server that will do a similar job for very much less than this, the computer skills required for this are very advanced, and well beyond the reach of beginners.

However you connect your network, you will find that spam can become a major problem. If you do not take precautions against spam you can expect up to around 20 per cent of all mail to your business will be junk. Fortunately there are ways to minimise spam. For the most recent developments search for 'spam kill' or 'spam block' using an Internet search engine.

## Using free web pages

Although you will be given space to create your own web pages when using a domestic connection, it is, in practice, of fairly limited use. The pages offered by ISPs and on-line services are suitable for a simple 'This is who I am and this is what I do' page, but more advanced sites, with such extras as video and sound, on-line trading, connections to a company database, electronic catalogues, and the ability to keep records of who has visited the site and what they did there, will not usually be possible. The limited amount of free space available prevents more ambitious site designs from being realised. (For further details on creating your own web site see page 221.)

Some ISPs specify that free pages are not to be used for commercial purposes. Others place limits on the amount of computer time they will devote to free pages, which either means that your page can seem extremely slow, or that you will be kicked off the free service if your site starts generating a lot of interest.

Another problem is that unless you use a web-forwarding service (see page 206) and plenty of other advertising, your pages will be well off the beaten track as far as visitors are concerned, and you will simply not get much interest.

An alternative to ISP-based free pages are free web services such as Geocities (*http://www/geocities.com*) and Tripod (*http://www.tripod.com*). These provide free web pages to all comers, but ply visitors with advertising. Geocities is experimenting with its virtual shopfronts, known as 'GeoShops', and other free web companies are likely to follow, but in practice they are even less useful for businesses. The computers behind these facilities are often somewhat overburdened, and sites may take a long time to appear. Moreover, the advanced web facilities listed earlier are unavailable.

## Cutting the cost

Although dial-up connections are the cheapest way to get on-line, with some forethought they can be made cheaper still. A useful first step is to consider all the different discount-pricing schemes that the telephone companies offer. For example, adding your ISP's number to BT's Friends and Family scheme can lead to significant savings. While the schemes offered by BT and Cable and Wireless are complex and require serious research (and are an ideal job for a spreadsheet) the possible savings make the effort worthwhile.

Another way of saving money is to schedule Internet connections away from peak periods. While impractical for web use, email and news can be sent and received automatically rather than manually, perhaps three or four times a day. An automatic service prevents 'single-message syndrome' where someone connects for a short period every time they want to send a message, which can increase a quarterly bill by 10 to 20 per cent. Windows 98 includes a scheduler, which can start software automatically.

It is also worth noting that the web is much quicker before about midday and becomes very slow during the evenings. Most web traffic is based in the United States, and most people are still asleep there during our mornings.

Another way to save on browsing bills is to use an *off-line browser*. This can pull information from a site to your computer while you view it. You can then disconnect and view the rest of the site, which will have been stored inside your computer for quicker access. Off-line browsers are a good idea, but some sites are very large, and in any case you may only want to view a page or two, which limits their usefulness.

**Web-caching** software keeps copies of pages you have already seen on your computer, and makes it possible for you to see them again without having to connect to the Internet. This is a rather more useful facility. Both web-caching tools and off-line browsers are available for free on the Internet.

ISDN connections have to be watched carefully. If routers and connection-sharing software are not set up properly, they can leave a link permanently connected. This can lead to ruinous bills, and telephone companies are unlikely to be sympathetic. When starting out with ISDN, you should make sure that connections are broken properly when you no longer need them. Usually there is a *time out* setting somewhere in the relevant software that can ensure this happens after a set period of inactivity.

## Business-specific services

The different business-specific Internet services available can help an enterprise in three ways. They can provide customised Internet addresses (for example, customers can send email to *someone@yourcompany.com* instead of *someone@an_anonymous_ISPname.com*). Secondly they can provide a permanent home for your company's web pages, which is available all the time, but does not require an expensive permanent Internet connection and all the technology that goes with it. Finally a company can, if it feels the cost is justified, link itself directly to the Internet, and become in effect its own ISP.

### Customising your address

If you use the email and web facilities offered by an ISP or on-line service, their name always appears in your email and web-page addresses. This makes it obvious that you are using their services. While this is perfectly adequate for some kinds of work, some businesses will benefit from having customised addresses based on the business name. The latter are more distinct and easier to remember, and also create the impression that a company may be bigger than it actually is. Customised addresses, which are the Internet's equivalent of headed notepaper, are known as *domain names*.

There are two steps involved in setting up a customised address. The first is to *register* your intended name with an Internet-naming authority. This provides a legal record that the name is yours. The second is setting up *forwarding* facilities, so that email sent to your customised address is forwarded to your real address (your real address can be anywhere, including an ordinary ISP mailbox).

### *Registering a domain name*

The biggest problem with registering a domain name is finding one that is not already in use. The second problem is dealing with trademark registrations; it is possible to register a name, use it, and then be sued for trademark violation by a larger company with a similar name that has arrived on the scene later.

Domain names fall into local and international groups. These are indicated by the last part of the name. In the UK the local designation is '.co.uk' ('.ltd.uk' and '.plc.uk' are also used, but are rare). The standard international designation is 'com' (a '.com.uk' variant is sometimes used, but this is *not officially sanctioned* and may cause technical problems if you try to use it).

Either '.com' or '.co.uk' appear on the end of the company name, for example 'ibm.com' is the domain name of International Business Machines, and 'tesco.co.uk' of the Tesco supermarket chain. Domain names are administered by naming agencies. These keep both paper records of domain names for reference, and electronic records, which the computers on the Internet use to make sense of addresses correctly.

The easiest way to register a name is to use a registration company. These advertise widely in the Internet trade magazines, and act as intermediaries to help you find a suitable name and to fill in the rather complex paperwork required to tell a naming agency about it. The naming agencies for the International and UK-based groups are completely separate, and you can register a similar name in either or both groups. For example, if your company is called Wild Footwear, you could register wildfootwear.co.uk, or wildfootwear.com. You could even register both, although this is probably unnecessary unless you have trademarked 'Wild Footwear' and want to make sure no one else can use it.

Unfortunately, the most popular and easy to remember names are already registered. If you have been trading for a while this can be a problem, although if your company name is complex and fairly unique you will probably still find that a suitable domain name is free. You can increase your range of options by cramming all the words in your company name into one long word (such as digitalaudioinnovations.com), separating the words with hyphens (digital-audio-innovations.com), using abbreviations (digaudio.com, or perhaps digaudioinnov.com), or by using an acronym (dai.com). More extreme variations include deliberate misspellings, such as substituting '8' for 'ate' (for example, cre8.com instead of create.com), using 'k' instead of 'c' and 'ph' instead of 'f' (lopht.com instead of loft.com). However, these tend to be the exclusive preserve of companies that like to appear more rebellious and creative than average. In general, the closer the name is to your original company name the easier it is to remember and the less trouble you will have with it.

If you are just starting up your business, you have more choices. You can choose an approximately suitable name at random from the list of domain names that are still available, and name your company after it. Meaningless 'off-the-shelf' company names that are often suggested for new startups by accountants (for example, startgrade, truecrest, wellwin, and so on) are also more likely to be available as domain names. If all else fails you may have to settle for a '.co.uk' or a '.ltd.uk name' when you would have preferred a '.com', or vice versa. Another alternative, if you have an offshore holding company, is to use its country code instead of '.uk'. Jersey, Guernsey and Isle of Man have their own codes ('.je', '.gg', and '.im' respectively). A full list of country codes is in the Appendices.

If you already have an Internet connection, or perhaps access to a connection at a local library or cybercafe, you can search for free names on-line. Virtual Internet is one of the larger registration companies, and its site at *http://www.vi.net* includes a live search facility that can check whether or not a name has been taken. You can search for words (for example, 'testing') instead of specific domains ('testing.com'). This will produce a list of all possible domain names that use that word, showing which ones are already taken.

If you are not yet on-line, you can ask a registration company to find a name for you. This is likely to take much longer, as you may need to provide a list of suggestions to them first. The on-line approach is much quicker and more efficient.

Once you have your name, you can inform the registration company that you want to register it. This involves paying a one-off set-up fee, followed by annual charges, which vary, depending on which group your name falls under. For example '.com' names cost $70, which covers rental for a two-year period. Note that names are only *rented*. If you let your registration lapse, you may lose your name to someone else.

## Names and trademarks

If your chosen company name is close, but not necessarily identical, to an existing registration you may have problems. UK-based registrations are only liable to trademark actions for trademarks registered in the UK. International ('.com') registrations are liable to action from any country at all, although the most likely source of problems is the US.

You can search for US trademarks at the US Patent and Trademark Office site at: *http://www.uspto.gov/tmdb/index.html*. There is no on-line equivalent for the UK, or for most other countries. This kind of search can be time-consuming and expensive (with the employment of a solicitor to search for you), but if you are at all unsure about a name, it is worth doing this if you can, as it may save you a lot of legal difficulties later. Just because a trademark exists does not mean that you will have legal problems, but it does make it more likely. In the future, as more and more businesses, both large and small, start to use the Internet, the potential for legal challenges (with the threat of damages) to your registration increases.

## Using web and email forwarding

A domain-name registration is a legal formality, and on its own offers you no advantage whatsoever. To actually claim a domain in practice, the behind-the-scenes computers that deal with Internet addresses have to be told where they can find you.

If you have a permanent connection to the Internet, the company that installs the connection will do this for you. You simply present them with your name registration, and they set up both your computer network and the Internet itself so that all information that uses your domain name goes straight to you.

If you do not have a permanent connection you can use a *forwarding service*. This acts as a halfway house (a little like a PO box, except that instead of an anonymous number it has your domain name on it). Email directed to your domain name is first sent to the forwarding service, and then forwarded automatically to your real address. This means you can use an ordinary ISP for email, but still take advantage of a domain name. The forwarding process is invisible to non-experts. Advanced forwarding options that are sometimes offered include the ability to forward email to fax machines and pagers.

To use email forwarding you *must* have use of an ISP connection. An on-line service like AOL does not allow you to set a suitable return address, and so even with mail forwarding, you will still appear to be 'someone@aol.com' whenever you send a message. An ISP connection lets you set whatever return address you like. If you set this to reflect your new personalised email address, you will appear to be sending and receiving messages directly at that address, even though your email is really being sent via an ISP and a forwarding service.

Web forwarding works in a similar way. When someone tries to see web pages that include your domain name, they are directed to a forwarding computer. The forwarding computer then connects them to the computer where the pages are actually available (which can be free web space anywhere on the web). If you have a number of pages you can 'camouflage' them, so visitors need never see that you are using free web space.

## Web hosting

For many businesses, web hosting is a better alternative than web forwarding. With this option your web pages are held on a computer at the offices of the hosting company. You have more space with which to use advanced features to make your web site more appealing and therefore more likely to result in sales. To use the service you simply copy a web design from your computer to the hosting computer. This is a straightforward procedure with which the hosting service will be able to help you.

Note that you will usually need to use an existing ISP for this and also for sending and receiving email. Most hosting companies do not have the racks of modems required to offer their customers a dial-up connection to the Internet. Instead, customers have to make their own arrangements.

Web hosting can be bought from perhaps £100 per year for a 25Mb site. Hosting services vary in the range of services they offer and, to a much smaller extent, by how much they cost. Features to look for include:

- **Web space** How much space is available? Although 25Mb should be enough for an effective site, up to 100Mb may be required if you plan to put a catalogue or database on-line.
- **Cost** This is usually quoted as an annual rental fee. Check to see what exactly is included. Are there any set-up costs?
- **Domain name registration** Sometimes this is included as part of a package deal.
- **POP3 email addresses** Again, this is often included. If you have a domain name, you only need a single mailbox, as mail sent to your domain can be sorted according to the information before the '@' sign in the address, and you can define different addresses however you like.

- **Connection speed** You want to be sure that your pages appear as quickly as possible. You can check for speed problems by asking for the URLs of other sites that are being hosted by that company, and then test how long they take to appear when you try to visit them. Some companies quote the speed of their own connection to the internet (for example, 155Mb/s), but this can be irrelevant in practice as the actual speed at which they can deliver web pages depends on the proportion of bandwidth to traffic.
- **Reliability statistics** There should be a readily available summary of 'down time' – periods when the hosting service was not working properly.
- **Server logs** These provide a detailed and complete list of everyone who has visited your site, and what they did when they got there.
- **Server statistics** These are a more useful version of server logs, which provide a useful summary from the information that the server logs provide.
- **Telnet and FTP** These allow you to connect to your site remotely and transfer information (such as design changes and updates) to it and from it.

Web-hosting services may also offer 'extras', which provide added options. Typical extras include:

**Common Gateway Interface (CGI) scripts** are special types of software that do the web hosting and add useful extra features to web pages. These include a counter that shows the number of visits made to a page, or the creation of on-screen forms that can take information and orders from visitors. Some hosting services provide *prewritten* scripts. These are the only ones you will be able to use. *Customised* scripts are a more useful option and will let you do very much what you like with your site, such as adding search facilities, web chat rooms, or other special features. Scripts for specific purposes can be either bought commercially, copied from the Internet, or written to order. Working with CGI scripts is a job for an expert, although a good, if more expensive, hosting service will be able to offer help in finding useful scripts, or may even create them for you.

**FrontPage extensions** provide extra features that work with pages designed with Microsoft's FrontPage web-design software. These are only useful if you use FrontPage for your design work.

**SSL (Secure Sockets Layer)** is a way to secure web pages so that when customers send information to them the data is sent in secret code. SSL is often used for credit-card transactions.

**Mailing lists** and **autoresponders** make it easy to add mailing-list facilities to your business site.

### Is your web host secure?

Once your web site is on-line, it becomes vulnerable to attack from outsiders. These attacks include:

- **denial of service**, during which your site appears to become too busy to provide web pages (in reality a single connection is 'jamming' it)
- **unauthorised copying** of customer orders, perhaps including their credit-card details
- **hacking attacks**, during which outsiders break into your site and the pages are replaced with electronic graffiti.

Internet security is in a parlous state, as shown by the number of successful attacks against large organisations such as the CIA.

There are two ways to avoid attacks. The first is not to do anything that might attract attention, for example, keeping a bare minimum of customer records at the web site. Hackers tend to prefer high-profile web sites, and if your site is small you are less likely to suffer from unwelcome attention.

The second step is to check the hosting company's security provisions. These should have formally documented security measures, covering the hosting software itself as well as physical access to the premises where the computers are kept. At least one member of staff should be a security expert and keep track of security information, which is released regularly by software manufacturers and various security agencies. An excellent security track record, preferably showing that a small number of hacking attacks has been repulsed successfully, would be reassuring. A record with no attacks at all simply means that existing security measures are unproved. Regular attacks means that the service has been targeted, for whatever reason, by hackers, and a successful attack is more likely.

The service should include full backup facilities for all web sites. If a hacking attack happens, or there is some other computer failure, which leads to the loss of your site, how long will it take for the site to reappear? You should, of course, keep your own backups of your web site, whether or not you designed it yourself. If the site-design company goes bust at the same time that the site-hosting company has a serious problem, you may lose thousands of pounds worth of site design. While this may be unlikely, the serious outcome strongly suggests a 'belt-and-braces' approach.

### Business packages and business ISPs

Some ISPs advertise themselves as being 'for business users', but in fact only provide a simple domestic connection. True business ISPs offer web hosting, email and web forwarding, help with domain-name registration, and perhaps also extra services such as 0800 and 0500 telephone numbers (for the UK), and a web-design consultancy. A small minority also provides dial-up access to the Internet. While a useful option, this is quite rare, and instead most services expect customers to sort out their own Internet connections.

Some business ISPs offer an 'all-in-one' option that includes hosting and email facilities, together with web-site design for a set price. This can look appealing, but there are important issues to look at when deciding on site design that make this kind of package less attractive than it might be otherwise (for more details see Chapter 12).

### Permanent and high-speed Internet connections

The ultimate Internet connection for business use is a permanent link, known as a **leased line**. Leased lines are among the most expensive options, and usually out of the price range of most small businesses. A permanent link with a speed of 64kbps, which is no faster than an ISDN connection, costs between £1,000 and £2,000 to install and between £7,000 and £10,000 a year to run. Connections with speeds of 2Mb/s cost around £50,000 per annum. Faster links can have six-figure annual rental charges. Installations are permanent, as the line has to physically link your premises to one of a small number of regional Internet centres that can offer the service. The further you are from one of these, the more expensive installation will be. If you move, you will have to pay installation costs again. A speed of 64kbps should be enough for any small business with less than around fifty employees. It allows roughly ten employees to browse the web simultaneously before the speed at which pages appear starts to become unacceptably slow (this is for one-way traffic into your business). If you plan to host web pages on your own computers, then you can easily have ten people viewing your web pages from anywhere on the Internet. Once you become this popular, you will need a faster link.

With a leased line, you have, in effect, total freedom to do whatever you want on the Internet. You can create huge web sites, using whatever special facilities you want, or an infinite number of email addresses based on your domain name. Incoming email is sent directly to your network, rather than via an ISP.

However, setting up a leased line can be a complex task. You will need to link your company network to the leased line through a router, and also set up a local email server that can work with both internal and Internet email. More importantly, you will have to look into security, using a firewall to protect your company network from outsiders. Security is very hard to do well, and a proper security audit from an expert can cost thousands of pounds. The alternative is muddling through and hoping that no one will take advantage of your vulnerability, which would be rather like leaving your car unlocked in a car park and hoping no one steals it. You *may* be lucky, perhaps even for long periods. However, it is much safer and more professional to do the job properly.

Companies that supply leased lines can advise on all of these matters. Some go so far as to install routers and firewalls for you, and set up a connection to your network. This is the best possible option, and is worth paying a little extra for. The alternative is taking the DIY approach, which would be a major challenge, even for someone who is reasonably computer-literate, or hiring a consultant who can advise on the project.

## Satellite links and other alternatives

For those whose main interest is browsing the web or reading newsgroups, Hughes Olivetti and Eutelsat now offer high-speed satellite links to the Internet. These can only be used to *receive* information. Outgoing information is sent using a conventional POTS (Plain Old Telephone System) or ISDN dial-up connection. To use satellite links you need to have a special aerial dish installed, which may need planning permission in some areas, and a link to the dish fitted inside your computer. When you want to view a web page or look at the contents of an newsgroup, you send a request, and the information is beamed to your computer through a satellite. Speeds of up to 400kbps are possible, although realistically you can expect speeds of half this. The dishes are also prone to weather problems, and service is degraded by rain or snow. Payment schemes are based on the amount of information you use, rather than the duration of a connection. Typically you can have a certain amount of information free, and then you pay for the rest by the megabyte. For example, the cheapest tariff for the Hughes Olivetti system (which is called DirecPC) costs £15 a month for the first 30Mb, and 50p per megabyte thereafter.

Compared to leased lines, satellite links are excellent value. If you use the web a lot, they can soon pay for themselves compared to a dial-up connection. The saving in time is also considerable. However, because of the speed of the connection you may find yourself spending more time surfing than you would otherwise, so overall running costs may be higher. Even with this caveat, this is an option well worth considering for the more serious Internet user.

DirecPC also offers a number of related business services. For example, you can use the satellite system to send information in bulk to regional offices from a central location.

Another option is to use ISDN (Integrated Services Digital Network) dial-back. This provides a way to simulate a leased line for a fraction of the cost. When an ISP needs to connect with your computer, it dials a special number at your office, then hangs up after a single ring tone. Your ISDN terminal adaptor calls the ISP back and creates a temporary connection. Once information has been transferred, the link is broken again. ISDN's ability to create a link within a couple of seconds (as opposed the 30–45 seconds required by a modem) makes this a practical option.

Unfortunately, very few of the larger ISPs offer dial-back. However, some business-oriented ISPs do offer the service, and are worth tracking down. Dial-back can be a very cheap way to get your network on-line.

### The near future

Leased lines are likely to become obsolete in the not-too-distant future. New technologies will soon provide a high-speed link to the

Internet for a fraction of the cost. Once these are available, Internet use will explode, as live video and music services, home shopping, and a variety of other new technologies start to vie with TV, radio and print media for the attention of consumers.

**Cable** and **ADSL** will offer a next-generation high-speed combined phone and Internet service. Cable systems use optical fibre laid for cable TV systems. ADSL (Assymetric Digital Subscriber Link – part of a family of technologies that are collectively known as xDSL, where 'x' stands for the different variations that are available) uses existing telephone connections in a more efficient way. Both are already available in some parts of the UK (for example, ADSL is available from the small independent Kingston Communications company, which serves the residents of Kingston-upon-Hull), and nationwide trials are due in 1999, with widespread use a year or two after that.

Both cable and ADSL offer speeds between 1Mb/s and 2Mb/s, although faster links may be available at extra cost. However, this bandwidth may be shared between a block of consumers (for example, everyone on the same street). What this means in practice remains to be seen. Pricing schemes have not yet been finalised, and there is a chance that costs will be based on the amount of information transferred, rather than the existing dial-up system of charging for the duration of a connection.

Nortel (Northern Telecom, a communications and electricity-supply multinational company) has been experimenting with a system that sends Internet information over the mains. If the scheme works, it could provide a permanent fast connection of around 1Mb/s, using minimal extra hardware. In principle this could be distributed around a house using existing wiring. Technical problems, including the discovery that streetlights radiate the information very efficiently, which raises security issues, have so far meant that the scheme remains very much in the realm of theory.

Chapter 12

# E-commerce and the electronic economy

E-commerce (electronic commerce) is both the most exciting and the most experimental application of information technology. It is likely that over the next 15 to 20 years e-commerce will transform the economy, and make it possible for businesses to operate with previously unimaginable flexibility.

Instead of large centralised concerns with hundreds of employees, it is now possible to run a business with a global catchment area and a very large turnover with only a handful of staff. Instead of niches in a relatively stable marketplace, successful trading will rely on entirely new skills, such as information mining, on-line community creation, and flexibility. E-commerce also makes it possible to create completely new kinds of products and services. While it is certainly possible to sell traditional goods on-line – from CDs to brussels sprouts – there are also opportunities for creating completely new markets.

The big advantage to selling on the net is that it gives you access to millions – perhaps even billions – of potential customers. If the take-up rate for your advertising is a tiny fraction of one per cent, you can still find yourself with tens of thousands of sales. If your goods and services are popular, word of mouth (or word of email) can also help spread information about your business.

The biggest problem in e-commerce is getting noticed. Prospective customers have literally millions of business sites to chose from, all clamouring for their attention. To ensure they choose your site instead of someone else's, they have to be deliberately led to it. Once they have found it they need a compelling reason to shop there, and preferably to visit again and again.

However, setting up an electronic business, or adding an electronic branch to an existing business, need not be any harder than creating any other kind of business. The most important skills are knowledge of your market and your potential customers, and making sure that you can offer them something they want. From that point of view an e-business is very much like a traditional business. The differences are that the kinds of services you can offer, the kinds of advertising you can do, and the economic relationship between advertising spend and turnover are completely novel, and to a large extent no one is quite sure what the rules in this market are. Companies that succeed in this new market are likely to show an unusual degree of initiative, and an understanding of how to fit new kinds of business into an existing company framework.

There are four steps involved in creating an on-line business:

**Preparation** involves looking at what the options are, how much they are likely to cost, and what potential changes or other factors need to be taken into account before a business can go on-line.

**Getting connected** involves choosing a practical and affordable method for connecting to the Internet, and finding a permanent electronic shop front – in the form of a web site – for your business.

**Getting noticed** involves designing and promoting your web site so that it is attractive and works well, and people know that it exists.

**Getting paid** is about setting up a practical payment system so that customers can buy from your site directly.

## Preparation

A vital first stage in planning an e-business is to look at what the possibilities are, and at what sells well on-line and what does not. It is possible to expand slowly in stages to help keep risks and up-front expenditure to a minimum. The options include:

- using an email address as an adjunct to phone and fax orders
- creating a web site to advertise your goods and services
- creating a true e-commerce system, which enables customers to place orders on-line, and (optionally) handle transactions automatically, so that money goes straight from your customers' accounts into your account.

## Successful on-line products

Understanding what is and is not likely to sell well depends on understanding the kinds of people that use the Internet. At the moment, the Internet is mostly used by:

- computer, IT and other technology professionals
- business users, who have Internet access at their place of work
- students and academics
- small-business owners and home workers.

To a lesser extent, services such as AOL and WebTV (Microsoft's very simplified Internet service, which uses a box that plugs into a TV and does not require a computer at all) have created a way on to the Internet that is popular with family members. While they make up a sizeable part of the Internet's population, they may be less interested in buying things on-line unless the process is extremely quick, cheap and convenient. Because of this, the products and services that seem to sell well on-line include:

**Luxury goods** Any goods which are exclusive, unique, or fit the needs of a very specialised niche market, can do well on-line. These include 'status' goods which use a strong brand image to reinforce the buyer's sense of their own spending power; books and CDs; art and artworks, especially those with a theme that appeals to a niche market; fine foods and wines, especially if they are non-perishable and can handle long shipping times to destinations outside the UK; and film and TV memorabilia, especially science fiction, which is a perennially popular subject area.

**Software** The Internet is rapidly becoming one of the best distribution systems for new software, for both customers and software developers. If you have a new software product, the net is the ideal way to promote and sell it worldwide. If the software is large (more than around 1Mb) UK sales may be slow, because it takes too long and costs too much to download the software directly. But sales in the US will not be hampered in the same way, because local calls are free, and many net users have access to many more high-speed links.

**Bargains** Goods at very low prices are often popular, especially if they are significantly cheaper than they would be elsewhere. Internet auctions are a variation on this theme, and allow individual items to be sold via auction on-line. From a seller's point of view items of specialist interest can be sold on-line for more than they might fetch locally. From a buyer's point of view, it is sometimes possible to pick up genuine bargains at an on-line auction, although it is sensible to get as accurate an idea of the true value of an item first by checking to see if it is available elsewhere.

**Obscure or hard to find items** Internet bookseller Amazon (http://www.amazon.com) offers a 'we'll try to find it for you' service, which can help track down obscure and out-of-print books. Certain good traditional booksellers can offer a similar service, but they tend to be exclusive, expensive, and rather difficult to find themselves. Amazon offers the service to all of its customers, and because of its huge customer base its throughput of second-hand titles is much higher than that of a traditional small bookshop, which means that out-of-print titles surface more regularly.

**Information** There are two ways to sell information. The first is to sell on demand: customers pay a fee for an 'item' of information, which is then delivered to them electronically, either by email or by FTP (file transfer protocol). The second is the 'subscription model', whereby customers are charged a set amount and in return are given access to a stream of information. This can be made available on a web site (protected by a password) or can be sent by email.

The first type is used by some of the on-line services – notably CompuServe – and certain financial services, which will buy or sell stock at the current price for a fixed fee. (This counts as an information transfer, because in effect all that changes hand is information rather than any tangible product.) The 'per item' model is unlikely to be a good choice for a small business as it relies on offering an almost unimaginably huge amount of information, usually about some specialist topic. A typical small business is unlikely to have the resources to create a suitable library of facts or other information that could be sold on this kind of basis.

The subscription model also has to be handled carefully. Very cheap subscription to high-quality information may work well if the information is genuinely of value to people, and if there is enough of a market base to make it worth selling the service. Examples include Science Week, which delivers a weekly summary of important science developments by email for only $10 a year, and Which? Online, which offers a service that can help pay for itself by pointing people in the direction of high-quality consumer bargains. Definite gaps in the market exist for other money- or time-saving information.

However, the kind of information more usually found in traditional media, such as journalistic commentary or film, music and TV gossip, is less likely to do well. Large media companies that have attempted to sell this type of information have yet gain significant success. Similarly, 'ezines' (electronic magazines) traditionally make money by attracting visitors and then sponsoring the site by selling space to advertisers, rather than by charging a subscription. In general, this approach seems to be the best way to make money from supplying information. For example, a site that makes it possible to check flight details and book airline tickets will probably not succeed if people have to pay to use it. It may succeed, however, if the airlines that it 'advertises' on its web site can be persuaded that it is in their interest to fund the site or to take out advertising on it directly. In general, the sort of **information that sells well** on the Internet includes:

- information that changes regularly (for example, share prices, where the speed of the Internet makes it possible to follow these changes)
- summaries of available products that offer 'best buys' (again, these can be updated regularly, using the most recent information)
- topical information about trends
- historical information, which puts more recent information into a useful context (share-price histories and company details are a good example)
- information for niche markets, such as professional groups of various kinds and certain kinds of consumer.

The sort of information that **does not** sell well on-line includes:

- static information that does not need to be updated regularly and can be found – and bought – in books
- information that requires lots of graphics or diagrams (unless customers have high-speed links)
- journalistic commentary and editorials, such as 'Sunday supplement' general-interest features, gossip and information that relates to entertainment

- subjects that are already covered well by the traditional media, or are available for free on the net (although these are sometimes suitable for the creation of sites that attract advertising revenues).

**Books and music in electronic form** A sub-set of the 'information' category, books and music in electronic form have both been sold experimentally by some small businesses. Currently, however, they suffer from practical distribution problems that make it hard for them to succeed on anything other than a small scale. At the moment paper books are far more accessible, convenient and cheaper than any electronic implementation of the same idea, although experimental 'e-books' are already available, and may become increasingly popular over the next few years. It is perfectly possible, however, to sell correspondence courses by email, and this can work very well indeed.

Similar practical restrictions apply to the distribution of music in electronic form. With the current speed of the net, true CD-quality distribution of a whole CD of music is impractical. It would take more than a day to copy all of a CD from one computer on the Internet to another over a modem link. But a system known as 'Mpeg 3' or 'MP3' has made it possible to distribute recordings with slightly poorer sound quality much more conveniently and efficiently. It takes only a few minutes to copy a three-minute song, and one company, Diamond Multimedia, has produced a hardware MP3 player that can copy music from a computer connected to it. The music can then be played anywhere. Because there are no moving parts, the system is immune to nudges and jogs and is more robust than a personal tape or CD player.

In reality, MP3 is often used to distribute pirate versions of copyrighted recordings. Music distribution is likely to change dramatically over the next five to ten years, and it is possible that the current system will mutate into some variety of 'music shareware'. This means that anyone will be able to publish their music on-line, and people will pay for it only if they think it is worth something.

## Unsuitable products and services for e-commerce

Tradespeople that gain their business from restricted local areas, such as hairdressers, garages, builders, and perhaps doctors, accountants and lawyers, are unlikely to benefit from on-line trading. The advantages of on-line selling simply do not apply to these kinds of work. For example, there is little point in advertising in Missouri if the trading area of the business is limited to 30 miles around a small town in Hampshire.

However, it may still be worth setting up a web site if (and only if) it is possible to get it listed in a national or local directory. Without this kind of exposure the web site will languish unvisited, and is likely to be a waste of time and money. For those for whom a listing is possible and potentially useful, it is worth noting that the UK's Electronic Yellow Pages (EYP) site at *http://www.eyp.co.uk* has a search facility that lists traders that advertise in the *Yellow Pages* by geographical area. An on-line listing is free (although at the discretion of the EYP staff), but the information offered about traders is sketchy and there is no facility for linking to a trader's web site. Nonetheless, as the service is free, and the main Electronic Yellow Pages site, known as YELL, is sometimes used by people looking for traders, it makes sense to have a listing.

Any item on sale that needs to be looked at close up physically, such as a used car, is unlikely to do well, although this has not stopped people from trying to offer these kinds of goods on-line, with varying degrees of success. Perishable goods are also unlikely to be successful, unless delivery is unusually prompt and efficient. Some supermarkets arrange on-line food orders, but here the doorstep delivery is as much part of the service as the availability of the food itself.

## Practical options for getting on-line

Having looked at what types of businesses are suitable for on-line trading, the next step is find the best way to get on-line.

### Using an email address

Using an email address is a very simple and cheap option for e-commerce if you already have a computer, and will cost perhaps £15 to £30 a month over and above your current overheads. You simply sign up for an Internet service that offers unlimited email accounts, perhaps buy a custom domain name if you feel you need one (see page 203) and create suitable email addresses for your business. For example, *sales@ukwidgets.com*; *info@ukwidgets.com*; *faq@ukwidgets.com*; and *support@ukwidgets.com*.

The main practical disadvantage to this approach is that many people are wary of giving their credit card numbers in an email. You could, in theory, use a system such as PGP (pretty good privacy; see page 180) to create a secure email link, but the complexities involved in doing this will be beyond people who do not have a technical background. But more importantly, this approach conflicts with the golden rule of e-business, which states that *the buying process should be as simple and streamlined as possible*.

Another problem is that, unless you already have a comprehensive print catalogue, people will need to ask you questions before they order. Fielding questions before you can close a sale can take up a surprising amount of your time. Ways to deal with this problem are either to create a 'frequently asked questions' (FAQ) document, or perhaps an electronic catalogue, and email them to prospective customers when they make their first enquiry. In the example above, the *faq@ukwidgets.com* address could be set up with an autoresponder, so that any email to that address will send back an automated reply with a list of typical questions and answers.

The email-only approach is suitable for small businesses with very limited budgets, for companies that would like to test the water before committing themselves further, and for anyone who would like to create a token electronic presence while working on a more complex, long-term e-business project. The main business drawback is that it is unlikely to lead to a huge increase in turnover, although any increase would be enough to cover the relatively modest costs without too much difficulty.

## Creating a web site

The advantage of creating your own web site is that it makes it much easier to create appealing and informative electronic advertising. An emailed FAQ document is likely to be text only, while a web page can include text, graphics, and even sounds and animations.

It is important to emphasise that the existence of a web site is not a guaranteed way to generate more business. Any web site design has to be carefully planned to make it accessible, appealing and easy to find. Plenty of businesses have failed to follow this advice and spent thousands of pounds on something that has had very little impact on their bottom line. So the point to remember here is that a web site is far more likely to become valuable when it is part of an integrated advertising and promotional strategy.

Even then a site is a gamble, and whether or not it is successful depends on the kinds of products and services being advertised, and on how well the practicalities of on-line advertising are handled as a whole.

## Creating an e-commerce system

In spite of all the jargon surrounding it, e-commerce simply means being able to sell products directly on-line. A web site acts as your shop front, and customers can place orders from it. In its simplest form, these orders are sent to your office via email and then dealt with in the usual way, just as if the order had been placed by phone or fax. More sophisticated systems will arrange for money to be transferred automatically, as long as customers pay by credit card. In effect the site acts as an on-line 'card swipe.'

Because computers are involved at every stage of the process, it is possible to enhance and simplify a business using a number of options. For example:

- orders can connected directly to a company's accounts and stock-control package
- orders can be summarised and passed directly to suppliers, which keeps the working capital free (instead of being tied up in unnecessary stock items)
- company premises may not need warehouse facilities, which reduces overheads
- customers can be individually targeted based on their previous sales record, and by analysing their spending habits it may be possible to automatically suggest new products, as and when they become available
- special offers can be emailed to customers much more cheaply than by paper mail
- businesses can help each other by carrying reciprocal advertising, or by paying a commission to any site which takes advertising that leads to a sale (this can be tracked automatically by software)

- other advertising can be sold on the site if it becomes very popular, creating another source of income.

## CASE HISTORY: Ian

Ian Letters, who runs Crotchet Music, a small family-owned company that buys and sells mostly classical music and jazz, explains how he went about creating a text-book example of an on-line business.

'The original reason for creating the web site was because we wanted to expand, and I felt the Internet was the way forward. We hired a company called Paradigm in Hampshire, on the basis of a write-up they had in *The Times*, to do the web-site design. They quoted us £4,000 for the work, although we did have other quotes of £15,000. We then produced a 12-page document (they might have quoted more if they had seen that first). We decided to design the site with the idea that people like to browse, and we're in the process of splitting the site into sections: Baroque, early music, modern, etc. There are lots of images to click on, and people get information relevant to that section. We've used the same page format for each section to keep costs down. We can plug in different photos and create a completely new section, perhaps for a special promotion or to start selling to a new market with a different interest to the ones we cover so far.

'Physically, we don't keep the web site here, as that would be much too expensive and complicated. Instead we've hired space on a web server, which is actually based in the Telehouse complex in London – right at the hub of the UK part of the Internet. We connect to the Internet over the phone like everyone else. We still pay Paradigm to make changes sometimes. It's not a static site, and people should realise that if they get their own web site they're going to need to budget for regular updates.

'To launch the site, I went down to the library and looked at a copy of BRAD, which contains details of all the media outlets in the UK. I got details of all the computer magazines, newspapers and other publications that we thought might be interested, and sent them press releases. We got write-ups in the *Daily Mail* and *Daily Telegraph* as a result, which led to a big surge of interest. It actually caused a bottle-neck in our system, as we had more orders than we could cope with for a while.

'What the web site has done for us is create a completely new customer base. We now have around 4,500 new customers around the world, with very minimal overlap with our original ones. It's not making huge amounts of money, but the pay-back period is around six months, which isn't bad at all for an investment. It's been worth the risk as each month our sales increase.

'Looking ahead, we'd like to get more business through the web site. We're looking at partnership schemes that would work by allowing us to place an ad on some one else's site (say company B). If we get an order from that ad, we would pay a commission to company B. The web server can track where customers come from so it's all automated. We've done that with an Italian newspaper. We're also considering the shopping areas on the big on-line services, like CompuServe, AOL, and MSN. We've got our logo on the *Gramophone* (classical music magazine) web site, and we're also looking at deals with Warner Brothers, whereby people can click through to our site and see a special Warner Brothers sales area.

'One thing I will say is that people seem very worried about credit-card buying. Because we use a secure server, our system is as secure as it can be, and we've never had any problems. I actually think it's safer buying things this way than in a shop. In a restaurant your card disappears for a minute or two, and who knows what's happening to it? Here, all the transactions are in code, and it would be too much work for a hacker to try to break it.

'The other important thing is integrating the financial side of things with the web and other sale outlets, so that we ensure positive cash flow. What happens now is that orders are keyed in either by email, fax, phone, post, or from the web store. If an item is in stock, the computer allocates it for delivery. If it's not, we raise a purchase order for it. We batch all of the latter together and once or twice a week we send off big orders to all our suppliers (we don't have enough room to stock all the thousands of CD in our database). The CDs are delivered the next day, or the day after. The software produces a picking list, which explains which CDs are due to go where. Once the CDs are ready to be shipped out, we charge the customer using a PC package supplied by Lloyd's. It's like a card machine, but more sophisticated. The money comes straight to our account via their system, which is called Cardnet. Then we produce a report for the post office, which picks up the parcels, signs them off, and away they go.

'Sales ledgers are updated, and the software produces a profit-and-loss account each month. Suppliers are paid at the end of the month, which means we have positive cash flow because money always comes in before it goes out.'

## E-commerce 'pitfalls'

An e-commerce system creates problems as well as opportunities for businesses, particularly currency complications. Fortunately, this is not as much of a complication as it sounds because currency problems can be dealt with quickly and simply by allowing credit-card orders. Credit cards are valid internationally, and can convert from one currency to another automatically. If your products sell well in the US, customers there will pay you in dollars even if you specify pounds in the prices on your web site, and the transaction will convert from one to the other without any further effort from you or the customer.

A more complex problem is allowing for delivery worldwide. If you plan to trade internationally, you must include information about a reliable (and preferably a quick) delivery facility on your web site, otherwise people may be reluctant to buy from you. Typically, this involves using an international courier, although for non-urgent deliveries surface parcel post is another option, even though it can take as long as a few months to reach some parts of the world. These details, complete with the delivery costs for customers, must be available on your site when you start trading on-line.

## Detailed preparations

At the end of the preparation stage you should have a clear understanding of what you are trying to sell, to whom you are trying to sell, and why it is likely to be successful. You should also have an idea of what changes, if any, your company needs to make in the ways that orders are accepted and processed, and in the ways that goods and services can be delivered. Finally, you should understand whether or not you will need extra staff to deal with the new business, and whether you will be able to do everything at in-house.

## Getting connected

The next step after preparation is to look at the different Internet connection options that are available. These are outlined in Chapter 11 (see page 194). For most small-business e-commerce projects, a custom domain name and a hosted web site, which are often available as packages, are likely to be the most convenient and cost-effective option. At this stage, it may be useful to invest in a cheap (or free) dial-up connection and do some research on-line to see how others have tackled the e-commerce problem. It can also be helpful to look through the computer press and prepare a shortlist of possible companies that may be able to help you. Preparing a formal document outlining your needs can be even more useful, and this will come in handy during the next stage.

## Getting noticed

When it comes to site design, you have two choices. The first is to hire in a design consultant, who will create your site for you and perhaps also arrange for the 'nuts and bolts' of an Internet connection at the same time. The second is to do it all yourself. The former approach is relatively quick and convenient, but can also be extremely expensive. You will probably have to pay either a four-figure or a five-figure amount for a typical web-site design. The second approach is much cheaper, as easy-to-use web-design tools are available for less than £100, and if you spend ten times that amount you can buy the very best tools that are available. The disadvantages to the DIY approach are that it will be hard work, take up far more of your time, and you may also create a result that is less satisfactory and effective than that created by a professional company. Whichever option you choose you need to follow up the design process with an integrated advertising strategy that makes sure that people who would probably like to see your site will know that it exists and where they can find it.

### Choosing a web consultancy

Consultancies advertise widely in the Internet press. When choosing a consultancy, many of the same criteria involved in choosing a consultant for any other IT project applies (see page 126). However, it is also important to look realistically at the business returns on a web-site project, and to draw up as realistic a business plan as possible. Your web site's main reason for existing should be to increase income and profitability, not to line the pockets of the designers. With that in mind, it can be very useful to ask for a proven track record of commercial success when shopping for a suitable consultancy.

It is also important that you choose a design company whose work you respect, and who you feel speaks the same language that you do. You need someone who understands you, understands your business and its needs, has a very clear idea of what you are trying to achieve, and is able to help you achieve it without compromising the way you work. What you do not need is someone who is more interested in creating an arty graphic experience that has little or no commercial relevance to what you are trying to achieve. This can be harder than it sounds, as many web-design companies are run by graphic designers who understand graphics and design but are less familiar with the needs of small businesses.

A good way to test the waters is to produce your own first attempt at a design and specification, and then discuss it with a shortlist of possible design companies. What you are looking for is a company that is helpful enough to correct any misapprehensions on your part without ever being condescending, and then has the design skills to create a firm and effective foundation for the site.

## DIY web-site design and e-commerce

DIY e-commerce can be tackled in two ways. The first is to create a home-made web page, and then add electronic trading features to it. The second is to use one of the 'pre-packaged' systems that make the job much more straightforward, but can also lack some of the flexibility of the home-made approach. Whichever route you choose, it is useful to understand how the web works, and how pages are designed.

### HTML
The codes and special letters and characters that control what appears on a web page are known as HTML (Hypertext Markup Language).

HTML is not a true computer language because it does not do anything apart from set the appearance of a page. In fact, it is more like a very advanced and complicated form of punctuation. Where English uses special characters to indicate that certain words are spoken ('He said') or are to be read as an aside (as in this phrase in brackets), HTML uses similar conventions to indicate when text is to be shown as **bold** or <i>*italics*</i>. Here the '' indicates that all text that follows appears in bold, and the '' turns off the bold effect, and the same for italics. In a real page, similar codes are used to define how large the letters are, what style of lettering they use, where paragraphs begin and end, where images appear on the page, where links are and what they link to, etc. HTML code words are known as 'tags' and always come in pairs. The first 'turns on' a text effect or defines the start of a section of HTML. The second, which typically includes a '/' character, turns off the effect or marks the end of a section.

The complete set of HTML definitions in common use is too complex and involved to include in this book. Books are available which explain the ins and outs of HTML in great detail, and naturally there is a very large amount of information on the web itself. (Try using a search engine to look for the words 'Beginners' and 'HTML'.)

In practice, this level of detail is rarely necessary. It is possible in theory to prepare HTML for web pages using a simple word processor (the code is typed in by hand). However, this is dull and tedious at best, and it is much better to use a WYSIWYG ('What You See Is What You Get') web-page editor. This allows you to produce pages by creating layouts, typing in text and positioning pictures directly on the screen, in a process which has a lot in common with desktop publishing. The 'raw' HTML that produces the page remains hidden away, unless you decide you want to work with it directly.

The best WYSIWYG editors can handle multiple pages, so you can use them to design an entire site at once. All the links between pages on the site will work exactly as they would if the page were 'live'. Links outside the site obviously will not work unless the computer is actually connected to the Internet while you are working, which is not usually recommended, as it is unnecessarily expensive. Editors are available commercially and in the form of shareware. Microsoft's Front Page and Adobe's Page Mill are relatively inexpensive commercial editors at about £100. AOLPress is a good example of a simple but effective shareware editor. AOLPress is designed to be used with the free web space provided by the AOL on-line service, but it can be modified, at the cost of some time and convenience, to work with any web-page hosting service.

## Getting pages to the Internet

Once a site has been finished, the information has to be copied to the Internet before anyone else can see it. Again, the best WYSI-WYG editors make this very simple for you. You connect to the Internet, tell the web editor the address of your web page, and they do the rest, copying all the information over and organising it so that your site appears whenever someone asks for it.

This can also be done by hand using an Internet facility called FTP (file transfer protocol). FTP is Internet jargon for 'copying' – all it does is copy information from one computer to another, although using an appropriate WYSIWYG editor is the simpler approach.

## Web-site design basics

Even the simplest site needs certain design basics, which include the following:

- **'Real world' contact details** These include a company's telephone number and postal addresses. If you want to give something more business-like than a home address, you can always use a PO Box number. Your post office can supply you with details of how to set up one of these.
- **Product information** If there is a lot of information in your web site, it can be very helpful indeed to include a 'search facility' to make it easier to find specific bits of information. On-line support, in the form of frequently asked questions about products, is another extremely helpful option, and can be applied successfully to almost any product or service.
- **Navigation bars ('navbars')** Traditionally these appear at the top left of the page, but should always be visible wherever they are on the page. Navigation bars make it easy to click straight through to a chosen page or facility.
- **A text-only option** This feature is for people who are looking at

pages using a palm-top or a very old or slow computer that cannot deal with pictures and audio.
- **A 'Last modified on' line** This optional feature indicates the date when the site was last updated.
- **A 'hit counter'** Also optional, this feature shows the number of times the page has been viewed.
- **Key selling point** The Internet equivalent of a Unique Selling Point, it may include free information that is useful to visitors, a prize draw, some other free or special offer, or something amusing and entertaining that changes regularly. The point here is to create something that persuades visitors to come back to your site repeatedly, even if it does not close a sale directly.
- **Strong image and branding** You can use graphics and fonts to create a consistent look and feel to your site that mirrors the kind of service you provide. The stronger the image, the more likely it is that your site will make an impression.

Things to leave out of a web site include:

- 'Under construction' signs as these look almost suicidally unprofessional on a commercial page
- very large pictures, which take a long time to appear.
- special effects that make it impossible to view the site without very specialised extra software, or which require a specific version of a web browser
- clichéd web clip art as this can look unprofessional, especially if it is animated.
- too many pages as you can expect to lose half your visitors for every extra page they have to click their way through on their way to finding what they want
- an overly complex site plan as it is essential that each part of the site is easily accessible from any other part, is clearly marked, and has content that is easy to understand.

Another point to remember is that before your site goes live you should test it as thoroughly as possible, preferably bringing in people from outside the project for comments and feedback. This applies whether you have done the design yourself or paid someone to do it. You can easily leave a site on-line unannounced during this process and be fairly confident about getting minimal passing trade.

Alternatively, you can protect the site with a password, which can be removed when the site goes live. In either case, testing should be an essential part of the process, and asking outsiders to look at the site is the best way to highlight its shortcomings.

## Designing with special effects

While a simple design is not necessarily a bad thing, it can be useful to know how to add special effects. The primary aim of a web site is to make it as easy as possible for customers to find what they are looking for. Bells, whistles, frills and bows should only be included if they help create a very strong image for the site that is likely to keep customers coming back. Too much window-dressing can make a site unwieldy. If the choice is between a simple and clear site that looks a little plain but works well, and an all-singing, all-dancing site burdened with so many special effects that it takes minutes to appear, the former is by far the preferable option. For all that, extras can make a difference for certain kinds of sites.

**Java** and **Javascript** software can be used to add special effects, such as **rollovers**, which are buttons that change or light up when the user passes his or her mouse pointer over them and **animations**, including text that changes automatically (for examples see the BBC site at *http://www.bbc.co.uk* and the Lotus site at *http://www.lotus.com*). The software can also be used to create **intelligent applications** that work with other information on the web (for example, graphing a share price which is quoted on another web page). Javascript is built into web pages, rather like an advanced form of HTML. Java uses applets, which are tiny software programs that are copied to the computer that is viewing the web page. Applets can be made very much more complicated than Javascript.

One problem with both of these options, which are collectively known as Dynamic HTML, is that different web browsers handle them in different ways. For example, a web page that works perfectly when viewed with a browser made by Netscape may produce problems when viewed with a Microsoft browser – and vice versa. This makes adding these Java and Javascript features a perennial headache for designers.

Creating special effects that use these systems from scratch requires some computer-programming expertise. Mastering this skill should not be beyond the reach of a dedicated beginner, but realistically this is not an option for anyone who does not have a talent for IT. However, pre-written 'extras' that use Java and Javascript are widely available for free on the Internet. These can be copied into any home-made project, and will then function correctly, even if their detailed workings remain a mystery. (For more details try searching for 'Java' and 'beginner' on the Internet and following the links that appear.) Alternatively, software such as Macromedia's Dreamweaver can be used to work with Dynamic HTML special effects in a way that hides the complexities away – rather like a WYSIWIG editor for web pages.

**Animated GIFs** are relatively small animations that comprise a series of still images shown in sequence so that they appear to be in perpetual cyclical movement. They are rather like electronic flick books. Unlike Dynamic HTML they cannot be made to respond to the actions of a user, and will simply repeat indefinitely.

**MIDI files** make it possible to add a musical background that will be heard by any visitor whose computer is fitted with a standard soundcard and software synthesizer.

**Streaming video** (notably from Real Media) offers a way to put both sound and video clips on to a web site. Quality is still poor for people who use a dial-up link.

### CGI (Common Gateway Interface) scripts

Normally, when a hosting service 'serves up' web pages for visitors, the pages are static. Even if special effects are used, the content of the pages themselves does not change in any way. CGI scripts makes it possible to modify what appears on a web page automatically, according to a set of rules. A CGI script is a computer program that lives and works on the server, rather than on the visitor's computer, and makes it possible for web servers to perform a variety of useful tasks with web-related information. A simple example is a 'hit counter', which shows how many times a page has been viewed. The server keeps track of the actual number, and then when the page is viewed again it 'fills in a blank' on the web page with the HTML required to display this number. The process is hidden away, so that all visitors see is a box that says, for example, 'This page visited 153756 times'.

CGI scripts can be very much more complicated than this. Search facilities are an example of a complex CGI script – for example, the site at Railtrack (*http://www.railtrack.co.uk*) uses a custom-written CGI script to scan through a database of train times and connections whenever a visitor asks for train journey details. Free and commercial CGI search facilities, which are available on the Internet, can help you add similar facilities to your own site. A good web-hosting service will be able to advise you where to find these.

One of the most sophisticated CGI facilities currently available, and one that is of particular interest to e-businesses, is called Actinic Catalog. This system costs under £400 and offers an 'all-in-one' CGI-based catalogue and secure e-commerce facility. It can keep track of an on-line product catalogue, provide visitors with an electronic 'shopping cart', which automatically keeps track of their purchases and maintains a running total of the cost so far, and includes secure email for transmitting orders to you.

Web-hosting companies are wary of CGI scripts because they can be a security risk if they are not used carefully. A CGI script effectively has full control of the server computer on which it runs, and this means that it could cause problems for other customers of a hosting facility. Some hosting companies deal with this problem by limiting customers to a fixed range of scripts that they know are safe. This is not an ideal solution, as you may find that their safe scripts may not allow you to do what you would like with your site. A better option is a company that allows any scripts, but reserves the right to vet them first. If you plan to use advanced CGI facilities you will have to liaise with your hosting company anyway, and it can be a very good idea to discuss your CGI requirements with them before you sign on the dotted line.

## Advertising your web site

The best web-site design in the world is useless if no-one knows it exists. Simply creating a site and then waiting for people to visit it is never enough. The site has to be publicised, and this involves electronic, print and perhaps other kinds of advertising.

To start with, integrate your web-site advertising with your existing paper advertising. If you send out a catalogue or a regular newsletter, include details of the site in it, and remind customers about it whenever your web site changes significantly. Similarly, if you are already paying for magazine advertising, make sure your site is included there, even if it is only a single-line mention, or just the web address. Paper and electronic advertising are complementary rather than mutually exclusive, and to get the best from either you need the support of the other. You may even want to consider a traditional mail shot.

If you have a company car or van it can sometimes be worth having email and web details painted on the side, especially if you can catch the eye of potential customers with something short but powerful that creates a strong image for your company.

If the service you offer is unusual or unique then consider sending out a press release to any relevant local and national newspapers and magazines, and perhaps local radio stations too. News editors are often grateful for copy and press releases are an excellent way to get effective free publicity. Consider contacting your local newspaper as well, as they are almost always happy to support local business.

## Advertising on the web

One possible on-line advertising option is to take space in a 'virtual mall' or other on-line shopping complex. In practice, this is just like being listed in a directory. You may get more business this way, but it is just as likely that the mall will remain anonymous and no-one will hear about it unless you do other advertising yourself, in which case your efforts will be subsidising the mall, rather than vice versa. In spite of that, this option can be worth considering if you run a very small business as a sideline and would like to make extra pocket money from it. A good example of a virtual mall is the shop-front system available on the Geocities site at *http://www.geocities.com*. Some UK-based IT consultancies offer the equivalent of local listings that work in a similar way. You should be wary of these even if they seem like a cheap way to get on-line, especially if site design is included in the package price. These sites are rarely advertised effectively, and you should ask searching questions about the financial benefits to your business before parting with any money.

A similar but slightly more successful approach to the same problem is offered by the Netopia Virtual Office product (at *http://nvo.netopia.com*). This lets you design a simple site using a set of templates, so that you never need to learn the intricacies of HTML. Your site is then posted on-line in an appropriate category. Netopia's clientele is almost uniformly based in the States, but the service offers a way to get on-line with the minimum of fuss and technical confusion and at a reasonable price.

Many other on-line advertising techniques are low cost if not completely free. An essential way to publicise your site is to make sure that it is included by all the main Internet **search engines**. You can do this by notifying the search engines directly. Most have an on-screen form that you can fill in with your details. A more sophisticated approach, which makes sure that your site is listed on both the popular engines and the obscure ones, is to pay a listing company a fee of about £30 to do the notification for you. These companies pass your details to the relevant people, and from then on you will be listed on-line with everyone else.

If you are planning to be listed, you should use meta tags on your web site. These are special HTML codes that list **keywords** to summarise your site. They also allow you to make sure that whenever anyone finds your site in a search a line or two of carefully written advertising blurb appears to describe it, instead of the first line or two of text on your site, which may not be as interesting. Meta tags are very easy to add, and there is plenty of information in most HTML handbooks, which explain how to use them to best effect.

A system known as Link Exchange (*http://www.linkexchange.com*) allows you to take out free advertising on other people's site, in return for carrying their advertising – for free – on yours. Most Internet advertising appears in the form of banner ads, which are effectively animated GIFs. To use Link Exchange you will need to hire someone to create a banner ad for you, or create one of your own using any of the popular animated GIF tools that are widely available for free on-line. To join the service you mail your banner to Link Exchange, and in return you receive a few lines of self-contained HTML that you will be asked to insert into your site. Your advertising then appears randomly on other Link Exchange sites as a banner ad with a clickable link that curious users can follow to see what you have to offer. Your site, in turn, will show a random banner ad from someone else using the system.

One problem with Link Exchange is that you get little or no say in who or what you are advertising. While you are very unlikely to find yourself advertising porn or other undesirable material, you may, nonetheless, advertise companies and services with which you might not want to be associated – perhaps even a direct competitor. The risk is small, but it does exist, and you should research possible problems in this area before signing up.

You can, of course, also take out paid-for advertising all over the Internet. The biggest and most popular sites, including the various on-line services, and the main search engines, are too expensive for small companies to consider. But it is possible to buy space on less popular sites for more affordable amounts. For example, the US version of *PCWorld* magazine charges from $50 for 1,000 views of your ad, to $2,500 (currently about £1,500) for 50,000 views. (Note that on-line advertising is often charged on a 'per view' basis – in other words, for the number of times a page is accessed by a visitor.) Comparable rates are available for UK-based magazines. The effectiveness of this kind of advertising depends very much on the overlap between the placing of the banner ad in terms of 'readership' and on the kinds of services you offer. From that point of view, it helps to try to quantify the usefulness of advertising. Assuming a visitor rate of 1 per cent and a sales take-up rate of around a tenth of that, you would need to make a clear profit of around £35 a sale to make a banner ad in the *PCWorld* site worthwhile.

Another option to consider is a partnership scheme. Here you team up with other companies with related interests and give each other reciprocal advertising space. You can turn this into a formal business proposition. Because it is possible to track where someone has come from when they visit your site, you can offer to pay partners a commission if someone comes to your site via theirs and then makes a purchase and vice versa. The electronic bookseller Amazon has pioneered this approach, and even small personal web sites now advertise Amazon because they know they will be paid a small amount every time they point someone towards the services that Amazon offers.

### *Mailshots and web newsgroups*

A convenient way to advertise on-line is to send out an email mailshot, or to send messages to a number of relevant newsgroups. The latter is not recommended because many ISPs (Internet Service Providers) treat bulk newsgroup postings as spam (unwanted bulk postings), and may react by banning you from their services. What does and does not qualify as spam is open to debate, but it pays to err on the side of caution.

Bulk email shots also count as spam and are another way to attract negative attention. Unsurprisingly perhaps, lists of millions of email addresses are one of the most widely advertised products offered by spammers (people who attempt to make a living by posting unwanted information on the Internet). It is very easy to get hold of these lists for a couple of hundred pounds or less. In theory, there is nothing to stop a company using these as a legitimate marketing tool. In practice any unsolicited bulk posting is very unwelcome indeed. Apart from possible problems with an ISP, repercussions may include death threats, vandalism and physical violence. For legitimate marketing campaigns, spam is most definitely not a recommended tool.

A more successful approach is to keep a list of past customers and to email information to them regularly. Typically, 'regularly' could mean less than four messages a year, because spam has given direct mailings such a bad name that even legitimate email shots can raise people's hackles. The most effective customer mailings are those that announce new products or services, rather than simply reminding customers of a company's existence. Very special offers, such as a sale with genuinely low prices, are also likely to be acceptable. Any bulk mailing should mention that customer requests not to receive further messages will be honoured scrupulously. Again, this is to try and distinguish such legitimate customer mailing from spam. Spammers claim to remove people from their lists when asked, but in fact a 'please remove me' message is often taken as confirmation that spam has reached that address, with the result that even more unwanted messages are sent there. Maintaining a list is easy if a database or contact manager (see page 25) is used.

## Getting paid

Although various 'digital money' systems are being developed (for example, the Mondex digital cash system, which went on trial in Swindon in the late 1990s), none of them are widely enough used as yet to be worth considering as the basis for an electronic business. As a result, the ability to take standard credit cards is rapidly becoming essential for on-line trading.

Credit-card payments deal with currency problems automatically. You specify an amount in your own local currency, and the card company debits the equivalent amount in your customer's local currency. Exchange rates are usually favourable, and, unlike travellers' cheques or other 'interchangeable' currencies, no commission charges are made. The disadvantage to you is that you will pay a surcharge of perhaps 2.5 per cent on every transaction. This is a 'card tax' that is currently unavoidable, but is justified in terms of the extra business you can create for yourself by being able to take credit cards.

Although you can, in theory, deal with cheques, postal orders, international money orders and even posted cash (although the latter is not recommended) you will get much more business if you apply for Card Merchant status, which allows you to trade with a credit card system. The first port of call when inquiring about becoming a card merchant is your bank. If you already have a business account your business manager will be able to advise you about what is involved. You may need to shop around, as transaction fees and starting conditions sometimes vary. For example, in some situations you will be denied an account unless you have been trading for more than a year and have a certain amount of stock on the premises. In situations like these you may need to talk to a bank's e-commerce specialist. Your manager should be able to put you in touch with the appropriate person (if they cannot, you should consider changing to a different bank). The actual process of becoming a merchant is relatively straightforward. In exchange for filling in some forms and offering suitable guarantees you will receive a card account, a manual card-swipe machine (the electronic models in shops cost extra to hire, but you may not need one initially) and some slips. From then on the process is similar to running an ordinary bank account.

If you are planning to accept orders that include credit card information, it is essential that you provide a way for orders to be placed securely, sidestepping the possible interference of hackers. The easiest way to do this is to suggest to customers that they fax or phone orders to you instead of using email, or that they disguise orders in some way – perhaps by splitting the card number across two emails, by using words instead of numbers, or by adding one to each digit on the card, and so on. Businesses do use these techniques successfully, but they obviously lack a certain professionalism and credit-card companies are not very keen on them.

A better approach is to use a **secure server** system. This passes orders to you in code. As far as both you and your customers are concerned, the process is completely transparent: they place an order in the usual way, and you receive an email that you have no trouble reading. But at all points in between information is encrypted, so that no-one else can read it. Your web-hosting service will be able to advise you on how to set up a secure server, and may even offer the service already. Actinic Catalog (see Appendix V) offers a related secure ordering facility. Alternatively, you should look out for a hosting service that offers Secure Sockets Layer (SSL) technology.

Even with a secure server, you may still have to deal with certain elements of the payments by hand. This is not a problem for certain kinds of business. If you are sending out goods by mail you can simply send customers the standard credit card confirmation slip through the post. However, it is more useful to be able to deal with payments electronically. The technology that can do this is still in its infancy, and there are a number of competing standards in use. They all offer the ability to transfer money for an order securely from your customer to your card account, and produce an automatic email acknowledging that payment has been received, which takes the place of the more common paper confirmation slip. (This part of the payment process is known as 'non-repudiation' and guarantees that neither party can back out of the transaction once it has been confirmed.)

The behind-the-scenes work needed to create an automated payment is complex, but is generally based on the digital certification and verification systems discussed in Chapter 11, and is hard for hackers to get into. Two systems are widely used. SET (Secure Electronic Transactions) is a joint effort by Visa and Mastercard, while OTP (Open Trading Protocol) is favoured by a number of computer companies, and is a more open-ended system that works with as-yet-unexplored digital-payment systems.

None of this matters very much from a business point of view, as the technology is hidden behind the scenes and does not have to be dealt with directly. For more information about practical digital payment systems you should contact the appropriate people at the credit card companies directly, talk to an e-commerce specialist at your bank, check the relevant trade magazines (notably *Internet Works* and *Internet Business*), or get the latest details from a relevant consultant or hosting company. This is a rapidly evolving field, and technologies that seem standard today may have become obsolete tomorrow.

# Chapter 13

# Dealing with the Year-2000 problem

On the 1 January 2000, an unknown number of computer systems around the world will stop working properly. This problem, known as the **Millennium Bug** or 'Y2K' (Year 2000), is caused by faulty software or hardware that are unable to cope with the change from a '1900' to a '2000' date. For the most part, computer books have so far concentrated on how the problem applies to desktop PCs. But in reality the problem may be far more serious. The larger computers used by airlines, banks, the stock market, air-traffic control systems, the various utilities, telecommunications and distributive trades (including food supplies) may all be affected. A small number of household electrical goods, such as videos and central-heating controllers, and perhaps even certain more recent car designs may also run into problems.

The scope of the problem is daunting. In addition to computers and software, problems may exist in 'embedded chips', which are simple computer chips that are used to control valves, lifts, heating devices and many other systems used in factories and businesses. In some cases these chips are very simple 'logic arrays' in which decision-making circuitry has been burned into the chip itself. Logic arrays are almost impossible to check for Y2K compliance once they have been fitted in place.

Professional estimates of the effects of Y2K are very variable, and range from the sanguine to the hysterical. Some IT professionals maintain that there may be a few failures, but on the whole it will be business as usual. Others, especially in the United States, fear the worst, and have literally taken to the hills after stocking up with enough supplies to live self-sufficiently indefinitely. If this sounds alarmist it is worth noting that in the UK, county councils have already held contingency planning meetings with representatives from the utilities and emergency services. Also, the relatively sober UK newsgroup uk.tech.y2k, which is used by IT professionals dealing with Y2K questions, suggests that readers should make plans for doing without essential services for at least a few days, on the grounds that this is 'only prudent'.

Further cause for concern is provided by the fact that with under 500 days to go, a survey by consultancy Regester Larkin showed that 41 per cent of companies were unaware of the existence of independently verified guidelines and definitions regarding the problem. Business analysts from the Gartner Group have estimated that worldwide compliance may be less than 50 per cent, with the 'emerging markets' in the Middle East, Far East and Latin America causing most of the problems.

Perhaps the most realistic assessment of the problem is that catastrophe is unlikely, but inconvenience – and possibly major inconvenience – is a serious possibility.

For the small business, there are two main issues to address: compliance and contingency. Compliance is the process of ensuring that your own systems and procedures will not be affected by the date change, and so, by implication, that any product or service you provide will not suffer from Y2K problems. Contingency is about limiting your dependence on anyone or anything that supplies your business with goods or services, so that if their systems fail your business will suffer as little as possible.

Note that for some businesses, *PCs may be the least of their worries.* Ensuring PC hardware is Y2K compliant is a relatively simple job. But if your business uses any machinery, office equipment, security systems, building control systems or other potentially date-dependent hardware, all of these have to be checked and repaired well before 1 January 2000. Alternatively, contingency plans will have to be made to deal with their potential failure.

## Compliance

DISC (**D**elivering **I**nformation **S**olutions to **C**ustomers through International Standards) is a department within the British Standards Institute and has produced a compliance document, which is available on the web from *http://www.bsi.org.uk/disc/year2000.html*. According to its definition: 'Year 2000 conformity shall mean that neither performance nor functionality is affected by dates prior to, during and after the year 2000.'

The first point to note about compliance is that not just your computer, but your business as a whole has to be made compliant. All of your hardware, software, office equipment, and even stationery have to be able to cope with the date change.

A more subtle point is that the Y2K problem has a wider scope than many businesses realise. Other dates can also cause problems, and these have to be checked as thoroughly as year-2000 dates. To achieve compliance you need to:

- examine which parts of your business may be at risk
- check to see whether any of these parts suffer from problems
- take remedial action, either repairing items or replacing them
- check again to see if all the problems have been solved.

Achieving absolute compliance may be impossible, because it may not be feasible to test absolutely everything. This is where contingency becomes important; you should be able to keep working even if there are serious problems with your hardware, software and other systems.

## Assessing the risk

Anything in your office that refers to a calendar may have problems. This includes:

- computer hardware
- computer software
- computer information
- printed stationery (cheques, for example)
- credit-card equipment
- other potentially date-sensitive equipment.

As a first step, list everything you have that falls into these categories. Then check thoroughly for all other equipment that may be date-sensitive. For example, some video recorders, answering machines and even telephones are date-aware.

### Checking computer hardware

A number of computer books and magazines have made the issue of Y2K compliance seem overly complicated, when, in fact, checking for hardware compliance is very straightforward. If you have **Apple Mac** computers there is no problem as they are fully compliant.

Most **PCs** are not fully compliant. They will 'roll over' to the correct date if they are left on at midnight on 31 December 1999, but the date is likely to become wrong if the PC is subsequently turned off and on again. To solve the problem, simply reset the date by hand, using the Windows date and time setting tool (double click on the clock at the bottom right of the screen to make this appear) or the MS-DOS date command if you are using an MS-DOS system. The date should be correct from then on. Strictly speaking this will not make your PC fully compliant. In most PCs the Real Time Clock (RTC) circuit is not year-2000 aware, and has to be reset by hand as described above to show the correct year after 1 January 2000. Only a tiny minority of applications uses the date calculated by the RTC directly, although Windows 2000 appears to rely on it, as do some other network-ready packages. If you are running a network it can be worth using extra software and hardware (described below) to ensure that your main server is compliant. In most cases other computers on the network will then be made compliant when they are next take a date from the network.

Non-networked PCs have to rely on their internal clock instead, which is the *BIOS* – Basic Input Output System. This is a different circuit that maintains its own clock once a PC is running. As long as your BIOS works properly and you have set the RTC by hand to show twenty-first-century rather than twentieth-century dates, your PC will maintain the date correctly.

A small number of PCs will need to be reset by hand every time they are started. To check if you have one of these, watch what appears on the screen after you turn your computer on. If it shows the words 'Award BIOS', check the date quoted, which is likely to appear at the bottom left of the screen. If the information flickers on and off too quickly to read, press and release the 'Pause/Break' key on the keyboard when the information appears. This will stop your computer in its tracks. Use the reset button on the computer's case to restart it. If the date shown is between 26 April 1994 and 31 May

1995, your computer will suffer from this problem (note that dates will be shown in the American format of MM/DD/YY). You then have a choice of ignoring the problem (an adequate solution if you mostly write letters, but one which may cause difficulties with bookkeeping and accounts software), setting the date by hand every time you start your computer, or 'repairing' the problem (for more details on the latter see page 250).

Rumours on the Internet have suggested that some PCs will stop working altogether. However, a detailed search showed that this was likely to be hearsay rather than a real problem. While the possibility exists, the likelihood of it happening is extremely small, and the rumour is only included here for completeness.

What is more certain, however, is the fact that a design fault in some PCs may cause an effect known as **time dilation** or the **Crouch-Echlin effect**. After 1 January 2000 the computer's clock may jump to an indefinite time in the future whenever it is started up. Very soon both the time and date become completely wrong. The problem is random, and mostly affects older computers. The 286 and 386 computers are quite likely to suffer from it, 486s are less likely, and Pentium computers onwards are very unlikely, although a small number of cases have been reported. To check for time dilation, you will either need to set the wrong date and leave your computer running (not recommended) or to buy a program called TDTools, which is available from Elmbronze Ltd (more details from *http://www.elmbronze.demon.co.uk/products/TDtools.htm*). TDTools includes a fix for the problem.

Other computers may or may not be compliant. In the case of powerful workstation computers, the easiest way to check is to contact the dealer from which you bought the machine, or check for relevant information on the web. For other computers, again check with manufacturer, but in general assume they are *not* compliant unless you are explicitly told otherwise.

You may, optionally, test your PC with Y2K-checking software. These are available commercially, and can also be copied from the Internet. They are unlikely to tell you anything that differs from the above, and may even cause you unnecessary problems.

Most checkers are simply advertising for various Y2K software fixes. They will state that your PC is not compliant, and therefore should be fitted with extra software. However, typical software fixes simply reset the RTC automatically, which you can do perfectly well manually with exactly the same result.

Nevertheless, if you would like to test your computer using any of the widely available software checkers, *do not* change the date and then start Windows in the usual way. Instead use a start-up disk, and change dates using the MS-DOS time/date command. When you have finished your tests, set the time back to the current time/date, remove the start-up disk, and only then start Windows again. This will prevent any problems with expired software licences, or confused book-keeping software. Information on how to make and use a start-up disk is included in the Windows help information. This will avoid problems with software licences that are renewed annually, or with time-limited free trial software. If you do not take these precautions you may find that setting the date forward to check for Y2K problems persuades the software that the license or trial period has expired.

## Checking computer software

The only foolproof way to check software is to set the date ahead and see what the results are. Unfortunately this can cause serious damage to your business records if you try it with 'live' information. Any date-sensitive package, such as accounting or book-keeping software, may become very confused. You may be able to get around this problem by backing up all of your records before any testing, although with a slow back-up system this will be very time-consuming.

An alternative is to rely on manufacturer's statements of Y2K compliance. The best place to find information about this is on the web. For example, *http://www.microsoft.com/technet/topics/year2k/default.htm* is Microsoft's listing of Y2K issues that affect its products. A patchy but useful list of links to compliance statements from various companies is available at *http://www.vendor2000.com*, and a selection of other sources of information is listed in Appendix VI. If you do not have an Internet connection, you can check with your suppliers by calling their technical support lines or writing letters to the correct department. The problem with compliance statements is that they are not foolproof and offer no guarantee that 'compliant' products will actually work properly. You are then left with a choice of either checking the software by moving the clock forward (which, as mentioned above, can cause problems) or taking the manufacturer's word for it and hoping for the best. Often neither of these is a satisfactory option.

There are a number of ways through this problem. One is to set up a dummy test using real information on an isolated test machine (licensing permitting). If you have a network, you can copy both information and software to it over the network, but should then *disconnect it from other computers when you perform any tests*. If you do not have a spare computer, consider hiring or borrowing one for a short period. This will work well for most off-the-shelf products. However, if you have specialised software with an annual licence, the licence will expire, and it is unlikely that the manufacturer will give you a special licence for testing. One way around this problem is to ask the supplier if they can supply a machine for testing at their own premises.

Finally, some Y2K-checking products claim to test for software compliance. These should not be considered foolproof, as there are a huge number of ways the Y2K problem can manifest itself in software. However, one area where checkers can be useful is if they offer a *database* feature – a list of date-related problems suffered by widely used business software. A list like this can help speed up manual checking by pinpointing products that may not work correctly. When checking software, remember to check the operating system too. For example, Windows 3.1 is, as Microsoft puts it, 'compliant with minor issues'. Again, information is available on the web.

Also, remember that you need to check for more than just the Y2K 'rollover' itself. In fact there are three kinds of sensitive dates, and correct operation with all of these needs to be checked where relevant:

**Precursor dates** rely on software being able to work with years 2000 and onwards directly, but have an effect some time before 1 January 2000. An example is the 1999 to 2000 tax period and financial year, which starts in April 1999. Financial software may need to be able to deal with dates in 2000 from April 1999 onwards. Another example is software that makes financial predictions, perhaps a year, a half-year or a quarter ahead. Again, it may be vulnerable to Y2K problems ahead of the main event. The 90-day, 60-day and 30-day predictions will also be vulnerable.

**Y2K dates** include dates after 1 January 2000. These are where the bulk of Y2K problems are likely to surface. The date 29 February

2000 is a leap-year special case. Software that uses the wrong rules to calculate leap years will ignore it, even though it exists in the year 2000.

**Other dates** that have nothing to do with Y2K can still cause problems. For example, the date 9 September 1999 (9/9/99) is used by some software as a 'signal' date, and is treated differently to ordinary dates. Popular off-the-shelf software is not likely to suffer from this problem, but if you use a bespoke system you should check it thoroughly, either with a practical test or by looking through the documentation. Your supplier should also be able to offer more information, and may, perhaps at a price, be able to repair the software so that signal dates work correctly and references to them are changed to a safe signal date such as 0/0/00.

## Information

If you have created databases or spreadsheets that use DD/MM/YY (two-digit year) dates instead of DD/MM/YYYY then you may already have a millennium problem.

What this means in practice depends on the software that you are using. For example, Microsoft's Access database always uses four-digit years internally, even if you only type in two digits. However, the version of Access in Office 95 assumes that two-digit years are in this century if the current date is before 1 January 2000, and in the next century afterwards. If you use it to create staff records that include a date of birth, or even date of first employment – perhaps for pension purposes – it may not work correctly. Other products simply assume that all two-year dates are in this century, and of course if you continue to use this software after 1 January 2000 you will get errors. To check information you have to:

- find any occurrences of two-digit years in your records
- check if the software you are using handles these correctly
- modify any forms that are used to enter data to make sure that either four-digit dates are used in future, or two-digit dates are corrected to four-digit dates.

A further problem is caused if you attempt to copy your information from one software package to another, perhaps because you would like to update your software before 1 January 2000 problems become likely. Software that works correctly internally may not necessarily be able to export information in a compliant way. To check, copy your information over and watch what happens in your new software when you attempt date calculations with dates both before and after 1 January 2000. If these do not work correctly you will have to take remedial action.

### Stationery and other equipment

A surprising number of cheque books still have '19__' printed in the date area. You should replace these before 1 January 2000. (You may be able to cross out the '19__', print your own date, and initial the change, but it is possible that certain bank staff may reject this.) Similarly, with pre-printed business stationery, check that there are no '19__'s visible.

Credit-card equipment will need to be checked before the event. You should contact your card company to check that both their hardware and their systems are compliant.

Some video recorders may have problems with timer recording after 1 January 2000. This is one item that you can check by setting the date forward without worrying about adverse consequences.

### Networks and the Internet

On many networks, client computers take their time from a central server. You should check if this is the case on your network, and make sure that the server is compliant. Other network components, such as hubs and routers, may or may not have date sensitivity built in. You should attempt to get a compliance statement from the original manufacturer if you are not sure, or, where practical, organise a test.

Network operating systems and software are likely to be date-sensitive. Email and groupware systems may be particularly vulnerable to date problems. At worst they may not work at all, at best you may have problems with messages appearing out of order when sorted by date. All of these should be checked in the same way as other software.

The Internet itself is unlikely to be fully compliant. Given its fault-tolerant nature it is unlikely to fail completely, although no one knows for sure what will happen to it on the first day of the year 2000. The underlying technical specifications that drive the Internet are compliant, but some individual computers that deal with email and web requests may stop working. In practice this means that some web sites will become invisible, traffic as a whole will become congested, and email may take longer to get through.

Many e-commerce systems are *not* compliant. The computers themselves are, but the way they exchange information with banks and other facilities may not be. You should check with your ISP and e-commerce providers to make sure that you will have no problems. This applies to other business services, such as mail forwarding and web hosting.

British Telecommunications is working hard to make sure that phone services are not disrupted, so the chances are good that you will be able to get a telephone connection to the Internet, as well as being able to do business by phone. But there may be temporary outages in some parts of the country if there are widespread power failures.

## Dealing with non-compliance

Armed with a list of non-compliant equipment, the next step is to look at what needs to be repaired or replaced, and what can be worked around. This will depend very much on your own requirements. If you mainly use your computer as a word processor, date problems may not bother you. If you use it as the basis of an e-commerce network, you will need to do remedial work. To tackle problems, you need to go through the same categories you used to check equipment.

### Non-compliant computer hardware

Most PCs can be fixed by hand simply by setting the date once when work starts in the New Year. If you have one or more of these PCs, you need to make sure that all staff are aware of the problem and will set the date when they need to.

PCs with more serious problems, including those that would otherwise need to be re-set every day, or which suffer from time dilation – require more work. One option is simply to replace them. Most new PCs are fully Y2K compliant and should give you no problems, although you should still insist on a formal compliance statement when buying. However, this is an expensive option and is not necessary, except perhaps as a last resort. (In any case some consultants are concerned that panic buying of new PCs in the run-up to 1 January 2000 will push up prices and make replacement an unrealistic option.)

Computers can be fixed in three ways. A **BIOS upgrade** will solve the problem by modifying the motherboard so that the BIOS works properly. Computers that have a flash BIOS can be reprogrammed simply by running a piece of software. Others may need to have the BIOS chip physically replaced. BIOS upgrades are fiddly, cost between £50 and £100, may cause other problems, and should only be considered if you use a PC for 'mission critical' work. A BIOS update is the only way to make a PC inherently and fully Y2K compliant. To obtain a BIOS update you should contact your supplier. It is possible to perform an update yourself by copying suitable software from the Internet, but there are technical issues involved, which are best left to experts.

**Motherboard replacement** has the same effect as a BIOS upgrade, but is rather more expensive. You should consider this option if your PC is due to be upgraded anyway. If you have an older PC, a suitable motherboard will no longer be available, so you will have to change the motherboard, processor chip, and possibly the memory at the same time. This will be the most expensive option short of buying a completely new machine.

**Software fixes** insert a software update into the computer that solves any Y2K problems automatically. Commercial fixes are typically less than £30. Most simply do the equivalent of setting the date by hand after 1 January 2000.

**Hardware fixes** add a completely new time/date system to the PC, in the form of an internal add-on card, which is supplied with suitable software. At around £150 for the card, it may be worth considering a replacement motherboard instead. Your supplier should be able to advise you which is the most cost-effective solution.

### Non-compliant computer software

Typically you have three choices when dealing with non-compliant software. **Patches** for Y2K problems are now being supplied by many manufacturers free of charge. These are small software updates that you install yourself, and correct existing Y2K issues. For example, patches for most versions of Windows are available from Microsoft. The Internet is usually the most convenient place to find patches, although some manufacturers also offer them on disk.

**Upgrades** are essential when dealing with an older version of software if a newer version is available that offers extra features and also solves all Y2k problems. Again, upgrades are often available on the web, or directly from software manufacturers. Unlike patches, not all upgrades are free.

**Migration** is the technical term for switching to a completely different software package. This is more expensive and can be fraught with complications. For example, copying all the information from one package to another can be time-consuming, and extra work may be required to make sure the information is correct. Migration is only required if a product will stop working properly after 1 January 2000, to the extent that it becomes completely useless to you. However, in some situations it is the only possible option.

## Information

Dealing with information that is sensitive to the date change is rather harder. The simplest if perhaps not the quickest way to modify information is to re-key it by hand. If you have a small number of records (perhaps less than 100) or are unusually patient, you can do this yourself. Alternatively, it may be worth hiring a temporary data-entry worker to do the job for you.

If you have tens of thousands of records this will not be practical. This is one of the few situations where knowing how to use macros and the programming languages that exist in office suites can be very helpful. If you can master these tools, it becomes relatively easy to create a simple piece of software that will, for example, convert two-digit years to four-digit years.

## Buildings and plant

Any number of date-sensitive machines in office buildings and plants may be a major headache. In fact, dealing with plant, buildings and manufacturing equipment can be far more of a challenge for a business than sorting out its computer systems. Problem items can include not just industrial equipment, but also office climate-control systems, photocopiers and other hardware that automatically signals maintenance requests after a set period.

As with other equipment, the choice is between contacting manufacturers for compliance statements and attempting to check for problems yourself. If a manufacturer is no longer trading you will have to improvise a test. Some systems will be able to limp along, even if they are not entirely compliant. For example, an automated vehicle emissions tester in a garage will still work properly even if it shows a two-digit date that starts with '19'. However, others will work erratically. And safety-critical equipment, such as medical items, may need to be certified formally for legal reasons.

If you do not have suitable expertise yourself to deal with these issues, your best option is to call in a suitable consultant or engineer to do the work for you. This, inevitably, comes at a price, but the alternative can be literally disastrous.

Similar problems apply to buildings and premises. If your building is 'dumb', with no automated systems, then you will have no problems. But 'smart' buildings with lifts, air-conditioning, heating and temperature control, sprinkler and other alarm systems, and automatic locks and security systems will need careful checking.

If you are renting, this is the responsibility of the landlord, who should supply a compliance statement. Failing to do so may perhaps go against the terms of your lease, leaving you with the option of legal action if something goes wrong on the day. You should check your legal position formally if your landlord is unwilling to provide a compliance statement.

If you are the owner, or are paying off a mortgage, these problems become your responsibility. If there are maintenance staff on hand they should be able to look into the issue for you. You will need to make a complete inventory of all the automated systems in the building, check for compliance with the suppliers of each one individually, and take any remedial action required.

If it is obvious that a building cannot have its Y2K problems repaired in time or within a realistic budget, then you have some tough decisions to make. Selling up or moving is one option, although potentially expensive and a major disruption. It may also leave you legally liable – although this is a case where *caveat emptor* ('let the buyer beware') is particularly relevant.

**Triage** of major systems is another. This is a formal procedure that divides systems into three categories: those which are beyond hope; those that have problems but are non-critical; and those that are critical but can be repaired in time. Performing triage helps focus on what you need to keep your business functional, even if it operates at reduced efficiency. For example, automatic locks are 'mission critical' because if they fail you will not be able to get into the building. Heating systems are not – you will be able to hire in other forms of heating temporarily, or organise some other system.

If after triage it is obvious that serious problems are still inevitable, then you may need to concentrate on contingency (see below) rather than repair plans, and deal with the repairs slowly after the event.

### Other items

The options for dealing with other, non-computer, items affected by the Y2K problem are, again, fairly simple: you can ignore the problems, you can have something repaired, or you can replace it. Deciding which option to take depends on the item and how it works. For example, a date-sensitive photocopier may stop working properly, or may simply light a 'maintenance' light. Similarly a video recorder may stop recording automatically, but will still play back correctly.

Realistically, the repair of many items will be impossible. It is fairly easy to upgrade a PC, because PCs are far more open-ended than other consumer goods. The software in other electronic products is fixed and very difficult to change, and in many cases is literally soldered in place. One useful trick that may work with equipment that falls into this category is to deliberately set the year to 1972. This has the same pattern of days as 2000, including an extra leap-year day in February. This can be used as a 'quick fix' with industrial machinery and building control systems, provided that they have a calendar that goes back far enough.

### Checking again

Once items have been checked and 'repaired', either properly, or temporarily, it is essential to refer back to your original list of non-compliant items and perhaps retest everything to make sure that systems really will work as planned. This stands you in good stead for the next stage: working out contingency plans.

## Contingency

Once a company's internal systems have been checked, it is essential to look at the way that products, services and information flow into the company to assess the likelihood of failure of any of these. A workable contingency plan has to consider *all the services that a company relies on*. These include: basic infrastructure supplies, such as power and water; distribution supplies, such as transport, post and courier services; financial services, such as banking, telecommunications, the Internet, and perhaps satellite links; and also any dependencies in buildings and plant. You will also need to be sure that whatever happens you will have access to all your business information.

Once you have a list of suppliers, the next step is to contact them for compliance statements. This will not be as straightforward as it sounds, because many companies are unwilling to specify full compliance for legal reasons. And some companies, notably some utilities, are unwilling to guarantee their service at all, although they will probably respond reassuringly if you query them about their services.

How you respond to this is a personal choice. For most companies it will be impossible to eliminate all dependencies. Creating a workable, bullet-proof contingency plan that ensures a business will keep running can easily use up all of a company's assets. A practical question to ask is when does a plan become good enough? No plan is foolproof, but you can gain greater insight into its possible effectiveness by:

**Listing your assumptions, and double-checking them** For example, if you expect power in your area to stay on (or perhaps go off) you should have good reasons for believing this, rather than relying on guesswork. If you have listed all of your suppliers and contacted them for compliance information, you will have at least some evidence to support your assumptions.

**Listing the rationale for each item on the plan** This can help you prioritise items if there are insufficient resources to complete the plan as a whole.

**Listing the implications for each item** What will the results be? Will they be the ones you expect, or are there other implications to consider?

Once this exercise is completed, it should be clearer how effective your contingency plans are likely to be, and how much they will cost. There is no overall right answer to the question of Y2K contingency, because some parts of the picture will remain unknown. But by identifying those issues that you think will cause you the most difficulty, you can make arrangements in advance of the date itself.

The best possible time to start this process is as soon as possible. If you need to buy or hire in extra supplies and equipment, you may find that they will become harder to get hold of later on as more and more businesses realise that contingency planning may be necessary. Examples of possible contingency steps include:

- creating paper copies of all your business records, including bank statements, contact details of suppliers and customers, and their respective financial positions
- investigating the practicalities of running your business without 'live' access to your computer records, and instituting procedures that can be used for this
- widening your list of suppliers. If you are dependent on one particular supplier, you should find at least two other companies that can provide the same service
- buying extra stock and supplies before 1 January 2000, which will provide a 'breathing space' if all your suppliers have catastrophic problems
- acquiring an adequate, but not excessive, cash float to pay for essentials
- liaising with other local businesses and your local Chamber of Commerce to discuss areas where local businesses can support each other.

## Insurance and legal issues

It might seem reasonable that your business insurance policies will cover you for Y2K problems. In practice, this is very unlikely. According to insurers, Y2K is a foreseeable event and therefore policyholders should have made plans for it, although this does not come under professional indemnity cover, which would normally cover you for the financial results of professional mistakes or misadventures.

If you are a director you are legally obliged to take all the steps in your power to make sure your company is not seriously affected by Y2K problems. Anything else may be considered negligence. In general, the legal questions around Y2K are not yet fully understood, and the issues are unlikely to become clear until after the event. It is probable that if you are a supplier, you will be asked to provide a certificate of Y2K readiness. Providing a certificate may leave you open to legal action later if your business has problems delivering to its customers, even if those problems are not your fault. Not providing a certificate may mean that customers refuse to continue doing business with you. Some companies have started offering loosely worded 'compliance' certificates, which state that every possible action is being taken, but services cannot be guaranteed. These are acceptable to some customers, but not all. Others companies have simply become secretive about their state of preparedness, and appear willing to take their chances in any aftermath. Still others, especially the larger utilities, have posted details of their compliance efforts on the web, and are willing, in some cases, for outsiders to come in and check their work. Negotiating a 'gentleman's agreement' with your customers, which provides them with evidence of your compliance efforts and general business best practice, but does not necessarily offer a full, legally binding compliance statement, is one possible way to deal with the situation.

In the US, the government has suggested a legal amnesty for companies to try and aid cooperation between companies in a mutually beneficial way. The same has not happened in the UK yet, although such legislation has been suggested. Until it appears, the legal issues will remain a complex headache for businesses trying to work through the Y2K rollover.

# Appendix I
# Making sense of specifications

The computer world is full of statistics and specifications. Newcomers can easily feel overwhelmed by the huge range of hardware advertised in the computer press. Details and differences are described in a technical language of numbers and apparently meaningless abbreviations. Choosing a system to buy can appear to be a major headache for those making their own buying decisions.

However, for average business use, it may not be necessary to understand all the jargon. Anyone who has no plans to venture beyond the 'bare essentials' outlined in Chapter 1 (see page 12) will find that the differences between the very best computer available and the more ordinary and affordable system are unlikely to be very noticeable. In practice any simple machine from a reputable manufacturer that costs between £500 and £750 should be adequate.

Buying a system through a consultant should, in theory, be another way to avoid having to learn about the finer points of computer advertising. A consultant or supplier will make buying decisions for you and, again in theory at least, you will be sold a system that satisfies your work needs without further effort. But even here, it is useful to know what different hardware options are available. Suppliers may go bust, leaving you without support, and systems sometimes need to be expanded. Being able to understand trade jargon also means you are likely to be treated with more respect when you deal with suppliers and their support staff.

It is true that some tasks do tax a computer fully, and when buying hardware for these kinds of work it really does help to understand the specifications that appear in advertising. Examples include the latest computer games, computer-aided design, illustration, image design and animation, very large spreadsheets or databases, and

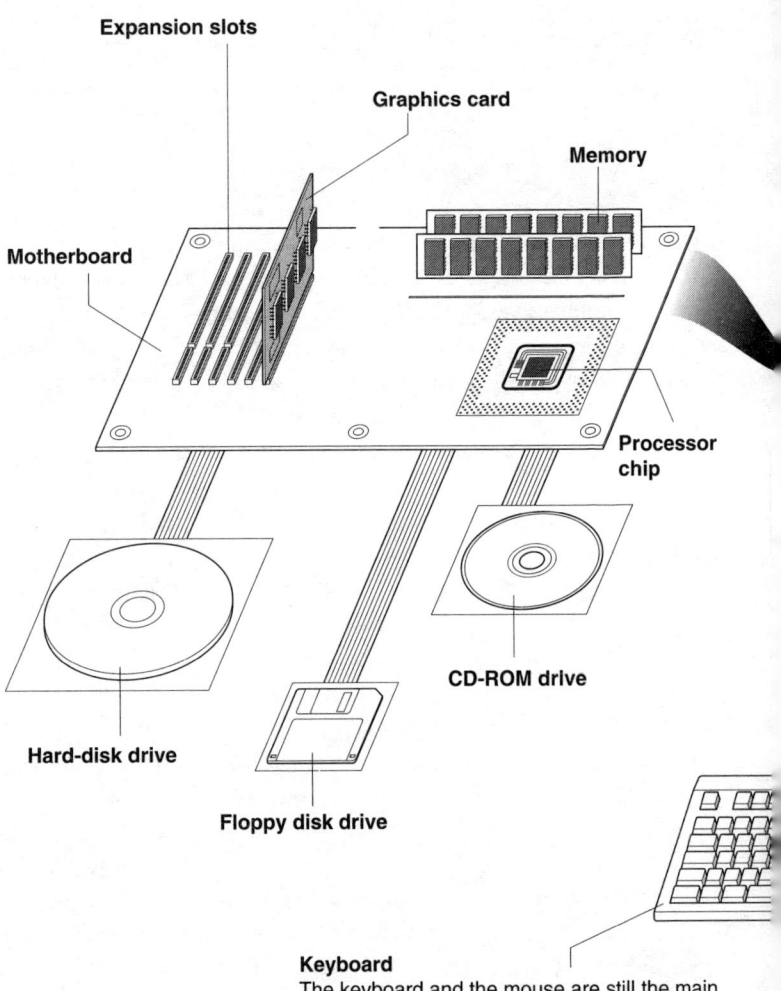

Labels on diagram: Expansion slots, Graphics card, Memory, Motherboard, Processor chip, Hard-disk drive, Floppy disk drive, CD-ROM drive, Keyboard

**Keyboard**
The keyboard and the mouse are still the main way of telling your computer what you want it to do. The keyboard is very much like the standard typewriter keyboard with an extra set of keys for numbers on the right-hand side and various other special keys, which are used by some software.

Making sense of specifications

**Monitor/screen**
The screen is where information is displayed and you can see what your computer is doing. Screens vary in size, but even the smallest are capable of displaying photographs clearly.

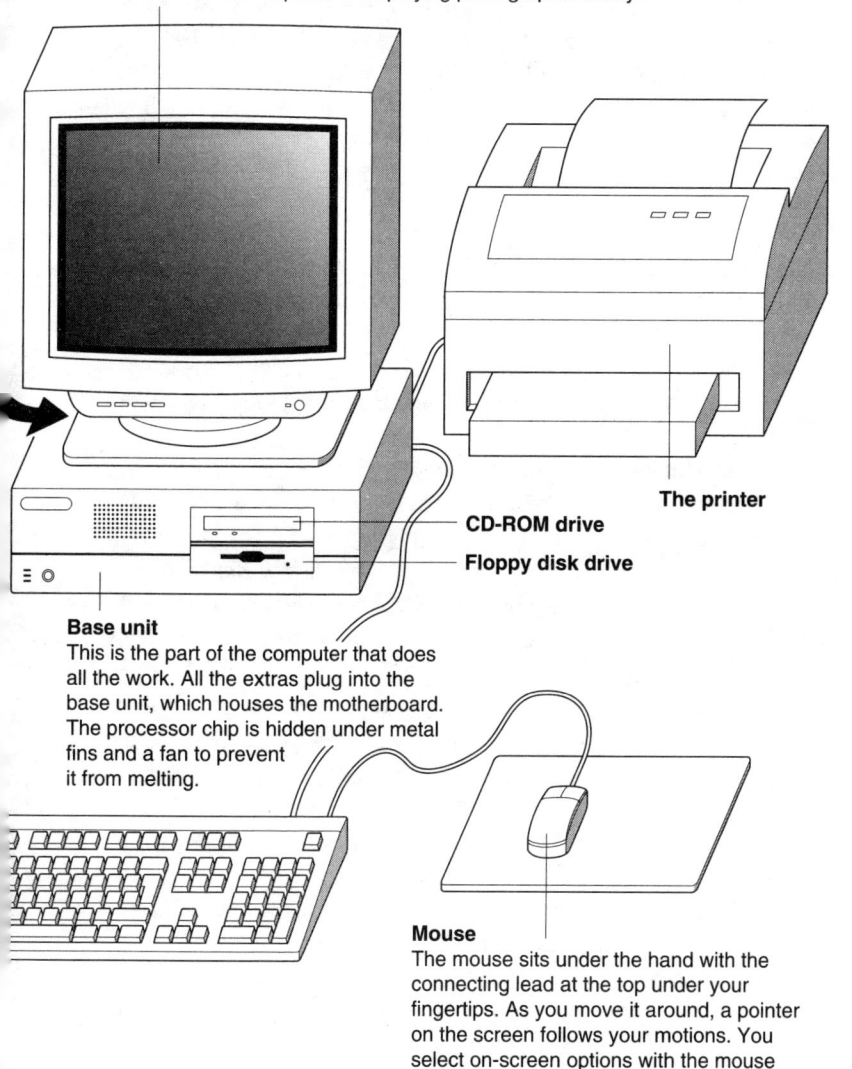

**The printer**

**CD-ROM drive**

**Floppy disk drive**

**Base unit**
This is the part of the computer that does all the work. All the extras plug into the base unit, which houses the motherboard. The processor chip is hidden under metal fins and a fan to prevent it from melting.

**Mouse**
The mouse sits under the hand with the connecting lead at the top under your fingertips. As you move it around, a pointer on the screen follows your motions. You select on-screen options with the mouse buttons, which are also under your fingertips.

specialised work, such as sound and video editing. For these kinds of applications it is worth spending extra money on more powerful hardware, because cheaper systems will seem frustratingly slow.

This appendix is a reference guide to the kind of hardware that is widely advertised in computer magazines, or which may be supplied when you order a complete solution. While mainly intended for reference, it can also introduce beginners to the language used when buying a computer.

---

**Anatomy of a computer**

- **Processor chip** The 'engine' of the PC, the processor does all the calculations, makes sense of your typing, controls what happens on the display, and produces useful results.
- **Motherboard** This is the 'chassis' of the PC. Everything is connected to the motherboard, including the processor chip and the RAM.
- **RAM (Random Access Memory)** This is the working area of a PC. It is rather like the desk space in an office where information can be held temporarily while being worked on. The bigger your desk or RAM, the more papers and projects you can keep on it at one time, and the more quickly you can switch between working on them. Unlike a real desk, all the information disappears when you turn the power off.
- **Hard disk space** (often shortened to **hard drive** or **hard disk**) This is used for filing information when the computer is off, and also as a slower temporary storage space if the main memory (RAM) becomes full. It is very much like the filing space in an office, with the difference that it contains both documents and a 'tool box' of the software applications.
- **Monitor** Just the technical term for the screen, the monitor is controlled by a **graphics card**, which converts information from the processor chip into shapes, pictures and words on the monitor.
- **CD-ROM drive** Now an essential extra, the drive is needed to make use of software that is often supplied in the form of a 'CD-ROM'. These CDs look exactly like a music CDs, but contain digital information that can be copied into the computer. CD-ROM drives can also play music CDs through a soundcard and speakers (see opposite).

> **Peripherals and extras**
>
> - **Peripherals** These extras – some optional, some essential – connect the computer to the rest of the world and make it possible to get information in and out of the system. The most important peripherals are the **keyboard**; the **printer**, which prints information on to paper; and the **mouse**, a small plastic object that fits into the palm of the hand, rolls horizontally and controls a pointer (called the cursor) on the screen.
> - **Popular optional extras** These include **soundcards**, which allow the computer to record and play music; **loudspeakers** and **microphones**, which plug into the soundcard; **network cards**, which connect the computer to a network; and **modems**, which connect it to the telephone line.

## What specifications tell you

From the outside, computers look more or less the same. Some may be housed in a bigger box than others, but this in no way relates to how well they perform. Instead, differences are distinguished in four ways:

- how quickly a computer works
- how much information it can hold
- what optional extras are included
- what kind of extras can be added in future.

The lists of numbers, letters and other jargon quoted in advertising give you some idea of how well the computer scores in these four different areas.

## The speed of a computer

The two indications of speed are the processor-chip specification and the overall system speed. The first of these is less useful, but is the only speed indication directly quoted in advertising. An example of a **processor-chip specification** is '450MHz Pentium II' or '300MHz G3'. The higher the first number, the faster the computer works overall. This figure is rather like those used for car-engine size; doubling the size of the engine will not make the car go twice as fast, but it does suggest that performance is significantly better. Technically, the number refers to the speed of an internal metronome (called a **clock circuit**) that synchronises the computer's operation. The figure '450MHz' means that the metronome beats 450 million times a second. In an older 66MHz computer it beats 66 million times a second. In the latest 1GHz designs, which become available at the end of 1999, the metronome beats 1 *billion* times a second.

The second part of the speed specification lists the type of processor chip that the computer is built around, such as Pentium II, AMD K6-II, Celeron, Cyrix 6x86MX, and so on. A company called

### General-purpose Intel Pentium chips

- **Pentium (75MHz to 200MHz)** Released in 1994, and now out of date.
- **Pentium MMX (150MHz to 266MHz)** Updated version of the Pentium, with added 'MMX' features, which help speed up software that uses video, animation and sounds.
- **Pentium MMO (150MHz to 266MHz)** A version of the MMX chip designed to run off batteries, for use in portable computers.
- **Pentium II (233MHz to 500MHz)** Updated, slightly faster and more efficient version of the original Pentium and which includes MMX features.

### Powerful Intel Pentium chips

- **Pentium Pro (150MHz to 200MHz)** Designed for work that concentrates on mathematical calculations, it contains no MMX features and is now obsolete.
- **Xeon (450MHz upwards)** Late 1990s replacement for the Pentium Pro. It is one of the more expensive options and contains MMX, but is not very much more powerful than the Pentium II.
- **Pentium III (450MHz upwards)** The latest generation of Pentium chips with better MMX features and other minor improvements.

Intel makes the most widely used chips, including the popular Pentium range. Competitors AMD (Advanced Micro Devices) and Cyrix are engaged in a permanent game of catch-up with Intel. Pricing and marketing policies are erratic and change frequently, which means that there is never an overall best chip to buy. In general, Intel chips tend to be better value for more demanding applications, and Cyrix and AMD are a better (cheaper) choice for small-business work. Technically, all the competing designs are more or less identical, and software designed to work on one machine will work as well on another.

---

**Budget chips**

Intel

- **Celeron** A crippled Pentium II, which is deliberately made to run very slowly and inefficiently. Although a cheaper option, it is best avoided.
- **Celeron II** This chip is slightly slower than a Pentium II, but significantly cheaper.

AMD

- **K6 (200MHz to 266MHz)** Although faster than a Pentium MMX, it is slower than a Pentium II.
- **K6-II (266MHz to 400MHz)** also known as **K-6 2**, and **K-6 3DNow!** A competitor to the Pentium II, it is faster for many kinds of work and better value, and it includes MMX-like features.
- **K7** (specifications unknown as yet) Competitor to Xeon.

Cyrix

- **6x86MX** Competitor to the MMX Pentium.

Winchip

- **Winchip** Very cheap chip, used in budget machines. It is slower than other designs, but still good value.

The only way to know which chips are the best is to keep up with the latest news in computer magazines. The table below is a summary of the chips available in autumn 1998, and the speeds at which they work.

## Older chips

Older chips are only available in the second-hand market. Listed below are Intel-made designs, as it is almost impossible to find designs from other manufacturers, and so they cannot be recommended.

- **The 8088 and 8086 chips** The Amstrad company made a popular range of machines in the 1980s, which used these very old chips. They are only suitable for MS-DOS software, and are very slow.
- **The 80286 chip** Again only suitable for DOS, these can be used for DOS-based business work at a pinch, but are quite slow.
- **The 80386 chip** It can run Windows 3.1 very slowly, but is fast for simple DOS applications.
- **The 80486 chip** This chip can run Windows 3.1 quite quickly, and Windows 95 slowly. It is useable, if not ideal, for connecting to the Internet. (Note that the 80286, 80386 and 80486 are usually known simply as the 286, 386 and 486 respectively.)
- **Slow Pentium (up to 100MHz)** Slow for Windows 95 and the Internet, it will, however, work with most modern business software.
- **Fast Pentium (100MHz to 200MHz)** Fast enough for Windows 95, it will also work more satisfactorily with the latest business software. These are the only obsolete models worth considering as an alternative to a completely new machine.

### Which chip, which speed?

For ordinary work the practical speed difference between a 200MHz AMD K6 and a 400MHz Pentium II is not as great as might be expected. In fact, for most office work it may be hard to tell the difference, although measurements will show that information appears on screen more quickly, and it takes less time to get information into and out of the computer's filing system. The difference between a 233MHz AMD K6 chip and a 266MHz Pentium II is negligible.

The exception to this rule is work that involves a lot of mathematical calculations, for example computer graphics, photo and video editing, and exceptionally complex spreadsheets. These are the only kinds of applications where chip speeds make a significant difference, and here the rule of thumb is: the faster, the better.

However, for most work it makes sense to get the cheapest computer you can afford. If you use a 450MHz Pentium II computer for writing letters, most of its power will be wasted.

Other factors, apart from the speed of the main chip, affect the apparent speed of the computer far more. These include the capacity of the working memory, and the speed of the other parts of the computer.

### Working memory

Working memory is known as **RAM (Random Access Memory).** As mentioned earlier, RAM is rather like desk space in an office. If you have too little RAM, the computer has to keep filing information away on its hard disk when you are not actively working with it. This is known as *swapping it out*, and can slow a computer to a crawl, no matter what kind of processor chip it uses.

For office work, RAM makes more of a difference overall than the speed and model of the processor chip. RAM capacities are measured in Mbs (Megabytes), and the more Megabytes, the better. Very big and powerful computers may offer Gigabytes (Gbs), which are thousands of Megabytes of memory; these are still rare, but are likely to become popular sometime around the year 2000.

How much memory you need depends on the kind of work you plan to do, and which operating system you use. The table below lists typical minimum, cramped, comfortable and generous amounts of memory. The first of these will be almost useless for serious work (see also Appendix III). The computer will start up, but information will be continually 'swapped out' to the hard disk, because the main memory will be full. This will slow work to a crawl. The 'cramped' amount will allow work to be carried out, but probably only when one kind of software is used at once. The comfortable amount is enough for most work. The generous figure will be suitable for more demanding work, during which you may need to have quick access to many different kinds of software tools at the same time.

The cost of computer memory has fallen markedly since about 1996. Then, 128Mb of memory would have cost around £700. In 1998 it was priced at just over £100, and some memory-chip manufacturers are facing bankruptcy because they are no longer able to generate enough income. If there is a global shake-out of memory makes, prices will climb again. If not, prices will continue to fall and by about 2001 computers with about 1Gb of memory will cost perhaps £200.

Different types of memory are available. The two most common types are SDRAM (Synchronous Dynamic RAM) and EDO (Extended Data Output) RAM. The former being slightly faster than the latter.

**Operating Systems and necessary memory**

|  | Bare minimum | Cramped | Comfortable | Generous |
| --- | --- | --- | --- | --- |
| MS-DOS | 512K | 1Mb | 2Mb | 4Mb |
| Windows 3.1 | 4Mb | 8Mb | 16Mb | 32Mb |
| Windows 95 and 98 | 8Mb | 16Mb | 32Mb | 64Mb |
| Windows 2000 | 32Mb | 64Mb | 128Mb | 256Mb |
| MacOS | 16Mb | 32Mb | 64Mb | 128Mb |
| LINUX | 4Mb | 8Mb | 16Mb | 32Mb |

### Cache memory

Cache memory is very fast memory. It is attached directly to the processor chip, which uses it as a notepad while it makes calculations. It is also sometimes quoted in specifications, and most computers today have either 512K (0.5Mb) or 1Mb of cache. More cache makes the computer work slightly more quickly, but the difference for simple work is slight. Pipeline-burst cache memory is slightly faster than asynchronous cache memory.

### Motherboards

The motherboard is the main circuit board inside a computer. All the other parts plug into it. Motherboards are also given a speed rating in MHz, and this too affects the speed of a computer, although it has most effect on the speed at which the hard disk (filing system) works. Motherboard speeds are rarely quoted. By 1998 the standard speed was 100MHz, although this will increase during 1999.

The **chipset** also has an effect on speed. This is the name given to the collection of ancillary chips that surround the main processor chip. Chipsets are usually defined by letters, for example, BX, TX and ZX. These seem to be decided more or less at random, and the only way to find out which ones are currently preferable is to read the relevant computer magazines.

A very small number of motherboards are **dual processors**. This means that they can be fitted with two processor chips instead of just one. This feature is only relevant for very specialised work, involving perhaps very powerful servers.

### Speed and benchmarks

The real speed of a computer when used for hands-on work depends on all of the above factors together. There is no standard way to measure this, although magazines often use benchmarks – special collections of speed-testing software – to give some indication of the relative speeds of different computers. Good benchmarks are hard to design well, and have to be tailored to specific situations. There is no single overall benchmark that can tell you how fast a computer is.

Computer advertisements often quote benchmark-like figures (typically with colourful names, such as MIPS, winstone, specINT and dhrystone) when it is unusually favourable to a product. It is best to ignore these figures and refer to independent magazine information instead.

## How much information can it hold?

The amount of room for information is defined by the size of the computer's hard disk drive. Many computer extras are known as 'drives'. This is simply a catch-all word used for anything that works with information that is not lost when the computer is turned off.

Like memory, disk capacity is quoted in **Megabytes** (Mbs) or, more often, in **Gigabytes** (Gbs; one thousand megabytes). Occasionally **Kilobytes** (Kbs; one-thousandth of a megabyte) are used. Typical capacities for a modern PC start at around 3Gb and go up to 9Gb for more expensive models (or tens of Gbs for an expensive server). Listed below are the typical storage requirements for different kinds of information (some based on the storage requirements of this book) to give an idea of what disk capacity means in practice:

- 100-word email (plain text, with no styling or page layout information) takes up 3Kb (which is the same as 0.003Mb)
- single-page business letter (including styling and page layout) takes up 35Kb
- chapter of a book (word-processor text file) takes up 120Kb
- complete book (word-processor text file) takes up 2Mb
- small compressed graphic takes up 35Kb
- medium-sized compressed graphic takes up 130Kb
- large compressed photograph takes up 1.5Mb
- large uncompressed photograph takes up 13Mb
- very large uncompressed photograph takes up 80Mb
- 10 seconds of CD-quality stereo sound takes up 1.6Mb
- 10 seconds of TV-quality video takes up 30Mb
- small software package (for example, an email program) takes up 3Mb
- large software package (for example, Photoshop) takes up 25Mb
- large office suite takes up 50Mb
- operating system takes up 140Mb.

In general, 3Gb should be enough for office work and 9Gb for more complex applications, such as software development or work with sound and video. For example, to install Microsoft's Office 97 Professional (which includes Access, Excel, PowerPoint, and Word), Windows 98, Corel Draw and three typical games takes up less than 2Gb. Powerful servers often benefit from as much disk space as will fit into the case, and it is possible to buy as much as 100Gb of space for very heavy-duty work. These were the standard disk sizes in late 1998, but the size doubles approximately every year. However, unless a new collection of very large software products arrives, it is hard to see why anyone would need more than 9Gb for an office PC.

## Types of disk drives

Disk drives come in two types. **IDE (Integrated Drive Electronics)** disk drives are slower than **SCSI (Small Computer Systems Interface)** drives. SCSI drives are significantly more expensive and are usually only available on 'peformance' computers.

The IDE standard has evolved through a number of generations, the most recent and fastest of which is known as Ultra-DMA, DMA-33, ATA-33 or Ultra ATA. A modern computer should be fitted with one or more Ultra-DMA drives as standard. (Note that on recent computers IDE is sometimes also known as EIDE or Enhanced IDE.)

SCSI has also evolved through a number of generations, including SCSI-2, Ultra-SCSI, Wide SCSI, Ultra Wide SCSI, Ultra Wide SCSI-2 and Ultra SCSI 3. 'Wide' drives can transfer information twice as fast. The standard for most drives currently is Ultra Wide ('UW'), although the faster drives may be available to special order. These are typically used in servers.

## RAID

To increase speeds further and to enhance reliability, disk drives can be connected together in complex ways. The technology known as RAID (Redundant Array of Inexpensive Devices) makes it possible for computers to survive the failure of a single drive with all their information intact, or to make information available two, three or even four times more quickly than standard drives.

Numbers 0 to 5 distinguishes the different kinds of RAID technology in use. Three of these, RAID 0, 1 and 5, are widely used. The others are either technologically redundant or too expensive to use except for very specialist applications.

RAID 0 is very fast and uses a scheme called 'striping', which distributes information across a set of disks. Each chunk of information (called a block) is written to and read from each disk in turn. As soon as a disk has dealt with a block it can start getting ready for the next one. This makes the technology ideal for servers and systems where a lot of information has to moved to and from the disk quickly. The drawback is that RAID 0 is less reliable than a single disk because the chances of failure are multiplied by the number of drives, and when a drive fails all the information is lost.

RAID 1 uses 'mirroring', during which information is copied to two disks simultaneously. If one of the disks fails, the other can carry on working until the first is replaced. This halves the effective disk capacity of an array, and provides no increase in speed. But it is a simple and cheap way to enhance reliability.

With RAID 5, information and error-correcting checks known as 'parity' are distributed across a number of disks. This gets round the bottleneck caused by a single parity disk. Writing to a RAID 5 array is still slower than writing to an ordinary disk, but reading from it is faster. This is the most popular system on the market today.

All versions of RAID apart from RAID 0 offer a 'hot-swap' facility, which means that faulty disks can be replaced with the power still on and a computer connected to the network. These are sometimes known as fault-tolerant (FT) systems. Of course, RAID only guards against failure to a certain extent, and if another drive fails while the first is being removed the system will stop working. In spite of that it provides an extra level of safety and reliability for 'mission-critical' work.

## Specifications for 'extras'

Computers are typically sold with a selection of 'extras', which are either part and parcel of the system, or can be purchased at an extra cost. Specifications for these are often given in computer advertising, and as such should be explained.

### Monitors

The monitor is just computer-speak for the 'screen' and there are currently two types available: cathode ray tube (CRT) and liquid crystal display (LCD) monitors. A third type, a flat panel plasma display, which hangs on a wall like picture, is currently being developed and will be widely available by about 2002. For the moment, monitors are still designed to sit on desks. Monitors are usually included when a computer is bought, but there may be the option to buy a better monitor for slightly more money. If your work requires this, it can be good value for money as any extras bought as part of a package are significantly cheaper than those bought later as an addition.

**CRT (Cathode Ray Tube) monitors** use TV-like vacuum-tube technology that has remained more or less unchanged for almost 60 years. They create images on a glass screen by electronically moving a dot of coloured light so quickly that the eye is fooled into thinking it can see a steady image.

Although CRT monitors are the current industry standard, they have a number of drawbacks. They are bulky, heavy (the largest need two people to lift them safely), fragile, and they consume a lot of power. They also produce heat and positive ions, which some people find difficult to work with for long periods. When placed on desks they can waste a lot of space, because they are deep as well as wide.

**Trinitron and FST (Flat Square Tube) monitors** offer better image quality. The former use an imaged tube supplied by Sony, similar to that used in popular Sony televisions. (These monitors are notable for the two very fine horizontal wires that stretch across the display area. Beginners sometimes complain about these because they assume they have a defective tube, but in fact they are a side effect of the manufacturing process.) FST monitors present a flat instead of a curved image surface.

**Dot pitch** is often quoted on CRT specifications. This is a measure of how fine and sharp the image is likely to be. In practice, it defines the size of the tiny dots on the surface of the tube. Dot pitch of 0.24in is a very good figure, 0.26in is average, and 0.28in is rather less satisfactory, although it may be useable on a very large monitor.

**LCD (Liquid Crystal Display) monitors** are also known as flat-panel displays, and use more recent solid-state technology. They consist of a thin, flat grid of cells, which can be individually changed to different colours. They are lighter and slimmer than CRTs, consume much less power, take up less desk space, and usually look more appealing too. They are also significantly more expensive, costing anywhere between four times and ten times as much as equivalent CRT designs. Some types are prone to 'smearing', which means the images move around the screen because the cells that make up the image cannot switch on and off quickly enough to prevent this. In extreme cases this means the mouse cursor can disappear while it is being moved. Video playback can also be problematic on some displays. For most applications however, many people find them easier to work with, especially for long periods.

LCD displays are standard on portable computers, and come in two types. Dual scan (DSTN) displays are cheaper, but less sharp, and the colours are less clear. TFT (Thin Film Transistor) displays are brighter, clearer and less prone to smearing, but also slightly more expensive.

## Monitor specifications

Both CRT and LCD monitors work by treating the screen as a grid of lights, each of which can have its colour and brightness set individually. The number of lights in each grid, quoted as the **resolution** across and down, is usually limited to a handful of standard settings. For example, '640 × 480' means the grid consists of 640 lights across and 480 lights down. For historical reasons these are in the ratio 4:3, which is the same ratio used originally on TV screens. The maximum possible resolution depends on the monitor's electronics and the size of the monitor's screen. Smaller monitors do not bother attempting to show the more advanced and detailed resolutions, as details and lettering become too small to see clearly.

For CRT monitors, sizes are defined by the diagonal width of the picture tube. The visible width is usually significantly less, and is measured from corner to corner on the glass area that is actually visible. A typical 21-in monitor may have a visible diagonal width of around 19.5in. While misleading to beginners, this is, unfortunately, a standard industry practice. LCD monitors are more consistent, and the width of the display that is quoted bears a much closer resemblance to reality.

Larger monitors are, not surprisingly, more expensive, sometimes very much so, but they are also more sophisticated technologically. Small, cheap monitors suffer from variable image size, image drift, bad focus and various other problems. In practice this means that you may have to keep fiddling with the controls to keep the image central on the screen, and to stop the edges from drifting out of sight as the monitor warms up. The image itself may not be very sharp, or may be sharp in one part of the screen but blurred in other parts.

Large, expensive monitors use sophisticated electronics that make sure that the image stays put. They also have more complex image settings, which can compensate for different kinds of visual distortions that may result from the electronics, or from the angle at which you look at the screen. The most expensive models have 'on-screen displays' (OSDs), which work rather like the tuning and record-time displays that some VCRs produce. Some of these features are available in smaller monitors too, but they will be absent on the standard small (14-in or 15-in) monitors that are supplied with a typical computer system.

The table overleaf shows the different standard sizes that are available and the kind of resolution (comfortable, cramped) produced by each size. It is worth noting that 'Cramped' displays may be suitable for short periods, but are unlikely to be comfortable for long durations. Moreover, LCD monitors may not necessarily be able to show the cramped resolution at all.

Another number to watch for is the maximum **refresh rate**, which applies especially to CRT monitors. These monitors produce an image by zig-zagging a dot of light down from the top of the screen. Each complete image, from top to bottom, is drawn many times a second. The exact number of redraws is known as the refresh rate measured in Hertz (Hz; redraws a second), and is actually controlled by the graphics card inside the computer. If this number is too low, the display will flicker noticeably. This can cause headaches and eyestrain over long periods of use. Larger monitors show flicker more clearly, and for user comfort the rate has to be equal to or larger than the one shown in the table.

CRT monitors have a maximum refresh rate, which is quoted for each display resolution. For example, a monitor's specification may include a list that says: '100Hz at 800 × 600, 90Hz at 1,024 × 768, and 85Hz at 1,280 × 1,024'. If pushed beyond this the monitors stop working reliably, with symptoms that range from scrambled displays to permanent physical damage (and perhaps even smoke and fire). Large, cheap monitors have a maximum rate that is too low for comfortable use. For example, a 21-in monitor may have a maximum rate of 60Hz at 1,280 × 1,024. This means the display will flicker terribly if you try to use the monitor at that resolution, and there is nothing you can do to improve the situation without endangering the monitor itself. As a result you can know for sure that this monitor is not the one for you.

## Standard resolutions and the necessary monitor sizes

| CRT monitor size | LCD monitor size | Comfortable resolution* | Cramped resolution* | Comfortable flicker | Possible uses |
|---|---|---|---|---|---|
| 14in | 12.1in | 640 × 480 | 800 × 600 | 72Hz | Letter-writing, accounts, spreadsheets (with difficulty) |
| 15in | 13.3in | 800 × 600 | 1,024 × 768 | 75Hz | Spreadsheets, simple desktop publishing |
| 17in | 14.4in | 1,024 × 768 | 1,280 × 1,024 | 82Hz | Image editing and retouching, large spreadsheets |
| 21in | 18in | 1,280 × 1,024 | 1,600 × 1,200 | 85Hz | Multiple applications at once, very advanced word processing, huge spreadsheets |
| 24in | N/A | 1,600 × 1,200 | N/A | 90Hz | Commercial design and publishing |

* resolution is measured in the number of lights across and down

### Graphics cards

Graphics cards act as intermediaries between a computer's processor chip and the monitor. They take instructions from the processor and convert them into a stream of electronic signals that create a picture on the monitor's screen.

With older cards it was possible to see the different bits of information on a screen appear individually whenever the picture changed. On newer cards changes are almost instant. The latest AGP (Advanced Graphics Port) cards plug into a special socket on the motherboard, which makes them very fast indeed. In fact graphics cards are now so good that, for business use at least, there is very little to choose between them. The main differences become most obvious when these cards are used for playing games. Many now offer '3D acceleration' of various sorts. This makes spaceships and aliens appear more animated and life-like, but has no effect at all on a typical letter or spreadsheet.

To check if a graphics card suits your needs, decide on a monitor resolution (and perhaps even a monitor) and then decide on a number of colours. The minimum number of colours is 16, which is fine for word processing and email, but photographs look very distorted (a 'psychedelic' effect) and may not be legible. The working minimum number of colours is 256, which can be used for general office work and photographs are legible, but look unnatural because of blotchy artificial shadings. With 65,536 colours, general-purpose work is fine and photographs look almost natural, although there will be colour inaccuracies and odd display side-effects. To reproduce photographs accurately, you need 16.7 million colours, although this is unnecessary for most business work.

After deciding on the number of colours, check with the manufacturers or suppliers if a graphics card can display the resolution you would like with the full number of colours. In practice this depends on the amount of memory on the card. This memory is separate from the main memory in the PC, and is used exclusively to produce the screen image. The more memory, the higher the maximum possible resolution with a given number of colours. Also check if the card can produce a usable refresh rate at that resolution. Finally, check for extra features and potential optional extras.

Some cards have a TV output facility, which means you can look at images on an ordinary TV, or, more usefully, hook up the computer to a TV-projection system when giving a presentation. Some also have optional TV- and video-editing facilities, or room for a plug-in TV tuner card, which lets you view TV programmes in a window on the computer's screen.

### Floppy-disk and LS120 drives

The 3.5-in floppy-disk drives are now supplied as standard with all computers and usually appear in specifications as a '1.44Mb FDD'. These disks are small square plastic wafers, which are rigid and not floppy, have sliding metal covers and can store up to 1.44Mb. They are now almost obsolete, although some software is still supplied in floppy-disk form. (Apple's iMac is the first widely available computer that no longer includes a floppy disk slot as standard, although a drive can be bought as an optional extra.)

LS120 drives can work with standard floppy disks, but can also use the LS120 disk system, which stores up to 120Mb inside a similar, slightly bulkier plastic wafer. Some manufacturers are supplying LS120 drives as standard on their machines, although they have not yet become a true industry standard. In the late 1990s these LS120 wafers were priced at about £30 each.

## CD-ROM drives

CD-ROM drives (sometimes shortened to CD-R) are used to 'play' information stored on CDs. This information includes software, music, and photographs that use the Kodak PhotoCD system. (This was once a good way to get photographs on to a CD, but seems to have become something of a commercial cul-de-sac, and is now used only by some professionals.) Any CD-ROM drive will be able to cope with all of these different kinds of information.

The two things that distinguish different drives are speed (quoted as a multiplier, for example '32X') and connection system. The multiplier refers to the speed at which the drive can copy information to the computer; a '1×' drive copies as fast as an ordinary CD player (which, in practice, means very slowly). Beyond around 20×, the variations between different speeds start to become more theoretical than actual, and there is little point in spending the extra on a 40× drive over a 32× drive. Both will be very fast, and both will copy information almost as fast as a hard disk can. In general, whatever CD-ROM drive your system is supplied with will be adequate.

The connection systems of drives are either IDE or SCSI. IDE drives will take up one of the available hard-disk slots inside a computer, and can sometimes interfere with the speed of the hard disk. SCSI drives tend to be more reliable, although they are slightly harder to set up, and they are rarely offered as an option on standard PCs. For business use IDE's limitations are not so important, and there is usually no good reason to pay the extra for a SCSI drive.

## Modems

Modems convert computer information into sounds that can be sent along an ordinary telephone line (sometimes known as POTS: Plain Old Telephone System). At the other end they are converted back, by another modem, into information that a remote computer can understand. Between them the modems create a workable but slow link between the two computers. Although it is possible to link any two computers together like this, modems are now most widely used for getting on the Internet. The main things that distinguish modems are speed, extra features and whether the modem is fitted inside the computer or is in a separate box.

## Modem speeds

All modems now work at the same speed: 56K (bits per second) or 56kbps. This is indicated in specifications by describing the modem as a '56K' or a 'V.90' model. Note that the two terms are not quite synonymous. The specification '56K' is an absolute speed measure, while 'V.90' is an international specification for modems working at that speed. Older schemes, known as 'K56Flex' and 'X2', were originally created for the 56K speed. Unfortunately these were incompatible, and this meant that some of their ISP customers were unable to connect to the Internet as fast as others. Manufacturers soon realised that a single standard was best for everyone, and so they agreed on the V.90 specification.

The specification 56K is only a guideline speed for V.90. In practice, connections are likely to be rather slower, perhaps at 50kbps, depending on the quality of the telephone line.

Modems described using other numbers, such as 'V.34' or 33.6kbps, are sometimes available second-hand, or in very cheap machines. These are a false economy, as they connect to the Internet much more slowly than V.90 modems, and so cost extra in both time and phone bills. Modems with other speeds are available in the second-hand market, but these are best ignored. Modems are now so cheap that the savings available by using a slower model are a false economy.

## Modem features

'Fax' modems can send and receive faxes. Instead of having to be printed on paper and run through a fax machine, faxes can be sent ('printed') electronically from any software that would work with a normal printer, and sent through the modem. Received faxes appear on the screen. 'Voice' modems include answering-machine facilities.

The latest modems offer voice and fax features that continue working even when the computer is turned off. Some even have playback and recording buttons on top of the modem's case. These features are very useful, as leaving a computer turned on simply to take messages wastes a lot of electricity.

## Internal and external modems

Internal modems are fitted inside the computer, while external modems have a separate case, and are connected via cables. In spite of the extra cabling required, which includes an extra power supply, external modems are far easier to use. They require less setting up, and are also easier to deal with if something goes wrong. An external modem can simply be turned off and on again to break a dead connection. To achieve the same with an internal modem, the whole computer has to be turned off and on again, which can be disruptive and waste time.

## Soundcard and loudspeakers

A **soundcard** can be used to connect microphones and loudspeakers to a computer. This is important for giving presentations, although for other office work soundcards and speakers are more of an interesting extra than a necessity. For example, it is possible to use a soundcard to play music on most computers from a standard music CD inserted into the CD-ROM drive.

As with graphics cards, typical soundcards are now so good that there is very little to choose between them. Recording and playback quality is good but not exceptional, perhaps equivalent to a cheap portable CD player or ghetto blaster. **Wavetable cards** have extra features, which make it possible to play back **MIDI** (Musical Instrument Digital Interface) music. This is sometimes included on web pages, and if you are designing pages of your own and would like to include MIDI music, you will need to use a wavetable card to get a realistic idea of what it will sound like to visitors. PCI soundcards use a faster connection system than ISA soundcards (see page 305 for an explanation of the difference between PCI and ISA). While a good thing in theory, in practice PCI cards can be prone to interference from non-AGP graphics cards and also some disk drives. ISA cards are older, cheaper, and perfectly adequate. But the difference is unlikely to be noticeable unless you plan to do a lot of work with sound. **3D soundcards** have extra features that make the sound 'bigger'. In theory, they can make sounds appear behind your head, as well as below and above you, although in practice these effects are very difficult to achieve.

**Loudspeakers** vary hugely in quality. Systems with a sub-woofer have an extra speaker for low sounds, which can create a more realistic effect. In general, most computer speakers are poor compared to even a good budget hi-fi, but are adequate for casual listening.

## Keyboard and mouse

Keyboards vary significantly in feel and comfort, but these differences are not usually advertised in specifications. **Cherry keyboards**, made by the German Cherry company, are highly regarded, and popular with users who do a lot of typing. **Natural keyboards** are designed with a slightly surreal look, and the keys are supposed to be in a more natural position for the typist's hands than the standard flat design. These are an acquired taste, and if you are used to a standard keyboard it may be worth asking if this can be substituted instead. Otherwise most keyboards are simply advertised as a '102-key Windows keyboard'.

Mice come in two main types: PS/2 and serial. There are minor technical differences between the two, but from a user's point of view there is little to choose between them. **Ergonomic mice** are shaped to fit the natural curve of the hand. As with natural keyboards, these may not suit everyone, although some people do find them more comfortable.

## Appendix II

# Choosing options and extras

Adding optional extras can extend the range of work that you can do with any computer. Some of the extras, such as printers, are essential for business use, but are only sporadically included in a package price.

If you buy all the extras you need at the same time as you buy the computer itself, you can usually make a significant saving, as they will probably cost more if bought separately later. Some advertising includes a range of options with **upgrade prices**, which can be added to the basic cost. Even where you do not see these, you may be able to negotiate a better package deal, especially if you add a large number of extras, or if your computer is more expensive than average. Not all retailers do this, but it can be worth asking all the same.

Even when ordering extras as part of a package, you will probably find that they will not be installed when the computer arrives. Typically you will receive a large pile of boxes and be expected to do the rest yourself.

> **Typical extras**
> - printer
> - removable storage for backups (zip drive, Jaz drive, etc.)
> - scanner
> - CD Writer
> - digital camera
> - DVD drive and DVD writer
> - multi-function peripherals
> - ISDN Terminal Adaptor (TA)
> - improved pointing device (i.e. better mouse or graphics pad)

When buying extras it is worth asking the retailers whether or not the system is delivered fully set-up and ready to go, or whether further setting-up will be necessary before all the extras can be used. Usually this will only be available at extra cost, although some retailers will do it for free if asked.

## Printers

Printers are available in all shapes and sizes, and to suit all pockets. There are many different printing systems available, each of which is suitable for a different kind of work.

**Dot-matrix printers** produce very rough output, and can also be very noisy. Originally they were by far the cheapest kind of printer, but the price differences have slowly eroded and now they offer little, if any, cost advantage over other types. They are suitable for inventory printing, billing and invoices (hotels and garages regularly use them for this kind of work), but not for high-quality professional business correspondence. They work by striking an ink ribbon with a row of tiny pins to leave marks on the paper. The number of pins varies; 9-pin types are very crude, although suitable for rough work such as simple billing. The 24-pin models are more sophisticated, give better results, but are also more expensive.

The main advantages of dot-matrix printers are their minimal running costs, their ability to work in non-office environments, such as warehouses and factories, and their compatibility with very old computer hardware and software. They are also the only kind of printer that can produce carbon copies directly (expensive models can produce up to six copies at a time). However, direct network connection is not usually possible.

Ink is supplied on ribbons that last for hundreds or even thousands of pages and cost less than £20 to replace. These printers are also the only kind of printer that can work with continuous paper (that is paper supplied as a very long single perforated and folded set of sheets). This makes them useful for situations where pages of related printed output need to be produced, but binding would be an unwarranted expense, for example inventory listings and computer programs. Some cheque-printing software also requires continuous paper. Tractor-feed dot-matrix printers use a row of sprockets to pull

281

paper through the machine. These are more reliable than friction-feed models, which can cause paper jams and snarls if the paper is not aligned with the printer very carefully.

**Ink-jet** and **bubble-jet printers**, which are more or less identical, are quiet, affordable, and can almost always print in colour. They work by squirting tiny blobs of ink on to a sheet of paper. Text quality is usually noticeably blotchy and never as sharp as the results from a laser printer. They are therefore adequate, if perhaps not ideal, for occasional business correspondence. On the other hand, colour output can be excellent, especially from the latest generation of 'photo' printers, which can produce results that compare well with professionally developed photographs. This makes them suitable for proofing in-house artwork, brochures and posters, which will then be printed by a professional printer, and for producing medium-quality artwork and promotional material for customers and for the public. Prices vary from around £100 up to around £500 for mid-range models that can work with A3-sized paper. Top-of-the-range printers cost upwards of a £1,000 and are suitable for work-group printing on an office network.

Ink-jets and bubble-jets have two drawbacks. Running costs can be high, especially for colour printing. Cartridges can last as little as a few hundred pages and cost between £15 and £40 to replace. Because colour printing uses three different inks (plus an optional black) the process is very wasteful. Partially empty cartridges may need to be thrown away, even if only one colour runs out, although some brands can be refilled. A single A4 page can cost up to 50p.

The other problem with ink-jets is speed. A full colour A4 page can take as long as 20 minutes to appear. While this is adequate for occasional use, it can create problems in busy offices, which need faster results.

As with laser printers (see below), print quality is related to dots per inch (dpi), although because of the completely different way in which laser printers and ink-jets work, their dpi specifications cannot be compared directly. A specification of 700dpi for an ink-jet suggests medium-quality output, but 1,440 (or more) dpi would give much better results. Output can be on ordinary photocopier paper, on high-quality paper (which is recommended to produce the very best results) or on overhead transparency film. Some printers can use special paper, which will transfer an image to a T-shirt when ironed.

Some ink-jets can be plugged into a car's cigarette-lighter socket and used on the road. Only the most expensive models have true network capabilities.

**Laser printers** are the standard for business correspondence. The cheapest models now cost around £150. They offer very good clarity for black-and-white text, although close examination shows that letters and symbols are not quite as smooth as those produced by a typewriter. More expensive laser printers overcome this drawback, and the top models can approach the quality offered by traditional typesetting machines. These more expensive designs can also print black-and-white photographs with passable results.

Laser printers use a tightly focused beam of light to 'paint' an image on to a special light-sensitive surface. This image is then printed to paper using a system based on photocopier technology. They can be very fast, with speeds for the cheap 'domestic' models starting at around 4 pages per minute (ppm), which is adequate for occasional correspondence. Faster, more expensive designs can serve the needs of an entire office, printing at speeds upwards of 20ppm and collating the results automatically.

Laser quality is specified in **dots per inch (dpi)**. Budget models start at 300dpi, which is perfectly acceptable for business use. Laser quality of 600dpi and 1,200dpi output is only required by those who want to make the very best possible impression, or who would like to include black and white images along with text. Some printers offer 'resolution enhancement', which is a halfway house between the standard dpi specifications. Since cost differences between these and the more standard designs are usually minor, it typically makes more sense to spend a little extra and get true high-resolution performance instead of the 'enhanced' version.

Running costs depend very much on the design. Pages typically cost less than 2p each, but one-off replacement charges for consumables (toner cartridges and printing drums) can still be quite high. **Toner cartridges** add to the supply of dry ink inside the printer and range in price from £15 to £75. **Drums** replace the actual printing surface. They need to be changed very infrequently, perhaps once every two or three toner cartridge changes, and cost anywhere up to £200, although prices of under £100 are more common. Not all printers have replaceable drums; if drum-related problems appear (such as smearing, blank areas, or streaking) the whole printer may need to replaced.

A handful of laser designs are only compatible with PCs running Microsoft Windows. These are known as GDI (Graphical Display Interface) models, and they off-load the computations they require on to the computer to which they are connected. While this makes for a very cheap printer, it can also slow even the fastest system to a crawl while printing takes place. The mouse will typically freeze for a short period while each page is produced, which can be annoying if you are trying to work on other things at the same time. Another issue is memory. Because the printer relies on the memory installed in the PC, it is possible for it to stall if there is not enough available to finish a job. (In practice this is only likely to be a problem with pages of tiny text or very complex diagrams as a typical letter can be printed on a PC with 16Mb of memory with no problems.) In general GDI designs are adequate for light-duty work, but cannot be recommended for larger printing projects.

Most other models are in fact stand-alone single-purpose computers, with their own memory and, in the case of high-end office-oriented machines, with their own local hard-disk storage. They work by pulling an outline description of a page's layout from a computer or network and then independently calculating where the dots that make up the image of the page should go. What goes on each page is defined by a special set of computer instructions. The two most common sets are called Printer Control Language (PCL) and Postscript. Postscript costs extra and is only really of value if printed output is being prepared for a professional print shop. For in-house printing PCL is perfectly adequate, and it is usually installed for free when a printer is set up. Both PCL and Postscript can be 'emulated'. This means their features are simulated in software. There should be no practical differences between emulated and standard PCL and Postscript, except that emulated designs may be slightly cheaper, because manufacturers do not need to pay licensing fees for the technology.

Some laser printers can be connected directly to a network. This means they can be put somewhere accessible, but out of the way, without having to be linked to an ancillary PC – a useful feature in an office.

**Colour lasers** are still very expensive. Prices start at around £1,500 and go up to five figures. Genuine colour lasers, which work like monochrome lasers but use four colours instead of one, offer good-quality results but cannot quite match the output from a photo-realistic ink-jet printer. **'Solid ink' printers** use crayon-like sticks of solid colour instead of colour toner. These can compete favourably with ink-jet output, as colours are very sharp and very rich.

The big advantage of both these designs is their speed. They can produce a page in around 15 seconds, while an ink-jet printer may take 15 minutes. Running costs for colour output are also much lower – between 5p and 20p a page. Colour lasers are ideal for high-speed proofing of colour output before sending the results to a print house, for in-house presentations, and for advertising materials.

## Other printers

Microdry printers are a more sophisticated reincarnation of the dot-matrix idea, although they often appear in the 'ink-jet' section of equipment catalogues. They use three or four ribbons instead of one and print each colour individually, rolling back the paper each time. Results for normal printing are poor; the colours are often washed out and if the roll-back is not done accurately, colours can be smeared or shadowed. However, these printers offer the unique option of output with metallic inks. While just a gimmick for most businesses, this can add an extra eye-catching detail to posters and other artwork. Microdry printers are also particularly suitable for T-shirt printing.

**Label printers** are specially designed to work with small labels, such as ID badges, floppy-disk labels, address labels, video-spine labels, and so on. They are much more convenient than trying to print labels in a more standard printer, and at less than £200 they are worth investing in for businesses or departments that find they are printing a lot of labels. Some offer optional software for lobby work, which prints labels for visitors and keeps a track of who has been in and out of the building.

**Line printers** use a line-at-a-time technology to print very quickly. Speeds up to 1,800 lines per minute are possible. (This is equivalent to around 300,000 pages per month.) Print quality is usually similar to that of dot-matrix printers, although those models at the top of the range can produce slightly better results, and some can even cope with graphics. Prices start at about £3,000 and go up to about £10,000. These printers are suitable for heavy-duty industrial printing when high throughput is essential.

**Poster printers** use ink-jet technology on a large frame that can handle paper sizes up to A0 (841 × 1,189mm). They are useful for large-scale advertising, although their relative slowness makes them less efficient for this than a print shop. Prices start at about £2,500.

## Choosing a printer

Apart from the pros and cons of the different types of printers and their suitability for various kinds of work, it is also important to consider the following:

**Running costs** How many pages will the printer be doing a week? How much will a printer cost to run each year? This can be a surprisingly useful calculation to make, as in some cases it can be cheaper to buy a colour laser printer than an ink-jet – the ink-jet's running costs and slow printing speed wipe out any price advantage it may offer. Running costs are usually easy to work out. Simply divide the price of consumables (toner cartridge and printing drum) by the number of pages they can produce. Some companies, such as Kyocera, deliberately emphasise low running costs in their designs.

**Paper compatibility** Will standard office paper produce an adequate result? Can the printer handle rougher recycled papers, overhead transparencies or labels?

**'Footprint'** is industry-speak for 'size'. Some models are cleverly designed to stand vertically and take up as little desk space as possible. Others are housed in very big boxes that demand large amounts of space. Apart from the bare physical size of the printer, it is also essential to consider the working area around it, including access to paper trays, connections, and consumables.

**Memory requirements** All printers have to use memory for the intermediate calculations they perform while preparing a page for printing. GDI printers use the memory of an attached PC, and as such can only be expanded by adding more memory to the PC itself. Other printers use memory that is fitted inside the printer, and sometimes this is not enough for complex pages with lots of different typefaces and diagrams. It is useful to check whether or not a printer's memory can be expanded, and if so how much it would cost. It can also be useful to take a sample page to a shop and ask them to print it, to see if the standard amount of memory is enough.

**Network connections** Can a printer connect directly to a network, or will information have to be sent to it via a computer? If a direct network connection is possible, it is essential to find out what kind of networks and network speeds are supported.

**Compatibility with operating systems** As mentioned above, GDI designs can only be used with Microsoft operating systems, but other designs may also be limited. It is essential to check that 'drivers' are available for your choice of operating system. If your operating system is slightly unusual, for example LINUX (see Appendix III), this can mean that you will have to check with the manufacturer yourself (or check their web site). Most sales staff will not have the detailed knowledge required to deal with this kind of issue for you.

**Printer control languages** It is useful to know whether or not Postscript and PCL features are available, and whether or not they are emulated. Postscript is only essential for print-shop work. PCL is something of an office standard. There are a number of versions of PCL, the most recent of which is PCL 6. Older printers may not work properly if PCL 6 information is sent to them, so, once more than one printer has been installed, it is a good idea to standardise all the printers on a network to the same version of PCL.

## Removable storage

'Removable storage' is used to store information away from a computer and to exchange large amounts of information with other computers where no network connection is available. Typical uses include archives and safety copies, publishing (where page layouts and images require a lot of space, and somehow have to be transferred to a print shop), and work that handles unusually large amounts of information, such as video editing.

Removable storage is in no way standardised, and competing systems will not usually work with each other. If you are using removable storage for backups, this is not a serious problem, and you can choose whichever system most suits you. But if you plan to exchange work with other businesses, it is essential to find out which system they use and then buy hardware to suit.

## Zip drives and Jaz drives

Zip drives and Jaz drives are another form of storage for information, made by a company called Iomega. They are essentially removable hard disk units, in which information is stored in large plastic cartridges that contain more robust versions of the inside of a hard disk. Cartridges are plugged into the drive when they are to be used, and then removed again for storage. They are significantly slower than true hard disks, but much faster than floppies (see page 275) and all but the very fastest CD-ROM drives.

Zip drives can store around 100Mb on a small cartridge. Jaz drives can store either 1Gb or 2Gb, depending on the model. The price of a 1Gb-cartridge was about £50 in late 1998, while the 1Gb Jaz drives cost about £200. All these are Iomega drives and are available in a range of connection options, including SCSI, printer port (which are rather slow), and IDE. Although widely used, these systems are perhaps a little expensive for what they do. Reliability has also been a problem with these devices. Some units, especially those produced during 1997 and 1998, suffered from a syndrome known as 'click of death' (COD), which effectively broke the unit and ruined any information that was held on it. Iomega's quality control appears to have improved, but it is still best to avoid second-hand models.

## Tape drives

Tape drives store information on tape cassettes, of which there are a number of different formats, including Travan (TR1 to TR4), QIC, Ditto (various sizes), DAT, MLR, Exabyte/8mm and DLT. These vary according to the size and shape of the cassette, the amount of information that will fit on to a tape, the speed with which it can be copied, the price and size of each tape, and, crucially, overall reliability.

## Choosing options and extras

Tape is unlike other forms of removable storage in that information is stored on it in a long stream. If you want information at the end of a tape, you have to wait for the tape to fast forward to it, which can take a couple of hours with some systems. This makes tape a good medium for backups, where information is usually recorded and restored in bulk, in a fixed order.

For server use, some tape systems are available with auto-changers. These swap tapes automatically, making it possible to perform complete unattended backups of tens even hundreds of gigabytes of information. Changers are very expensive, and cost thousands or tens of thousands of pounds.

Individual tape drives come with the usual range of connection systems. IDE is popular for cheaper drives, and SCSI is used for more serious and expensive applications. Some drives can even be connected to the computer's parallel port, for slow but convenient transfers.

### Types of tape

The **Travan** tape system is a popular choice with users on a budget. The drives cost between £200 and £300, and the different sizes of tape can store between 1 and 4Gb, or 2 to 8Gb if compressed. Compression packs more information on to a tape by squeezing up the natural gaps that occur in most computer information. Although it adds extra capacity to a tape system, it also decreases reliability, and should not be used for very critical information.

Travan drives and tapes have to be matched, for example a TR4 tape will only work properly in a TR4 drive. A TR4 system will take around 7 hours to backup and double check 4Gb of information, making it suitable for backups that are left running overnight. The tapes themselves are fairly bulky and cost about £25.

**Ditto** is Iomega's attempt to produce a standardised backup system. From a user's point of view it is similar to the Travan system, with the difference that the largest tape size can hold 10Gb instead of 8Gb.

**QIC (Quarter Inch Cartridge)** tape drives offer very similar performance, but are perhaps slightly more reliable, and cost around twice as much as Travan tapes.

**DAT (Digital Audio Tape)** systems are the next step up in tapes and again cost around twice as much as Travan drives. They transfer information around four times as fast and can store up to 24Gb on tiny cassettes. Auto-changer systems (which swap tapes tapes automatically) are also available.

**MLR** tape drives are made exclusively by Tandberg (a Scandinavian company perhaps better known for its hi-fi systems). They can hold up to 32Gb on tapes that look very similar to standard audio cassettes. They can read certain kinds of QIC cartridges, a useful feature for anyone who already has an archive of these.

**Exabyte** systems are something of a special case. They are widely used in the publishing industry for storing images and page layouts. They are also used in CD manufacture. Prices start at about £700 for basic desktop models and go up to £2,500 for fast machines. Tape capacity varies from 7Gb to 40Gb, depending on the model.

**DLT** drives and tapes are mainly designed for use with servers. They can store up to 320Gb in around 8 hours. Prices start at around £2,500.

Both Exabyte and DLT systems are available in the form of multi-drive 'libraries'. These can work with a number of tapes at the same time and are useful for situations where a selection of archives needs to be easily accessible. Prices range from about £3,000 to £40,000 upwards.

## Scanners

A scanner takes an image, such as a photograph, a drawing, a blueprint, a page of text, or even a small object, and feeds it into the computer. The output from a scanner is a file of information that can be modified in an image-editing program.

Physically, scanners look and work rather like small, flat photocopiers. The object to be scanned is placed face down on a large glass plate under a lid. A moving light then scans the image, and the results are sent to the computer.

Many scanners come with software for 'optical character recognition' (OCR). This attempts to read a page of text, rather than simply grabbing it as an image. For example, the words on the page can be copied into a word processor as if they had been typed. Although the results can sometimes be rough and ready, OCR software combined with a scanner can be a useful time-saving tool for applications where large amounts of text would otherwise have

## Choosing options and extras

to be typed in by hand. Cheap OCR systems are unlikely to be reliable. You will need a good scanner and good OCR software if you want to use the system professionally.

Scanners vary hugely in quality and price. The cheapest now cost less than £75, while the most expensive cost many thousands. There are obvious diminishing returns once the cost rises over a few hundred pounds. The most expensive models are only needed by businesses that make a living out of working with high-quality images, such as print shops and magazine publishers. The main differences between scanner models depend on:

**Speed** Advertisements rarely quote speeds for scanners. Where they do, they are usually quoted as an absolute time (for example, 80 seconds) for each page. Speed is directly related to the way that the scanner is connected to the computer.

Printer port scanners are attached to the printer connector at the back of a PC, and can be tortuously slow. A page of A4 colour information can take up to 20 minutes to scan. These models are suitable for businesses that would like a scanner, but use it so rarely that a more expensive model would not be justified. Some printer port scanners include a 'pass-through' connector. This is a useful feature that renders the scanner invisible to the computer when the printer is being used; information passes through the scanner completely unchanged, and the printer works in the usual way. Scanners that do not have this feature need to be used with a switcher box. This connects the computer to either the scanner or the printer, depending on how a switch on the panel is set. A switcher costs less than £15, but can be inconvenient in practice, as most people forget to set them properly when changing from printing to scanning and vice versa.

SCSI scanners use the much faster SCSI system to pass information to the computer. An A4 colour page can be scanned in a couple of minutes. The downside of these models is that connection and setting-up are more complicated. Before they can be used, a SCSI adaptor card has to be fitted inside the PC. Some models are supplied with cards that have to be fitted by the user, others assume that a suitable card is already present. Fitting a card is a relatively straightforward process, and for those who do not wish to do it themselves most suppliers can be persuaded to do the job for about £50. SCSI scanners are the preferred choice for offices where scanning is done regularly. Although they cost slightly more, their superior speed is well worth the extra outlay.

**Image quality** Scanner image-quality is defined by two numbers. The first is colour resolution, which is listed as a number of bits, usually 30 or 36. The number of bits defines the absolute maximum number of colours a scanner can distinguish. A 30-bit scanner is perfectly adequate for casual use, while a 36-bit model, which reproduces colours slightly more faithfully and costs more, is only necessary when working in publishing, design or advertising. The 36-bit scanners have truly astronomical numbers of colours that they can distinguish, the subtleties of which are well beyond the sensitivity of the human eye. Grey-scale scanning produces black-and-white images. This is a standard feature on all colour scanners. The standard grey-scale resolution is 8 bits.

The second measure of quality for scanners is image resolution, given in dots per inch (dpi). This is a measure of how much detail a scanner can pick out. A resolution of 300dpi means that features smaller than 1/300th of an inch will disappear into a blur. While 300dpi sounds like it should be enough for almost any job, in practice the coarsest resolution that can be used for most work is 600dpi. Image resolutions of 1,200dpi and 2,400dpi give correspondingly better results for high-quality applications. Resolutions of 4,800dpi and 9,600dpi are sometimes used for very high-quality results, although you should be aware that these produce huge amounts of information, which can be unwieldy to work with.

Resolutions are often *interpolated*, which means the scanner mathematically reconstructs details that it would not normally be able to see. This inevitably loses some of the finer points of an image, but interpolated scanners are the norm at the affordable end of the market and produce perfectly adequate results. The *optical* resolution is also sometimes quoted. This is the resolution that the optics in a scanner is physically capable of before interpolation.

**Size and optional extras** Most scanners are for A4 paper. A3 models are sometimes available, as are slide scanners, which work exclusively with transparencies and are correspondingly smaller physically. Some scanners have sheet feeders, which feed paper through automatically when multiple pages have to be scanned.

**Software** All scanners are supplied with basic image-editing software. Often this is a 'cut-down' (simplified) version of a well-known commercial program, and is enough for day-to-day scanning work. More expensive scanners are sometimes 'bundled' with top-of-the-line products, such as Adobe's Photoshop. These can be very good value, offering substantial savings on the price of a scanner and software bought separately.

All scanners are now 'TWAIN compatible'. This means that they can scan directly into an image-editing package without having to be saved to disk first.

## CD-related drives

CD (compact disk) technology is now very widely used, and it is now possible to create your own CDs, which hold information, software, photographs, or music. Despite their versatility, they are limited from the point of view of information storage, as their capacity of 650Mb is relatively small compared to a 3Gb hard disk.

### CD-ROM drives

Most computers now come with a CD-ROM drive already installed (see page 276). Drives are fitted inside the case and are usually connected using the IDE disk drive sysem, but on more expensive computers the SCSI disk drive system is used instead. It is also possible to connect a CD-ROM drive to a computer's printer port. This allows the drive to be plugged in when needed and removed when not in use. It is particularly suitable for laptop computers where it may not always be needed, although this set up limits the speed of the drive.

### CD writers

CD writers (CD-R) are used to create ('burn') home-made CDs or CD-ROMs. They can store music (as standard audio CDs), software, and other useful information. (To create music CDs, extra software may be required.) Blank disks costs around £1 and store up to 650Mb of information, or 74 minutes of music. Note that once a disk has been burned, the information on it can no longer be changed. If something goes wrong during the writing process, the disk will be ruined. However, if disks are burned using the multi-session option – a feature that all good CD writers and writing software include as an option – it becomes possible to add new information to the disk at a later date.

For business use, CD-R can be a good way to distribute large amounts of information to employees who use portable computers. For example, it is relatively easy to create a CD-based catalogue, which perhaps includes extra features that can produce quotes and discounts on the spot.

## CD-rewritable drives (CD-RW)

CD-RW drives can do everything CD writers can, but they also work with special rewritable disks. These cost ten times more than ordinary CD blanks, but information can be written on to them again and again, up to about 1,000 times. CD-RWs are useful for trial runs of a CD-R project before a large number of CD blanks are burned. They can also be used as temporary backup storage for any project that does not take up huge amounts of space. (The text of this book was backed up on CD-RW while it was being written.)

Note that both CD-R and CD-RW drives read information much more slowly than standard CD-ROMs, with CD-RW drives being the slowest. Remembering that standard CD-ROM drives can read up to 40 times ('40×') faster than the equivalent speed of a music CD system, the best-read speed available for a CD-R drive is 12×, and 8× for a CD-RW drive. Writing speeds are much slower: 6× for a fast CD-R drive, and 4× for CD-RW. A speed of 2× is more likely to be used in practice for writing, as faster speeds may be unreliable.

Often these drives are fitted together with an existing CD-ROM drive. They can be connected to a computer by way of SCSI or IDE, and some CD writers include a SCSI card as part of the package. SCSI is preferable to IDE because it seems to produce more reliable results.

It is worth noting that CD-writing technology is often rather unreliable. It usually works well, but sometimes either the software or the hardware involved will start to behave unpredictably. At best this is annoying, at worst it can result in ruined blanks. Even successful blanks are rather less robust than commercial CDs, and are unlikely to survive for a long period without more careful handling. Blanks also vary in reliability, and some CD writers seem to be more successful with certain brands than others. It can be worth discussing these issues with a dealer before buying a CD-writing system.

## Digital Cameras

Digital cameras are very similar to ordinary cameras, but use computer memory instead of film to store images. When the camera is full, photographs are transferred directly to a computer. This can be done by way of a cable, a floppy disk, or a thin plastic wafer that holds the information, according to the model. The camera is then ready for use again.

The theoretical advantages of digital cameras are obvious. There are no developing costs, and images can be viewed on a computer, and perhaps edited and corrected, instantly. If a permanent record is needed, the images can be printed out on a 'photo-quality' printer.

The practical uses are less easy to quantify. There are very few businesses that need images to order immediately. Architects and estate agents may be able to find a use for digital cameras, as may journalists, but in general these cameras are still rather gimmicky, and poor value for money for the features they offer. The optics on cheaper cameras are noticeably inferior to those on equivalently priced traditional cameras. For those situations where image editing is essential but speed is not an issue, it makes much more sense to buy a good conventional camera and a good scanner. Very few digital cameras have facilities for lens swapping, gel filtering, single-lens reflex operation or triggers for professional flash systems. Most are really snapshot holiday-style cameras with added digital facilities.

For all that, digital cameras have an appeal, and for some kinds of work they can be very useful indeed. Prices are now falling, but a good-quality digital camera still costs between £500 and £1,000. Truly professional digital cameras, which are suitable as replacements for the kind of very high-quality film cameras used in advertising and magazine photography, can cost up to £20,000.

The main differences between good cameras in the affordable price brackets are image quality, resolution, storage space, and ease of connection.

Megapixel cameras are strongly recommended for serious use. These offer a resolution of more than a million dots, which is the bare minimum needed for images that compare in quality with traditional photographs.

Storage space for digital cameras is usually quoted as a number of images. Some cameras offer 'high-quality' and 'average' images. High-quality images take up far more space, and so the camera will be able to store fewer of them.

*Connections* from the camera to the computer are usually via one of the computer's serial ports. More advanced models offer SCSI connection facilities, which are very much faster.

## DVD drives and writers

DVD (Digital Versatile Disk, although sometimes the words Digital Video Disk are wrongly used as well) is a next-generation CD-like system. The disks themselves look very similar to CDs but can hold far more information. A number of types are available: DVD5 (4.7Gb), DVD9 (8.54Gb), DVD10 (9.4Gb) and DVD18 (17.1Gb). Although DVD9 and DVD10 have very similar capacities, they work in completely different ways. DVD10 and DVD18 are double-sided versions of DVD5 and DVD9 respectively (this does not mean that the disks have to be turned over like vinyl LPs, but that the DVD drives can read from both sides of the disk at the same time).

DVD is capable of playing back music that uses a more advanced system than conventional CDs, and should sound as near perfect as possible. Up till now it has been used only to produce high-quality videos and CDs, but has yet to prove itself commercially. In any case most computer-based DVD players cannot play videos without extra hardware or software. So far no software is available on DVD. Apart from certain games, which are sold on multiple CDs, most software comes nowhere close to filling up an ordinary CD, so there is no good incentive to start supplying software in the DVD format.

While a standard DVD drive is probably unnecessary for business use, DVD-RAM is more promising. A DVD-RAM drive can write around 4.7Gb of information on a DVD blank. Blanks cost around £30, and writing times are comparable to a medium-speed tape drive. When reading back, however, any item of information can be copied immediately because DVD does not suffer from fast forward or rewind delays. This makes DVD a good choice for backups. DVD-RAM can also copy all of the functions of a CD-RW drive (see above). Currently DVD-RAM drives cost around £400, which is not very much more than a CD writer. If the format becomes popular, prices are likely to fall sharply.

## Multi-function peripherals

The computer industry's marketing teams have yet to come up with a more catchy title for these all-in-one products, which include a printer, fax machine, scanner and photocopier in a single box. Some also include a modem and an answering machine. The main drawback to these units is that better quality results are available from separate stand-alone units. The copying quality is usually quite poor compared to that of a true copier, and the copying process can be very slow, especially for colour copies. However, for situations where this is not a major problem, the advantages of these units – their low cost, convenience, small size and value for money – make them an excellent choice for small offices. For businesses running on a tight budget they can be the only way to afford colour copying, since stand-alone colour copiers are still very expensive. Scanning results are also poor compared to stand-alone machines, but are still adequate for everyday document scanning tasks that do not demand photo-realistic quality.

These products can be used without a computer to provide basic fax and copying services. In fact they can still work in a stand-alone way even after they have been connected to a computer, which makes them useful for staff who are not technology-trained. Fax output is always on plain paper, which does not fade. Faxes can also be stored on the computer's hard disk, which helps save paper (they can be viewed on-screen and only printed out if they are unusually interesting or important).

By keeping everything inside a single box, it is also possible to cut down on consumables. Instead of the multiple sources of toner and paper that separate fax machines, copiers and printers require, these devices only need one.

Print quality varies, depending on the print technology used. The best models use a laser-based system. As with standard laser printing, this gives very high-quality black-and-white text output but cannot be used for colour. Colour models use ink-jet technology and suffer from all the relevant advantages and disadvantages: relatively high running costs and slow output, but reasonably good colour results. Some brands can also send and receive colour faxes.

Most models come with a range of software that includes optical character recognition (OCR; see page 290), image editing and perhaps simple document management. OCR tools can 'read' a fax or a page of text and convert the characters into words that can be sent in an email or pasted into a word processor. The image-editing tools supplied are usually quite crude, and better results are available by spending modest amounts on more serious software. Document management is very simple, sometimes no more than a fax-management system.

## ISDN terminal adaptors

ISDN (Integrated Services Digital Network) is a next-generation telephone system being pushed by British Telecommunications (BT) as a fast connection to the Internet. BT's Business Highway service offers an ISDN connection that can be used to provide two ordinary phone lines, two linked data lines (providing a connection speed of 128kbps) or one phone and one data line. ISDN is also available separately from the Business Highway promotion, but the technology used is similar. For more details see BT's web site at *http://www.bt.com*.

The fact that ISDN is digital means that office telephone exchanges and handsets will not work with it directly. Instead connections are made via a **Terminal Adaptor** (TA), a small box which converts the digital information to and from sounds in a handset, and, in many cases, connects to a computer as well.

For Internet use, the TA takes the place of a modem. As with modems, TAs are available in internal and external forms. Again, the external form is more useful, if sometimes also slightly slower in practice and more expensive. Currently the cost of a TA seems to have little to do with features or quality. A £600 'business' TA may not necessarily be any better in practice than a £75 model. The best way to get up-to-date information on TAs is to read the industry magazines and to ask some searching questions of various mail order suppliers. It is also a good idea to talk to your existing ISP to see if there is a list of ISDN features that they recommend.

Where ISDN has become the new standard in other countries, BT's pricing policies in the UK have meant that it has remained an optional extra for certain types of businesses. As a result it is mostly used for a small range of specialist applications. Apart from its Internet applications, it is popular with print shops that can receive print-ready electronic descriptions of books, magazines, posters and brochures directly over the line from their customers' computers. It can also be used by recording studios to create a high-quality audio link between one studio and another, so that a busy singer can find the time to add a contribution to a piece of music without having to travel to another country. Radio stations also regularly use ISDN to connect together visiting guests in different studios. For this kind of work, ISDN is ideal, as it is an international system and offers an affordable, reasonably fast, general-purpose connection.

While ISDN is very much cheaper than it used to be, it is about to be leapfrogged by new technologies like ADSL (see page 213) and cable, which offer much faster connection speeds, often at lower costs. This means that BT's three-year and five-year discount schemes are probably best avoided.

However, ISDN does offer certain minimal advantages in a business setting. For a small fee a range of telephone numbers can be reserved and 'mapped' to the two lines. And some fax machines, answering machines and other equipment can be set up to respond to a given number from the set, instead of answering whenever either line rings. Some TAs also make it possible to 'bundle' the two lines together to double the speed (note that this doubles the cost of a call).

## Pointing devices

For most work, a standard, cheap mouse is perfectly adequate. However, more sophisticated mouse designs can help with productivity by making the mouse easier or more comfortable to use, adding extra buttons and other features, or removing cabling. Alternative pointing devices, such as graphics pads, as used for very specialised applications.

## Mice

The standard two-button mouse supplied with most computers can easily be improved upon, although mice with special features are not widely advertised. They are sometimes available from large computer stores or listed in product catalogues.

**Ergonomic mice** are designed to fit comfortably under the hand. Some designs are more successful than others, and these have to be assessed individually, as what works well for one person may literally cause pain for another.

**Scrolling mice** add a central wheel between the two standard mouse buttons. This can be used to move through a document without moving the mouse. Most people find this an improvement, although its value depends on the kind of work they do.

**Three-button mice** simply add an extra button, which can be useful for controlling an extra facility, for example clicking on the central button starts up a particular piece of software. Three-button mice are the standard on UNIX/LINUX systems. Some mice even have four buttons: three at the top, and one at the side for the thumb.

**Wireless mice** use radio to eliminate the mouse cable. An interesting gimmick, it is useful in some work situations, such as when giving a presentation.

**3D mice** are also useful in presentations. Instead of being rolled, they are controlled by being waved around.

**Designer mice** are ordinary mice with a special finish, for example simulated mahogany or leopard print.

## Trackballs

Trackballs are inverted mice: the base stays fixed to the desk, and a ball on its surface is moved around. They have obvious applications in cramped working areas, and some people prefer them to standard mice. A variety of designs are available, some with one or two extra buttons.

## Graphics tablets

Of obvious interest to artists and designers, graphics tablets (also known as graphics pads or art pads) provide a large flat area and a 'pen' instead of a mouse. Moving the pen over the pad moves the mouse cursor on the screen in the usual way. When used in a graphics program or an image editor, it becomes possible to 'draw' with colours, or to outline shapes, much more conveniently than with a mouse. Some graphics pads also supply a mouse-like object called a 'puck' that works in a mouse-like way on the pad.

Advanced pads offer pens with an electronic 'rubber' at the top, and perhaps also some special areas on the pad that can be used to call up useful editing operations, such as cutting and pasting areas on the screen. Pad sizes vary from A5 to A3, with prices from about £100 to £1,000.

Experimental designs, which place an LCD screen under the drawing area, are also available. This combined pad/monitor must surely be the ultimate tool for artists. Unfortunately commercial models have yet to appear.

# Adding other extras

All computers can be improved with extras, although the more recent the model, the easier and cheaper this will be. There are two ways to add extras to a computer; internally, by adding extra memory, a larger hard disk, changing the processor, or fitting a new graphics card; and externally, by plugging in extras into the computer's *ports* (the connection sockets at the back).

## Adding memory

If your computer seems to spend a long time with its hard disk clicking and whirring, and if it takes a very long time to switch between one software tool and another, you can solve these problems by adding more memory.

Memory is very easy to add. It is supplied in the form of long, thin wafers, which plug into slots on the motherboard. Wafers are available with different memory capacities, typically 16Mb, 32Mb, 64Mb or 128Mb. Sometimes these are supplied as pairs.

Some computers are supplied with all the available slots filled. To add more memory, the old memory wafers have to be removed, and new ones with more capacity put in. Always check if there are any free slots for memory when buying a new machine. If not, when you pay someone to add more memory make sure they hand the existing wafers back to you. Some suppliers will keep the old chips for resale unless you ask them.

Also, when buying a computer, ask what the type and speed rating of the memory is. If you want to add more, you may need to quote these figures to the engineer or consultant. Adding more memory will typically cost you between £50 and £100 for labour costs. Costs for parts vary, depending on the amount of memory involved. In late 1998, 128Mb of memory cost about £100, but memory prices fluctuate rapidly.

## Adding hard-disk space

A new hard disk is unnecessary unless your computer starts sending messages that the existing one is full. Once this happens, you can usually free up space on the existing disk by removing software and information you no longer need. If you do this and still see messages saying that there is not enough room, you need a larger hard disk. Note that some computer cases offer very little room for a new disk. If your case is very small, you may need to check, or pay someone to check, that there is enough room available first.

If your computer uses the IDE system, then it will have four spaces for a hard disk. Two of these spaces will be used by the factory-installed disk and the CD-ROM drive. An extra hard disk can be plugged into one of the free spaces. Computers that use the SCSI system can have between 7 and 15 disk drives fitted altogether, depending on which variant of SCSI is used. As long as a new disk uses the same variant of SCSI as the one inside your machine, fitting it should not present any problems. SCSI drives are also available in *external* form, in a box of their own. This makes it possible to add a SCSI drive to a computer even if there is no room inside the case.

Once the disk is working, you need to rearrange the information in your computer so it is spread across two disks instead of one. This may not be as easy as it sounds. If you simply copy your favourite software from one disk to the other, your computer may not be able to find it any more. You may even have to remove and then reinstall some of your software on to the new disk. The best approach is to copy information instead, as this is usually more 'portable', or to create a completely new collection of information on the new disk, which you can then fill up from scratch.

## Adding a faster processor?

Processor chips are harder than many other components to upgrade. You can, in theory, take out a slow chip and fit a faster one from the same family. For example, a 233MHz Pentium II could be replaced with a 333MHz Pentium II. However, unless you suddenly find you need the extra speed for more demanding work, the difference in performance is likely to be negligible.

In general it is not worth changing a processor chip unless one that is twice as fast from the next generation is available. The difference between a 133MHz Pentium and a 266MHz Pentium II should be noticeable, even for simple work. However, this requires changing the motherboard as well as the processor chip. A complete upgrade like this will cost perhaps £500 to £750, depending on the new kind of processor chip used. With these prices it may be worth considering a completely new machine – perhaps keeping the old one, connecting it to the new one on a simple network, and using it as an archive.

**Overdrive chips**, which are speeded-up versions of an existing chip that are guaranteed to fit as a replacement, and other kinds of chip updates suffer from the same problem, and are best avoided for the same reasons.

## A new graphics card?

The need for a new graphics card is unlikely to arise unless you also buy a much larger monitor and discover that your existing card is slower than you would like it to be or it cannot show enough colours at the larger screen resolution. Another possibility is that you would like to fit a video-editing option, which is only available for a different graphics card to the one inside your computer. (The other reason for buying a new graphics card is to play games.)

To fit a new card, you will need to know whether your existing card uses the PCI or one of the AGP systems (see page 305). If the latter, you will need to know exactly which variant of AGP is used.

With that information, adding a new card is also easy, and, again, a qualified engineer should be able to do the job in an hour or two.

## Extras for ports

Ports are sockets that live on the back of a computer. You can connect extras to them without having to open up the computer itself. Typical ports include:

**Serial ports** There are usually two of these, and they are used for a modem, some kinds of mice, and certain other extras, such as graphics pads (see page 100).

**Parallel ports** Usually only one of these is available. Apart from connecting a printer, they can also be used to add scanners. Printer ports are completely standardised, so there are no variations between different computers.

**PS/2 ports** These ports are used for keyboards and mice. Older computers used a different type of connector for the keyboard (one that looked like a large circular plug with pins). If you have an old keyboard with this type of connector and you would like to continue using it when you buy a new computer, you will need an adaptor, which your supplier should be able to include for free, or at nominal cost.

**USB (Universal Serial Bus) ports** The latest port system, these are much faster than any other kind of connector, and are also easier to use. In theory, it should be possible to connect everything that is outside of a computer – speakers, monitor, modem, etc. – to a single USB port. In practice, very little USB-compatible hardware is available yet, although this is likely to change during the course of 1999.

**Firewire IEEE1394 ports** These are similar to USB, although currently they are most often used to connect video cameras to a computer.

**MIDI and joystick ports** are standard on most soundcards. MIDI ports can be used to connect a music synthesizer so that performances can be recorded and played back (software known as a MIDI sequencer is used for this). MIDI ports may, perhaps, be useful for certain kinds of presentations. Joystick ports are used to connect a joystick (a games accessory).

## Using expansion slots

Expansion slots are literally plastic slots on the computer's motherboard (inside the computer case) that are used to hold soundcards, internal modems, graphics cards, SCSI cards (for connecting high-performance hard disks), and other specialised extras, such as professional equipment for working with sound or video. The expansion slots are only accessible by opening up the computer's case. The insertion and removal of cards in and out of the slots is quite straightforward, although some care must be taken not to crack the motherboard.

There are three kinds of slots currently in use, and two obsolete types, which are no longer widely available. The ISA (Industry Standard Architecture) slots were designed using technology that has not changed since the mid-1980s. Moves are afoot to make ISA obsolete, and from about 2000 onwards, ISA slots will no longer be available on new computers. PCI (Peripheral Connect Interface) is a more recent and more efficient slot design, which is now becoming the new standard.

AGP (Advanced Graphics Port) is a type of slot used specifically for graphics cards, and AGP X2 and AGP X4 are even faster designs, although the difference in normal business use is negligible. VLB (VESA Local Bus) slots were used on computers made in the mid-1990s but have been replaced by PCI slots on new machines. Cards that work in VLB slots are no longer being made or sold. MCA (MicroChannel Architecture) slots are another old system that is very occasionally used on servers, but is now all but obsolete.

# Appendix III

# Operating systems

From the user's point of view, an operating system ('OS') is the 'face' of the computer. It defines what happens on the screen, how appealing (or otherwise) it looks, and which key presses and which mouse movements you have to make before something useful happens. In the industry the combination of the different elements of an OS is sometimes known as the 'look and feel'.

Technically, an operating system is the piece of software that acts as the user and computer hardware go-between, and makes it possible to write standardised software that will work on all kinds of machines without problems. Dealing with different kinds of hardware is a major problem in the computer world, and many of the difficult and annoying problems with which users have to deal are caused by standardised hardware not working as it should. The operating system does its best to hide these differences. For example, the user need not worry about the fact that their floppy-disk drive is made by manufacturer X instead of manufacturer Y, and works in a slightly different way.

Operating systems come in two types. The first is the **'command-line'** system. Users have to learn a small number of cryptic words and messages, and type them in by hand from the keyboard whenever they want to do something. For example, a user may need to type 'DIR' or 'ls' to list the information on a hard disk. Mistakes are easy to make and the messages that appear when users make mistakes are terse and unhelpful. Command-line systems are now almost obsolete. However, they are still in use in some commercial situations, because there are occasions when they are all that is required to do a given job. Their minimal complexity also means they can work well on very cheap hardware.

The more modern alternative is the **Graphic User Interface** (GUI). This presents information in the form of pictures, which can be controlled and manipulated with a pointing device, usually a mouse. Information is shown in different 'windows', which can be laid on top of each other, rather like pieces of paper on a desk. The different tasks that can be done in each window are shown as 'menus' – lists – and these are kept out of sight at the top of window, only appearing on demand (drop-down menus). Various other enhancements make the GUI experience easier for beginners to learn, and also much more efficient in an office setting. These include toolbars, which provide a shortcut to different menu items by hiding them behind tiny graphics, and dialogue boxes, which appear when the computer has to explain why there is a problem or when it needs more information from the user.

A more technical distinction is whether or not an operating system is **'multi-tasking'** – in other words, whether or not can it do more than one task at once. From a user's point of view, a multi-tasking system can be used to write a letter, print a different letter, pull information off the Internet and check a colleague's diary to arrange a meeting, all at the same time. Without multi-tasking, each of these would have to be done sequentially, which would take significantly longer.

A multi-tasking system can deal with many requests for information simultaneously, while perhaps sending out requests of its own to various other systems within a company. Multi-tasking is essential for serious business use. All modern operating systems now offer full multi-tasking facilities, although this is not true of older systems. A half-way house approach used for a while in the early 1990s is called task switching – the computer is not able to do more than one thing simultaneously, but it can be made to switch between different tasks very quickly by hand. Before that, older systems, especially desktop computers, were resolutely single-tasking.

Advanced operating systems allow **clustering** and **multi-processing.** The former allows the workload to be divided up between a number of different computers that have been connected together. The latter does the same for a single computer that has more than one processing chip inside it. Both of these features become important for high-performance work.

From a computer manager's point of view, two other qualities are just as important as multi-tasking and ease of use, and these too are affected by the choice of operating system. Reliability is a key factor in a business setting. Computers should not stop working, and they should not lose the information filed away inside them. If they do, the consequences can vary from the irritating to the commercially disastrous. The other issue is 'cost of ownership', which is the cost of maintaining, upgrading and repairing a computer. For example, it is possible to connect some computers to a network simply by plugging in a cable at the back. With others, the case has to be opened up and a card has to be fitted (although once the case is closed, the card will work immediately). However, some models baffle users and force them into a time-consuming struggle that demands plenty of experimentation and coaxing. Time is wasted and productivity is lost, and when multiplied by the number of computers in an organisation, the amount of damage done to a business soon becomes significant. To some extent these are hardware questions, but this cost of ownership is also affected by operating systems.

What follows is a guide to the different operating systems that are in use today, with information about how useful they are in a business context.

## MS-DOS (PC only)

MS-DOS is sold by Microsoft, and is now technically obsolete. The last version available was 6.22, although earlier versions, which are best avoided, are still very occasionally advertised in the trade press. MS-DOS is a command-line system and has no multi-tasking facilities, although it can sometimes be coaxed into printing a letter while the user gets on with something else.

In spite of its drawbacks, MS-DOS is still widely used, and is a good choice for certain kinds of businesses. It is relatively cheap, it works with simple and low-cost hardware, and it is an ideal base for a simple bespoke (tailor-made) system. A good example would be a job-tracking and stock-control system used by a garage. With these kinds of applications the details of the operating system remain out of sight, and the settings required to make it work will never be changed. This means that the contribution it makes to cost of ownership is negligible.

MS-DOS becomes less suitable when large amounts of information need to be exchanged within a business. It is adequate for systems in which a branch office automatically passes, through a modem, a summary of a day's trading to head office once a day. However, it is totally unsuitable for groups of people managing a complex project together (with a need for more sophisticated forms of communication), for serious Internet use, or when a computer network has to keep track of multiple transactions as they happen.

## Windows 3.1 (PC only)

Windows 3.1 was the successor to MS-DOS, and the first operating system made by Microsoft that caught the public imagination. (Windows 1.0, 2.0 and 3.0 were all commercial failures.) It was the first true GUI system offered for the PC, but was only able to offer task switching instead of full multi-tasking. In effect Windows 3.1 simply added a GUI to make MS-DOS more useable. (It is impossible to use or install Windows 3.1 without installing MS-DOS first.)

Although technically obsolete and no longer sold (except to special order) Windows 3.1 is still widely used in business today. It is less robust than Windows 95, but is also less complex and easier to manage. Some people find it easier to understand and work with. Cost of ownership is variable. For stable systems that have hardware that is not going to change, it can work reasonably well. But it is unsuitable for anyone who would like to expand his or her computer system significantly after buying it. It is also worth noting that new software that will work with it is now becoming scarce. On the plus side, the fact that it was designed for much older and slower hardware means that it can be almost ridiculously fast on today's more powerful machines. In addition, it will work well on very cheap computers. A 'workgroup' version of Windows 3.1 called Windows 3.11 allows for the sharing of information and printers in an office.

Overall, Windows 3.1 is a good choice for a sole trader on a tight budget who wants to use a computer solely for business and will be doing nothing more complex than word processing and accounts.

## Windows 95 (PC only)

Windows 95 (Win95) is the successor to Windows 3.1. Although, in theory, it uses computer hardware more efficiently, in practice it is a larger and more complex piece of software and demands a more powerful machine to function at its best. Even then it can seem sluggish on very cheap models.

Windows 95 looks rather different to Windows 3.1, and some people find it overcomplicated. Nonetheless, it is a workable semi-standard system for light business use, and also includes network facilities so that computers can be connected together easily. More software is available for Windows 95 than for any other kind of system.

The main problem with Windows 95 is its lack of reliability. In typical use you can expect something to go wrong approximately once a day, ranging from the minor to the more serious 'crashes' where the PC either turns itself off or shows a cryptic message that says the PC has stopped working.

Some of these problems are due to software and hardware issues related to the products of other manufacturers rather than Windows 95 itself. But, for whatever reason, Windows 95 seems more prone to them than other modern PC operating systems. On that basis it is suitable for light office work, but not for more critical applications, such as those where an entire office needs to rely on the continued operation of a machine. Also, cost of ownership can be quite high, even for light use.

## Windows 98 (PC only)

Windows 98 (Win98) is essentially Windows 95 with one or two new features (such as the ability to use more than monitor at the same time), some cosmetic changes, a few fixes for known Windows 95 problems, and a built-in copy of Microsoft's Internet Explorer Version 4 web browser. Win98 is now included with new machines, so if you buy a PC for general-purpose use this is likely to be the operating system you are given. Like Win95, Win98 is not suitable for 'mission critical' applications although it does seem to be more reliable in general use. (It has been popular with support departments, who get fewer calls from people who use it.)

# Operating systems

If you are using a Windows 95 as your operating system, there is no compelling reason to upgrade to Windows 98. In fact there may be good reasons *not* to do so. According to reports in the computer press and in Windows-related newsgroups on the Internet, Windows 98 may have problems completing an upgrade of certain Windows 95 systems. This depends to some extent on the software originally installed. At best this means that certain items, such as modems and Internet or network connections, may stop working. At worst you can be left with a useless computer that needs to have all the information and software reinstalled from scratch. For an office system this is clearly unacceptable. Unless there is a compelling reason to upgrade, Windows 95 should continue to be sufficient. Microsoft may address these problems with a 'service pack' – a collection of improvements and fixes for problems – during the life of this book. For the latest news, check with your dealer.

## Windows 2000 (for PC, PowerPC, DECAlpha)

Windows NT ('New Technology') is the Microsoft product designed for serious professional use. In the long term Microsoft is planning to kill off Windows 95 and 98 and move everyone to a version of NT called Windows 2000, which will be available in domestic and professional variants.

NT (currently up to version 4) is more demanding of computer hardware, especially memory, than other versions of Windows. However, it is also more robust, and unlike other varieties of Windows it can work on computer systems that have more than one processing chip.

Microsoft is keen for NT to become the de facto business standard for virtually the entire range of businesses that have IT needs, from tiny companies with a handful of employees all the way up to banks and building societies.

The system is closely tied to Microsoft's other business-oriented products. NT and applications such as BackOffice are often sold together as complete packages. (Software not written by Microsoft is of course also available, if not quite so widely advertised.)

By late 1998 the future of NT was still confused and Microsoft had plans to rewrite NT completely to create a robust new version with important new features. The release date for this version – known as Windows 2000 – has slipped repeatedly. Originally slated for release in 1999, the new name suggests that the product will not be available until the year 2000 at the very earliest.

In the meantime, businesses have to decide whether to wait for the latest version, whether to continue using NT version 4, or whether to use a completely different system such as LINUX (see below). The decision is a complicated one. Because Windows 2000 will be a radical new release, there is no guarantee that upgrading from NT version 4 will be easy or problem-free.

NT is available in two versions, known as NT Client and NT Server. NT Client offers the improved robustness of NT on a single machine, and is intended for anyone who wants a more stable version of Windows for their own private use. NT Server is designed to function at the centre of a network. It costs nearly four times more than NT Client, and it is sold on a 'per-licence' basis, so that the more people use the network, the more expensive it becomes.

## UNIX (various)

UNIX was originally designed as a test project, but emerged from the research lab into a commercial product. This operating system is very technical and gives the impression of having been created by computer experts for computer experts. On the plus side, it makes far more efficient use of computer hardware than the varieties of Microsoft Windows, and is also more robust. Commercial UNIX systems are reliable enough to work for years on end without failing. On the down side, UNIX can only be described as complex and obscure, especially for those without a background in computing.

At its most 'nuts-and-bolts' level, UNIX looks very much like the kind of very simple operating system that was available on large computer systems back in the late 1970s and early 1980s. It can be controlled from the keyboard by typing commands, rather like MS-DOS, although the command syntax is far more complex and almost deliberately obscure. For example, where MS-DOS uses 'TYPE' to show a document on the screen, the equivalent command in UNIX is 'cat' – an abbreviation of 'catenate'. This is a made-up word based on the idea of concatenation, and in turn reflects the way that UNIX handles information internally. While apparently bewildering, prolonged exposure to UNIX makes it clear that the train of thought that led to this abbreviation does make sense, albeit in a very lateral way. However, anyone used to Microsoft Windows will find that not only are all the commands hard to remember, but the philosophy of the system is completely different.

In a typical business setting this complexity will be invisible to most users because UNIX can be equipped with a variety of Windows-like GUIs, which help make it far more approachable. In any case, business software written for UNIX is often offered on a bespoke (tailor-made) basis (see Chapter 7). All that users ever see are a small number of different screens full of information and text, each designed to do a specific job. General-purpose UNIX machines are only likely to be found in scientific and academic settings, where the complexities are tolerated and even welcomed because of the flexibility and power they offer.

UNIX is available in a number of commercial versions. Manufacturers of very fast computer hardware often supply their own variants designed to work specifically with their products. For example, Sun supplies SOLARIS, and Silicon Graphics supplies IRIX. Another popular commercial product is FreeBSD UNIX, which is for general-purpose use and can work on both PC and Mac hardware.

## LINUX

One of the most interesting developments in the UNIX world is LINUX – a full version of UNIX that is completely free. LINUX is maintained and developed over the Internet by an international network of computer enthusiasts who contribute to it in their spare time. Versions are available for all kinds of hardware (PCs, Macs, and even obscure and obsolete computers such as the Commodore Amiga), and the software can be downloaded from the Internet. A number of semi-commercial variants of LINUX are available on CD-ROMs, which can be bought on their own or with accompanying explanatory books for around £40. (Note that, unlike commercial operating systems with complex licensing deals, this is a one-off payment, and no further licensing fees are required, even if the system is subsequently used on a network with thousands of computers.)

The most common semi-commercial varieties of LINUX are called Red Hat, Slackware and SuSe ('Susie'). Red Hat is perhaps the most popular, although the differences are marginal. Occasionally these are given away free on magazine cover disks.

LINUX is growing in popularity and has been used successfully for commercial applications. It is also compatible with Novell's Netware, which means that it can be used for business networking. For a long time LINUX suffered from a dearth of commercial applications, but this is now changing. A version of the popular WordPerfect word processor became available in 1998, and other commercial applications, including spreadsheets and databases, are following suit.

LINUX's main drawback is the fact that it may not be completely compatible with every kind of hardware. For example, it may not work with a given graphics card because the software that links the card to the rest of the system (known as the driver) has not been written by anyone. While this can be an insurmountable problem for anyone who has non-standard hardware, widely used hardware almost always has drivers available, although getting hold of them may require a detailed search on the Internet.

For commercially supplied, ready-to-run, bespoke applications, the suppliers will do all the setting-up, and hardware compatibility should be less of a problem. In this kind of setting LINUX is an excellent way to make use of the reliability and robustness of UNIX without paying a fortune in commercial licence fees. An example of its popularity is the use of Apache, which is a free web-server application supplied as part of the LINUX package. Apache is now more widely used on the web than any other kind of web-server software, commercial or otherwise.

In the long run LINUX may turn out to be the wave of the future. Because it is free, companies such as Microsoft have no commercial leverage against it. At the moment it is still too complex for beginners to set up, but if this changes it could well start to become the new standard from about 2000 onwards.

## MacOS (Apple Mac only)

Although Apple has a relatively small market share, MacOS tends to be more popular with its users than Windows. It is a fully multi-tasking system with a similar – if perhaps more mature and sophisticated – set of features as any version of MS Windows. It is usually easier to add new hardware, and Mac software seems to be more robust. Cost of ownership is also lower.

In the mid-1990s, Apple introduced various OS-like products, and projects appeared and then disappeared again before coming to fruition. Its latest plans are to introduce a hugely improved version of the MacOS – called MacOS X – towards the end of 1999. This will be a combination of a UNIX-like core (based on a system called Rhapsody that Apple originally developed as a stand-alone product) with a new Mac look and feel. As an interim measure MacOS 9 is due to appear in the first half of 1999. This is an improved version of the current MacOS 8.5.

Mac users are advised to watch the trade press carefully to see if it is worth upgrading to any of these products. In the past, Apple has occasionally produced systems that were more trouble than they were worth. On the whole though, most versions of the MacOS are stable and easy to use.

## BeOS (Mac and PC)

BeOS was created by a former manager at Apple, and is an interesting new product that is currently the only commercial alternative to the 'big-name' operating systems. It is fast and well designed, and commercial applications are starting to appear for it. However, Be (as the company that makes it is known) is unlikely to have the marketing ability to compete effectively with more established products. Currently little more than a curiosity, BeOS is included here for the sake of completeness.

## Network operating systems

Unlike standard operating systems, network operating systems (NOSs) are designed to work 'behind the scenes' to maintain a network. Some standard operating systems include simple network features that are adequate for networks that have perhaps five computers on them. If there are between five and ten computers, these facilities start to show their limitations. Beyond ten computers, a true NOS becomes essential.

## Novell IntraNetware

More usually known as NetWare, this system has become something of a business standard for network operating systems. NetWare is server-based, which means that you have to buy a server if you want to use it. This server will not be available for any other kind of work – its sole job is to run the network. A standard desktop PC will work as a server, but more expensive and advanced server hardware is recommended for best results.

NetWare can work with Btrieve, a popular software development system also made by Novell. A number of business-specific packages are available in Btrieve.

## LANTastic

LANTastic is a simple peer-to-peer system (connects two or more similar computers together) that was popular until recently. The arrival of peer-to-peer features in the various versions of Windows has meant that its popularity has waned.

## Java

Java is not so much a network operating system, as a universal system. It takes a completely new approach to the way that computers can be used for both business and pleasure. Software written for one kind of computer should work on any computer that has a version of Java installed. This is very interesting to software developers, who usually either have to concentrate on one kind of computer and ignore all the others, or else have to translate ('port') software between machines – a process that is time-consuming and expensive. Java does away with this.

Java works best on networks, and is built into all of the popular web browsers. But Java's true potential probably goes beyond web browsers, and its real talents may become more obvious when networks become much faster than they are now, and many more people use the Internet (or whatever its descendants are called).

At the moment all software is large, bulky and clumsy because users have to buy and install all the options in a package just in case they may need them. In general, most of a package simply takes up space on a hard disk. Java makes it possible to spread both information and tiny, but usable, fragments of software around a network, which are then assembled 'on the fly' according to the needs of a user. On a fast network this is potentially a more efficient way of working, as much less storage space is required overall.

Interest in Java peaked towards the end of 1997, and since then there has been something of a backlash, as computer programmers have become more familiar with its current limitations. However, in the medium term this remains a system to watch.

## Network features in standard operating systems

Many everyday operating systems have basic networking facilities built-in. For a small network of perhaps five computers or fewer, which is used for simple business work, these systems can offer all the network facilities that are needed. Larger operating systems (such as Windows NT) offer more complex network-ready facilities.

### Win95, Win98 and Windows for Workgroups

Win95, Win98 and Windows offer simple network facilities that are suitable for sharing information and printers. Simple security features are included. Users have to identify themselves ('log in') when they start using the network. The name under which they work defines the 'privileges' they have on the network – for example, which individuals and groups are allowed to share information on the network, whether they can delete and move other people's information, or whether they can only read it. Windows 98 includes basic Intranet facilities, so that collections of information can be presented on a network with background graphics and web-type facilities, rather than as simple lists.

### NT Server

The NT Server is designed to run a large network and includes extra security features that are missing on smaller network systems. User activities can be logged, so that someone managing the network can keep track of potential problems. The state of the network as a whole can be monitored from a single computer. NT Server also includes Virtual Private Network (VPN) facilities, which make it possible to create a private company network over the Internet, hiding transmissions between offices with a secret code so that they remain secure.

## MacOS

MacOS includes built-in basic information and printer-sharing facilities. All but the very cheapest Apple computers have network hardware included, and building a network becomes very simple. An almost ubiquitous email package called QuickMail is often used on Apple networks to provide email facilities.

# Appendix IV
# Internet addresses explained

Rather like postal addresses, Internet addresses are put together using specific rules. To make addresses easier to remember, and also to make it more likely that an address is passed on to someone correctly, it helps to know what these rules are.

Note that in general all Internet addresses are lower case. Capitals are sometimes used to make an address easier to read, but, as far as the computers on the Internet are concerned, addresses are always interpreted as lower case.

Also note that there are never any spaces in an Internet address. Words are usually separated by dots ('.'), although other punctuation is used in certain circumstances. Addresses always have to be typed in *exactly as they appear*. Using a '/' instead of a '\', or getting a single letter wrong means an address will not work. There is no Internet equivalent of that department in the UK Post Office which tries to make sense of obscure or miswritten addresses.

Finally, note that *every Internet address is unique*.

## Email addresses

Email addresses take the form '*someone@somewhere.sometype*'. 'Someone' can be anything at all. A long word, a short word, a number of words separated by dots or underscores ('_'). The symbol '@' is the 'at' sign, which is present in all Internet email addresses. 'Somewhere' can be a single word or a number of words separated by dots. It usually refers to the name of a company or an organisation. 'Sometype' tells you more about the kind of company or organisation it is, and also sometimes includes a country code that tells you which

319

country it is in. (For more information see Appendix V for a list of all the codes used in email and web addresses.)

In Internet jargon anything after the '@' is known as the 'domain'. For example, the address *someone@exeter.ac.uk* would tell you that this was the address of someone in the UK ('.uk'), at an academic establishment ('.ac'), in this case Exeter University ('exeter'). Similarly, *someone@bbc.co.uk* would be the address of someone at the BBC, and *someone@which.net* would be the address of someone who uses Which? Online.

Similarly, *mark@idris.com* would be the address of someone called Mark working at a company that included the name 'Idris' and was either based in the US or traded internationally ('.com'). Note that there may or may not be a direct link between real company names and domain names. Because competition for domain names is fierce and they are alloted on a first-come first-served basis – at least until trademark lawyers get involved – companies sometimes have to resort to using part of their full name, or comvert their full name into one long word – for example, 'digitalaudioinnovations.com'

Note that on-line services use different schemes. AOL, for example, uses **screen names**, which are simply unique ten-letter names (e.g. 'richard136'). AOL users can send email to each other simply by typing in the screen name. As long as the email stays within AOL's computers, '@'s and dots are unnecessary. To send an email from outside of AOL to someone in AOL, you simply add '@aol.com' after their screen name. Someone sending email from AOL to someone on the Internet also needs to use the full Internet address.

## Web addresses

Addresses used in web browsers are known as **URLs** (Uniform Resource Locators). These come in two parts. The first defines what kind of information the browser is looking for, thus **'http://'** is a standard web page and **'https://'** is a secure web page. Usually 'http://' is used. (The letters stand for 'Hypertext Transfer Protocol', a technical term, which simply means 'web page'.) Note that to save time, some browsers will add an 'http://' automatically if it is not typed in.

The rest of the address is simply a unique identifier for a web page. The smallest possible identifier is two words separated by dots, for example, *http://somename.com*. The largest is an interminable string of letters, slashes, and other punctuation, for example:

*ttp://news.bbc.co.uk/hi/english/business/the_company_file/ newsid_181000/181404.stm*,

which was the URL for a BBC news article about the crash of a major Japanese bank.

If a long URL does not work for any reason, it is sometimes possible to try to find related information by backtracking. This is done by repeatedly leaving off groups of letters between '/' signs. In the example above

*http://news.bbc.co.uk/hi/english/business/the_company_file/*

leads to 'The Company File' on the BBC's business pages,

*http://news.bbc.co.uk/hi/english/business/*

jumps to the main list of stories on the main business pages, and

*http://news.bbc.co.uk*

is the main BBC news summary.

Many web-site addresses start with the letters 'www'. This is a convention rather than a necessity as the examples above show. However, it does mean that it is easy to guess the web address of a well-known company. For example, the address of IBM's web site is simply *http://www.ibm.com* and similarly, the address of Dell's site is *http://www.dell.com*. If a company is based in the UK or has a UK subsidiary, it can be helpful to replace '.com' with '.co.uk'. Thus, *http://www.dell.co.uk* gives the address of Dell UK's web site.

Note that browsers can be used for much more than looking at web pages. The starting codes for other options are:

- **ftp://** An FTP site
- **gopher://** A gopher facility (an antiquated text-only information indexing system that is very rarely used now)
- **localhost://** A web page kept on the user's own machine
- **file:///** (note the three slashes instead of two) A file of information on the user's own machine
- **news://** A newsgroup.

The only one of these that is used regularly is 'ftp://', and even this is not common.

## Newsgroup names

Newsgroups have names rather than addresses, because they are global discussion areas that do not have a single location, and do not rely on a single computer. Names are always made up of words separated by dots, for example, 'uk.tech.y2k'. The first word defines a master group, the second a sub-group, the third a sub-sub-group, and so on. There are rarely more than five or six subdivisions, although there is no limit in practice. For example, the joke group 'alt.a.b.c.d.e.f.g.h.i.j.k.l.m.n.o.p.q.r.s.t.u.v.w.x.y.z' takes the subdivision process to a silly extreme. The main master group types are:

- **rec.** recreation
- **biz.** business
- **sci.** science and technology
- **comp.** computer-related subjects
- **soc.** societies and cultures
- **misc.** miscellaneous
- **talk.** chatter and repetitive debates
- **news.** information about the newsgroup network (but *not* news in the usual sense)
- **alt.** anything and everything (a free-for-all)
- **<company name>.** groups created by companies – for example, Microsoft, 3Dfx (who make graphics cards) and the on-line service AOL
- **<geographical location>.** US states, countries (including 'uk.' for UK-specific groups), sometimes cities and other areas
- **<university name>.** many colleges, especially in the US, have their own groups – for example, 'utexas.' for the University of Texas, and 'ucam.' for Cambridge University
- **<others>.** various more or less obscure groupings, most of which are usually of little interest to most people. For example, 'fido7.' for users of 'fidonet', a very crude precursor of the Internet, or 'slac.' for scientists who work at the Stanford Linear Accelerator (an atom smasher).

Finding useful groups can be hard, because the structure of Usenet (the network for newsgroups) is something of a mess. Many master groups are so obscure that it is impossible to guess what they are for without reading their messages (and even then it may not be obvious). In general, Usenet is a little like a shortwave radio, with hundreds of competing voices, many in foreign languages, clamouring for attention, while all manner of morse code signals, transmissions from satellites and other noises serve to make it harder to find useful stations.

The best place to look for helpful information is in the main master groups, especially biz., comp. and perhaps rec. and alt., and also in the various uk. (UK-specific) groups.

## International codes

.org     a non-commercial organisation, such as a charity
.com     a commercial organisation that trades internationally
.co     a company that trades in a single country
.gov     a government department or other related facility
.net     an organisation or company that provides Internet access
.ac     an academic institution
.nato     a NATO installation

### UK-specific codes

.ltd     a UK limited company
.plc     a UK public limited company
.sch     a school
.police     for the police (not much used)
.mod     anything run by the UK Ministry of Defence
.nhs     anything run by the National Health Service

### US codes

.edu     a school or university
.mil     a military base
.k12     a school
.(state)     a two-letter state abbreviation (always followed by .us)

In 1998 plans were afoot to extend these codes to include:

**.firm**  a business
**.store**  a trading establishment
**.web**  related to the World Wide Web
**.arts**  related to arts and culture
**.rec**  related to recreation and hobbies
**.info**  an information service
**.nom**  a specific private or business name.

Note that there is no pan-European code yet.

## Domain Country Codes

| | | | | | |
|---|---|---|---|---|---|
| ad | Andorra | bj | Benin | cx | Christmas Island |
| ae | United Arab Emirates | bm | Bermuda | cy | Cyprus |
| | | bn | Brunei Darussalam | cz | Czech Republic |
| af | Afghanistan | bo | Bolivia | de | Germany |
| Ag | Antigua and Barbuda | br | Brazil | dj | Djibouti |
| | | bs | Bahamas | dk | Denmark |
| ai | Anguilla | bt | Buthan | dm | Dominica |
| al | Albania | bv | Bouvet Island | do | Dominican Republic |
| am | Armenia | bw | Botswana | | |
| an | Antilles | by | Belarus | dz | Algeria |
| ao | Angola | bz | Belize | ec | Ecuador |
| aq | Antarctica | ca | Canada | ee | Estonia |
| ar | Argentina | cc | Cocos (Keeling) Islands | eg | Egypt |
| as | American Samoa | | | eh | Western Sahara |
| at | Austria | cf | Central African Republic | et | Ethiopia |
| au | Australia | | | fi | Finland |
| aw | Aruba | ch | Switzerland | fj | Fiji |
| az | Azerbaijan | ci | Côte d'Ivoire | fk | Falkland Islands |
| ba | Bosnia and Herzegovina | cl | Chile | fm | Micronesia |
| | | cm | Cameroon | fo | Faroe Islands |
| bb | Barbados | cn | China | fr | France |
| bd | Bangladesh | co | Colombia | fx | France (European Territory) |
| be | Belgium | cr | Costa Rica | | |
| bf | Burkina Faso | cs | Czechoslovakia | ga | Gabon |
| bg | Bulgaria | cu | Cuba | gb | Great Britain (UK) |
| bi | Burundi | cv | Cape Verde | gd | Grenada |

# Internet addresses explained

| | | | | | |
|---|---|---|---|---|---|
| ge | Georgia | jp | Japan | mw | Malawi |
| gg | Guernsey (Channel Islands) | ke | Kenya | mx | Mexico |
| | | kg | Kyrgyzstan | my | Malaysia |
| gh | Ghana | kh | Cambodia | mz | Mozambique |
| gi | Gibraltar | ki | Kiribati | na | Namibia |
| gl | Greenland | km | Comoros | nc | New Caledonia (French) |
| gp | Guadeloupe (French) | kn | Saint Kitts Nevis | | |
| | | kp | North Korea | ne | Niger |
| gq | Equatorial Guinea | kr | South Korea | nf | Norfolk Island |
| gf | Guyana (French) | kw | Kuwait | ng | Nigeria |
| gm | Gambia | ky | Cayman Islands | ni | Nicaragua |
| gn | Guinea | kz | Kazakstan | nl | Netherlands |
| gr | Greece | lb | Lebanon | no | Norway |
| gt | Guatemala | lc | Saint Lucia | np | Nepal |
| gu | Guam (US) | li | Liechtenstein | nr | Nauru |
| gw | Guinea Bissau | lk | Sri Lanka | nt | Neutral Zone |
| gy | Guyana | lr | Liberia | nu | Niue |
| hk | Hong Kong | ls | Lesotho | nz | New Zealand |
| hm | Heard and Macdonald Islands | lt | Lithuania | om | Oman |
| | | lv | Latvia | pa | Panama |
| hn | Honduras | ly | Libya | pe | Peru |
| hr | Croatia | ma | Morocco | pf | Polynesia (French) |
| ht | Haiti | mc | Monaco | pg | Papua New Guinea |
| hu | Hungary | md | Moldova | ph | Philippines |
| id | Indonesia | mg | Madagascar | pk | Pakistan |
| ie | Ireland | mh | Marshall Islands | pl | Poland |
| il | Israel | ml | Mali | pm | Saint Pierre and Miquelon |
| im | Isle of Man | mm | Myanmar | | |
| in | India | mn | Mongolia | pn | Pitcairn |
| io | British Indian Ocean Territory | mo | Macau | pt | Portugal |
| | | mp | Northern Mariana Islands | pr | Puerto Rico (US) |
| iq | Iraq | | | pw | Palau |
| ir | Iran | mq | Martinique (French) | py | Paraguay |
| is | Iceland | | | qa | Qatar |
| it | Italy | mr | Mauritania | re | Réunion (French) |
| je | Jersey (Channel Islands) | ms | Montserrat | ro | Romania |
| | | mt | Malta | ru | Russian Federation |
| jm | Jamaica | mu | Mauritius | rw | Rwanda |
| jo | Jordan | mv | Maldives | sa | Saudi Arabia |

| | | | | | |
|---|---|---|---|---|---|
| sb | Solomon Islands | td | Chad | us | United States |
| sc | Seychelles | tf | French Southern | uy | Uruguay |
| sd | Sudan | | Territory | uz | Uzbekistan |
| se | Sweden | tg | Togo | va | Vatican City State |
| sg | Singapore | th | Thailand | vc | Saint Vincent and |
| sh | Saint Helena | tj | Tajikistan | | Grenadines |
| si | Slovenia | tk | Tokelau | ve | Venezuela |
| sj | Svalbard and Jan | tm | Turkmenistan | vg | Virgin Islands |
| | Mayen Islands | tn | Tunisia | | (British) |
| sk | Slovakia | to | Tonga | vi | Virgin Islands (US) |
| sl | Sierra Leone | tp | East Timor | vn | Vietnam |
| sm | San Marino | tr | Turkey | vu | Vanuatu |
| sn | Senegal | tt | Trinidad and | wf | Wallis and Futuna |
| so | Somalia | | Tobago | | Islands |
| sr | Suriname | tv | Tuvalu | ws | Samoa |
| st | Saint Tomé and | tw | Taiwan | ye | Yemen |
| | Príncipe | tz | Tanzania | yu | Yugoslavia |
| sv | El Salvador | ua | Ukraine | za | South Africa |
| sy | Syria | ug | Uganda | zm | Zambia |
| sz | Swaziland | uk | United Kingdom | zr | Zaire |
| tc | Turks and Caicos | um | US Minor | zw | Zimbabwe |
| | Islands | | Outlying Islands | | |

## Appendix V

# Useful addresses

## Business software manufacturers

**Adobe Systems UK**
Waterview House
1 Roundwood Avenue
Stockley Park
Uxbridge
Middlesex UB11 9AE
Tel: 0181 606 4000
Fax: 0181 606 4004
Web site: http://www.adobe.co.uk

**Best!Ware (UK)**
The Software Centre
East Way
Lee Mill Industrial Estate
Ivybridge
Devon PL21 9PE
Tel: 01752 201901
Fax: 01752 894833
Web site: http://www.myob.co.uk

**Corel**
268 Bath Road
Slough
Berkshire SL1 4DX
Tel: 01753 708406
Fax: 01753 708839
Web site: http://www.corel.com/International/uk_ireland/

**CSSA FITS SERVICE**
Hanover House
20 Red Lion Street
London WC1R 4QN
Tel: 0171–395 6700
Fax: 0171–404 4119
Web site: http://www.cssa.co.uk/

**Elmbronze Ltd**
PO Box 8361
Largs KA30 8YA
Scotland
Fax: 0870 055 7834
Email: TDsales@elmbronze.demon.co.uk
Web site: http://www.elmbronze.demon.co.uk/products/TDtools.htm
(Elmbronze Ltd is the UK distributor of tools that check for Y2K time dilation)

**Inprise (UK) Limited** (formerly Borland)
8 Pavilions
Ruscombe Business Park
Twyford
Berkshire
RG10 9NN
Tel: 0118 932 0022
Fax: 0118 932 0017
Web site: http://www.inprise.co.uk

**Intuit Service Centre**
PO Box 139
Chertsey
Surrey KT16 9FE
Tel: (0800) 585058
Web site: http://www.intuit.co.uk

**Lotus UK**
Lotus Park
The Causeway
Staines
Middlesex TW18 3AG
Tel: (01784) 455445
Web site: http://www.lotus.com

**Megatech Software plc**
29 East Street
Epsom
Surrey KT29 1BS
Tel: 01372 727274
Fax: 01372 721414
Web site: *http://www.megatech.co.uk*

**Microsoft Ltd**
Microsoft Campus
Thames Valley Park
Reading RG6 1WG
Tel: (0870) 6010100
Fax: (0870) 6010200
Web site: *http://www.microsoft.com*

**Novell UK**
1 Arlington Square
Downshire Way
Bracknell RG12 1WA
Tel: (01344) 724000
Fax: (01344) 724001
Web site: *http://www.novell.com.uk*

**Pegasus Software Ltd**
Orion House
Orion Way
Kettering
Northamptonshire NN15 6PE
Tel: (01536) 495200
Email: *mailbox@pegasus.co.uk*
Web site: *http://www.pegasus.co.uk*

**Sagesoft Ltd**
Sage House
Benton Park Road
Newcastle upon Tyne NE7 7LZ
Tel: 0191–255 3000
Fax: 0191–255 0308
Email: *info@sage.com*
Web site: *http://www.sagesoft.co.uk*

**Serif (Europe) Ltd**
The Software Centre
PO Box 2000
Nottingham NG11 8AA
Tel: 0115 914 2000
Fax: 0115 914 2020
Web site: *http://www.spco.com/INTL/uk/INTLUK.HTM*

**Symantec (Europe)**
Customer Services
PO Box 5689
Dublin 15
Ireland
Tel: 0171 616 5600
Fax: 0171 616 5700
Web site: *http://www.symantec.com/region/reg_eu/*

## Internet software resources

Use the following URLs as a starting point, and follow the links at each site to locate the software that suits your particular computer and operating system.

## Web browsers

Microsoft Internet Explorer
http://www.microsoft.com

Netscape Communicator
http://www.netscape.com

Opera
http://www.operasoftware.com

## Email software

Qualcomm Eudora
http://www.eudora.com

## News software

Forte Agent and Free Agent
http://www.forteinc.com
News Archive Deja News
http://www.dejanews.com

## Image libraries and related organisations

*Digital Vision*
Chelsea Reach
78–89 Lots Road
London SW10 0RN
Tel: 0171 351 5542
Fax: 0171 351 6487
Web site: http://
www.digitalvision.co.uk

*ImageBank*
17 Conway Street
London W1P 6EE
Tel: 0171 312 0300
Fax: 0171 391 9111
Web site: http://
www.imagebank.co.uk

*Performing Rights Society*
29–33 Berners Street
London W1P 4AA
Tel: 0171 580 5544
Fax: 0171 306 4455
Web site: http://www.prs.co.uk

## Insurance brokers

*Association of British Insurers*
51 Gresham Street
London EC2V 7HQ
Tel: 0171–600 3333
Fax: 0171–696 8996
Web site: http:///www.abi.org.uk

*Burnett & Associates*
39–41 Victoria Road
Woolston
Southampton SO19 9DY
Tel: (01703) 442227
Fax: (01703) 442210
Email: info@burnett.co.uk
Web site: http://www.burnett.co.uk

*First Domestic*
Swan Court
Wimbledon
London SW19 4AA
Tel: (0990) 500500

*Royal and Sun Alliance Engineering*
(formerly National Vulcan)
St Mary's Parsonage
Manchester M60 9AP
Tel: 0161-834 8124
Fax: 0161-834 2394
Email: *marketing@eng.royalsun.com*
Web site: *http://www.royal-and-sunalliance.com*

*Tolson Messenger*
148 King Street
London W6 0QU
Tel: 0181-741 8361
Fax: 0181-741 9395
Email: *home-business@tolsonmessenger.demon.co.uk*

## Internet access providers

*America OnLine (AOL)*
Gilde House
East Point Business Park
Fairview
Dublin 3
Ireland
Tel: (0800) 2791234
Fax: (0800) 2797346
Email: *Ukgen@mail.tech.aol.com*
Web site: *http://www.aol.com*

*CompuServeUK*
1 Redcliff Street
Bristol BS1 6NP
Tel: (0990) 000400 (customer support), (0990) 000200 (sales)
Email: *mail.compuserve.com*
Web site: *http://world.compuserve.com*

*Demon Internet*
Gateway House
322 Regents Park Road
London N3 2QQ
Tel: 0181-371 1234
Email: *sales@demon.net*
Web site: *http://www.demon.net*

*Direct Connection*
Martin House
1 Tranquil Vale
Blackheath Village
London SE3 0BU
Tel: 0800 072 0000
Faxback info: 0181-852 8800
Email: *sales@dircon.net*
Web site: *http://www.dircon.net*

*Freeserve*
Details and software available in the UK from any Dixons, Currys, the link or PC World store.
Tel: 0990 500049
Web site: *http://www.freeserve.net*

*Which? Online*
Freepost
Hertford X
SG14 1YB
Tel: (0645) 830256
Email: *freeCD@which.net*

## Pre-printed computer stationery

*Paper Direct*
Freepost (LE6296)
Hinckley LE10 0BR
Tel: (0800) 616244
Email: *sales@paperdirect.co.uk*

*Viking Direct*
Bursom Industrial Park
Tollwell Road
Leicester LE4 1BR
Tel: (0800) 424444
Fax: (0800) 622211

## Others

*Data Protection Registrar*
Wycliffe House
Water Lane
Wilmslow
Cheshire SK9 5AF
Tel: (01625) 545745
Fax: (01625) 524510
Email: *data@wycliffe.demon.co.uk*
Web site: *http://www.open.gov.uk/dpr/dprhome.htm*

## Y2K resources

Countless Y2K-related web pages are available on-line. The following are a small sample of the more useful or relevant sources of information.

**Official government millennium bug site:**
*http://www.open.gov.uk/bug2000*

**Microsoft:** *http://www.microsoft.com/technet/topics/year2k/default.htm*

**Lotus:** *http://www.lotus.com/year2000*

**Corel:** *http://www.corel.com/2000.htm*

**Sage:** *http://www.sage.com/year2000*

For a list of links to compliance statements (not comprehensive) go to *http://www.enablis.co.uk/swwp/y2k/investigation/index.html*.
For a Y2K mailing list go to
*http://www.onelist.com/subscribe.cgi/sme2000*.

## Virus and virus hoax resources

Department of Energy Computer Incident Advisory Capability
*http://ciac.llnl.gov/ciac/CIACHoaxes.html*

Computer Virus Myths page
*http://www.kumite.com/myths*

IBM's Hype Alert web site
*http://www.av.ibm.com/BreakingNews/HypeAlert*

Symantec Anti Virus Research Center
*http:///www.symantec.com/avcenter*

McAfee Associates Virus Hoax List
*http://www.mcafee.com/support/hoax.asp*

Dr Solomons Hoax Page
*http://www.drsolomon.com/vircen/vanalyse/va005.html*

Datafellows Hoax Warnings
*http://www.Europe.Datafellows.com/news/hoax.htm*

## E-commerce Internet resources

These are useful jumping-off points for further exploration:

**Visa's web site** *http://www.visa.com*

**Mastercard web site** *http://www.mastercard.com*

**More about the SET system** *http://www.set.com*

**Shop@assistant** *http://www.floyd.co.uk*

**Secure trading** *http://www.securetrading.com*

**WorldPay** *http://www.worldpay.com.*

**Actinic Catalog** *http://www.actinic.co.uk*

# Appendix VI

# Further Reading

## Magazines

Although most computer magazines cover the same territory, there is a huge difference in readability, usefulness and value. Some are aimed at readers who already have a good grasp of the subject, while others cater specifically for the uninitiated. Generally, they are an invaluable source of information and free software. What follows is a brief survey of the magazines available in November 1998.

### Monthly professional PC titles

*Computer Buyer* (Dennis Publishing)
An all-round general-purpose title, although sometimes perhaps too technically advanced for complete beginners. The main emphasis is on hardware and software news, comparisons and reviews. The comprehensive Buyer's Guide is unusually good.

*Computer Shopper* (Dennis Publishing)
There are useful sections devoted to computers other than the PC and Mac but much of the content is highly technical. A regular beginners' featire ('Ivan Iwannado') does its best to demystify a different part of computing each month, but is perhaps still a little technical for absolute beginners. The large question-and-answer section is a reliable source of technical hints and solutions. *Computer Shopper* has a very low cover price.

*PC Direct* (Ziff-Davis UK)
This magazine is aimed particularly at mail-order buyers of PC

333

equipment. Otherwise it is very much a typical PC enthusiast's monthly title.

*PC Magazine* (Ziff-Davis UK)
*PC Magazine* specialises in in-depth comparative reviews. Hardware reviews are presented in simple bar-graph form and software reviews include usability and productivity studies.

*PC Plus* (Future Publishing)
This magazine has the usual opinion, news, reviews and educational sections. Like the others, it is best suited to readers who have a grasp of the basics rather than absolute beginners. It has recently started to include regular free booklets, which can be extremely useful, and there is an informative, if not comprehensive, buyer's guide which lists most of the widely available software and hardware products in any month.

*PC Pro* (Dennis Publications)
This title is aimed at the computer-literate professional user. It includes a comprehensive buyer's guide and a list of industry contact numbers and addresses.

*Personal Computer World* (VNU Publications)
This is one of the longest-running computer titles on the market. Apart from the usual blend of industry news and product reviews, there are also company profiles and interviews, as well as occasional more general computer or information technology-based features.

*What PC?* (VNU Publications)
This is a very basic and straightforward monthly, which is unusually useful to beginners. Each month a new topic, such as printers or portable computers, is covered in some detail. While not as thorough as some of the more professionally oriented monthly magazines, it is a good place for complete novices to find explanations of jargon and other useful information.

*Windows Magazine International* (CPS Publications)
Another US title which, in spite of the name, is very much a typical PC monthly. The advertising is mainly US-based, making it less than useful for UK readers. It is better suited to the intermediate reader who already has a good grasp of PC basics.

## Others

*PC Mart* (Maze Media)
A fortnightly paper containing classified ads. It is a good source of bargains and computer book reviews but not much solid buying advice.

*MacFormat* (Future Publishing)
This monthly magazine covers the full range of Mac software from business to games and creative applications. There is a wide range of reviews, hints and tips, and the content is suitable for beginners.

*MacWorld* (IDG Communications)
A good choice for the professional Apple user, this monthly magazine tends to cover the traditional Apple areas of image-processing, desktop publishing and creative design.

*TotalMac* (Paragon Publishing)
Essentially a CD-ROM of shareware with a monthly magazine attached, *TotalMac* includes plenty of low-cost and trial software, although the accompanying descriptions in the magazine are perhaps a little minimal.

*MacUser* (Dennis Publishing)
*MacUser* is one of the more informative Apple titles. Every fortnight it covers a wide range of software, not just the usual graphical and artistic applications, and there is even a 'getting started' section for beginners, although this tends to be aimed at Apple users with some basic experience rather than complete novices.

*MicroMart* (Trinity Publications Ltd)
Printed on cheap paper, this inexpensive weekly includes some of the best computer bargains around. This is one of the best available sources for cut-price hardware and software bargains. It also has pages of free classified ads.

*Internet* (EMAP Publications)
*Internet* includes features aimed at both beginners and more experienced users, although the style is always approachable and non-technical. The title is distinguished by its comprehensive directory section, which includes an Internet glossary, full details of UK service providers and a huge selection of Internet locations and services.

*InternetWorks* (Future Publishing)
A business-oriented Internet title that concentrates on setting up Internet facilities for a medium-sized company, and other topics of business interest. Rather specific and technical for beginners, but can occasionally be a source of useful tips.

*Internet Business* (Internet Business Magazine Ltd)
Aimed squarely at business users, this title includes a variety of business-related features, many of which cannot be found elsewhere. It is perhaps best thought of as a monthly manger's Internet briefing: strong on business ideas and background, but lacking practical 'nuts and bolts' details.

*Wired* (Condé Nast)
An attempt to produce an Internet lifestyle magazine, this US publication tries to inspire a vision of what the Internet should be about. It has topical and futuristic stories about what may happen next on the net. It does not have any 'how to' articles, and even the web listings are short and stylised. Beginners may find the style of this magazine heavy going, but some of the more forward-looking and topical articles may be thought-provoking.

*Computing* (VNU Publications)
This weekly publishes regular news on all things corporate and computer-related. It includes news about products for large businesses as well as smaller ones, recent industry gossip, and advertising from more professional suppliers and those offering more complex services, such as hard-disk recovery. It is quite technical, very definitely business-oriented, and includes a very large selection of IT jobs.

*PC Week* (VNU Publications)
Very similar in approach and editorial style to its sibling, *Computing* magazine, it does, however, concentrate specifically on PC-related news, products, companies and services.

# Glossary

Words or phrases in italics have a separate entry in the Glossary.

**AMD (Advanced Micro Devices)** Computer manufacturer that competes with *Intel*. AMD chips are usually cheaper, not quite as fast of Intel chips, but much better value for money.

**Apple** Sole successful personal computer company that uses its own proprietary technology instead of conforming to the *Wintel* standard. It is best known for its *Mac* computers.

**BIOS (Basic Input-Output System)** Part of a computer that controls the hardware directly, and also stores essential settings that define how the computer works.

**bit** Smallest unit of information in a computer. It holds information by being either on or off.

**blank** A CD-recordable or CD-rewritable disk with no information on it.

**bridge** *Hardware* used on a *network* to link two different sub-networks together.

**bubblejet** See *inkjet*

**byte** The smallest useful unit of information inside a computer. A byte is made of eight *bits*.

**cache** Very fast memory which is used by a *processor chip* to speed up its calculations.

**Cat5** The highest-grade cable that can be used to create a *network*. It is considered essential by most network designers.

**CD-R (Compact disk – Recordable)** A CD that can have information written on to it only once, but can be played back in any player, including a hi-fi.

**CD-RW (Compact disk – Rewritable)** A CD that can have information written on to it up to about 1,000 times, but information can only be written on to the disk or played using a special drive.

**CD-ROM (Compact disk – Read-Only Memory)** Software or other information supplied as a CD.

**CD-ROM drive** A computer extra used to read the information on a *CD-ROM*.

**CD writer** A computer extra that can write to *CD-R* blanks or, in some cases, *CD-RW* blanks.

**Common Gateway Interface (CGI) script** A way of automatically producing *web pages*, perhaps using information from a *database*.

**chipset** Collection of ancillary chips that surround the main *processor chip* inside a computer. The chipset has an influence on speed and efficiency.

**client** A computer that connects to a *server*, which lets the user see and work with the information that the server holds.

**CMOS (Complimentary Metal Oxide Semiconductor)** Very specialised memory which is used to store the settings for the *BIOS*.

**colour depth** The maximum number of colours with which an item of hardware can work. The most common numbers of colours include 16, 256, 65,536 and 16.7 million (the last being more than the human eye can see).

**command** A single word that makes a computer do something specific when typed in. See also *Command line*.

**command line** An antiquated system under which computers are controlled by commands that are typed in from a keyboard. The system is now superseded by *GUI*.

**contact manager (CM)** An electronic address and appointments book.

**Cyrix** Computer company that competes with *Intel* in the manufacture of *processor chips*. So far it has not been as successful as Intel's other key rival, *AMD*.

**database** An intelligent filing cabinet within a computer that can organise almost any kind of information, create summaries of what it contains to order, and pick out information according to different criteria.

**desktop** A computer that sits on a desk and is not portable in the same way as *laptops* and *palmtops*.

**Dial-up** A temporary connection to the *Internet*, usually made over a telephone line.

**digital** Information in the form of numbers, which is how information is stored in computers.

**domain** On the *Internet*, the name given to the unique address of an organisation. On a smaller *network*, it is the name given to a sub-section of the network.

**drive** Any computer component that can exchange information with the computer's main memory.

**driver** A small piece of software, supplied with many computer extras, which tells the computer how the extra works so that the computer can use it.

# Glossary

**DVD (Digital Versatile Disk)** A 'next-generation' CD that can store between 5Gb and 17Gb of information, depending on the type.

**DVD-RAM** A *DVD* disk that can have up to 5Gb of information stored on it by a computer. This transfer of information is possible only with a DVD-RAM drive.

**E-commerce** Trading over the *Internet* by way of *email* and the *World Wide Web*.

**E/IDE (Enhanced IDE)** An improved and faster version of the original *IDE* system. *UltraDMA* now supersedes it.

**email (electronic mail)** messages that can be sent directly from one computer to another.

**fax modem** A *modem* that can also send and receive faxes. All modern modems have this facility.

**Firewire** A very high-speed link (external connector) offered on some recent computers. It can be used to link extras such as a video camera.

**floppy disk** A small, removable plastic wafer with a sliding metal cover that can hold up to 1.44 *megabytes* of information.

**frames** A special effect used on *web pages*, which divides them up into independent panes of information.

**G3** The computer *processor chip* used in Apple *Macs*. It is faster and more efficient than a *Pentium*.

**gigabyte (Gb or 'gig')** A unit of measure for the capacity for information of a *hard disk*. It is approximately a billion *bytes* (1,073,741,824 bytes exactly).

**graphics card** The part of the computer that converts information from the *processor chip* into electronic signals that make an image appear on a *monitor*.

**groupware** Software used to help people work together on collaborative projects.

**GUI (Graphical User Interface)** A system that lets users control a computer by selecting pictures and selecting tasks from a *menu*.

**hard disk** The main filing system in a computer. It is used to store software, and to keep information safe when the power is turned off.

**hardware** The physical parts of a computer that you can touch.

**hits** Term used to describe the number of visitors to a *web site*.

**HTML (Hypertext Markup Language)** The set of special words and letters used to create pages for the *World Wide Web*.

**hub** A piece of *hardware* used on a *network* to link three or more computers together.

**IBM (International Business Machines)** Formerly the largest computer

339

company in the world, and the developers of the original *PC*. It competes with *Microsoft* and *Intel*.

**IBM-compatible** Another term used to describe a *PC*.

**IDE (Integrated Drive Electronics)** A very popular system used to connect *hard disks* to the rest of the computer. See also *SCSI*.

**image editor** A digital darkroom in the form of software that can work with photos and other images to correct exposure mistakes and create special effects.

**inkjet** A kind of *printer* that creates images by squirting tiny bubbles of ink on to a sheet of paper.

**infra-red link (IrDA)** A wire-less link that uses infra-red light (as used in TV remote controls) to exchange information. It is often included with *laptops* and *palmtops*.

**Intel** Makers of the most popular *processor chips*, including the *Pentium* range.

**Internet** The world's largest public-access computer network.

**intranet** Internal computer network used within an organisation. It appears as a small and private version of the Internet.

**ISDN (Integrated Services Digital Network)** A 'next-generation' telephone service that offers improved facilities for working with computer-friendly digital information.

**Java** A system used on the *World Wide Web* to create *web sites* with special effects.

**Jaz drive** A popular, if perhaps slightly expensive, system used for backups and other work involving large amounts of information that has be stored for safety reasons or swapped in and out of a computer.

**kilobyte (Kb or 'k')** A measure of the size of *cache* memory, approximately 1,000 *bytes* (1,024 bytes exactly), in a computer.

**LAN (Local Area Network)** A *network* that connects computers that are physically close together – in a single building or office.

**laptop** A portable computer with most of the facilities of a *desktop* model but in a much smaller box (usually around the size of a medium telephone directory).

**laser** Type of *printer* that draws an image on paper with light, and then 'fixes' it using photocopier-like technology

**LCD (Liquid-Crystal Display)** Type of thin screen which consumes little power in the production of light. It is often used in *laptops*.

**leased line** An expensive but permanent connection to the *Internet*.

**link** A word, phrase, address or image that appears on a *web page*, underlined or in a different colour, that links to a different but related web page, an email address or a *newsgroup*.

# Glossary

**LINUX** A free *operating system* based on *UNIX*, which is designed and maintained by enthusiasts and is rapidly growing in popularity.

**LS120** A variant on the *floppy-disk* drive. It can hold up to 120Mb of information.

**Mac (short for Macintosh)** A popular family of computers produced by *Apple*. They are not as widely available as IBM *PCs*.

**mail merge** A facility offered by most *word processors* that can prepare a general form letter and then fill in names, addresses and other distinguishing details from a list of contacts to produce personalised letters. The facility is much used for mailshots.

**megabyte ('Mb' or 'meg')** A unit of measure used to describe the size of a computer's main memory and *cache* memory. Each unit is approximately one million *bytes* (1,048,576 bytes exactly).

**menu** A list of tasks (that a computer can do) from which a user can select.

**Microsoft** The largest software company in the world and the creator of a wide range of popular small-business products including *Windows* and *Microsoft Office*.

**Microsoft Office** A popular *office suite* sold by Microsoft, and often supplied with new computers.

**millennium bug** A problem with many computer systems, which may stop working properly after 1 January 2000, because of their inability to recognise the '00" in the year date.

**modem** A computer hardware extra that connects the computer to the *Internet* (or to another computer) over the telephone line. See also *fax modem* and *voice modem*.

**monitor** Term used to describe the computer screen.

**motherboard** The large circuit board that holds the main *processor chip*, and a selection of other chips. Everything inside a computer is connected to the motherboard.

**mouse** A small rolling plastic object that fits snugly under the palm of the hand and can be moved in two dimensions to control a pointer (cursor) on a screen. It is an essential part of any *GUI*.

**MS-DOS (Microsoft Disk Operating System)** A *command line* operating system popular up until about 1995. Now obsolete, it is still sold and used in cases where a *GUI* would be unneccessary.

**Netware** A popular *operating system* used to create *networks* built around a *server*.

**network** Two or more computers connected together so that they can share facilities and information electronically.

341

**newsgroups** Public discussion areas on the *Internet*, noted for their huge range of subjects and colourful, aggressive debates.

**OCR (Optical Character Recognition)** A facility used with a *scanner* to read printed text and to convert it into text on screen, which can then be edited in a *word processor*.

**OSR2** A *version* of Windows 95, produced in 1997, which includes subtle enhancements over the original. It was included in the software of new machines, but was never sold directly to the public.

**ODBC (Open Database Connectivity)** A system for sharing database information with other *software* tools, such as *word processors* and *spreadsheets*.

**office suite** A collection of *software* intended to be useful for business. It usually includes a *word processor*, *spreadsheet*, *contact manager*, *email*, and perhaps *presentation software* and a *database*.

**operating system** The *software* that defines how information appears on the screen, and what steps users have to take to get the results they want.

**palmtop** A computer small enough to fit into a jacket pocket or a handbag.

**parallel port** The socket at the back of a computer which is most often used to connect a *printer*.

**PC (Personal Computer)** Also known as the IBM-compatible computer, it is the most widely used type of computer in the world (more common than the *Mac*). It is based on a specification originally created by IBM in the mid-1980s and is usually built using cheap off-the-shelf parts from the Far East.

**Pentium** The *processor chip* family used in most of today's computers.

**POST (Power On Self Test)** The process which a PC undergoes when the power is turned on.

**presentation software** Software that produces charts and viewgraph (overhead projector) slides. Popular in large companies, it is of less use to most small businesses.

**printer** An essential *hardware* extra that produces printed letters and other documents on paper.

**processor chip** The chip inside a computer that does the most important work, making sense of what a user types, calculating results, and controlling what happens on the screen. The speed and power of a processor chip largely determine the capabilities of the machine as a whole.

**PS/2** One or two connectors at the back of a computer which are used to connect a keyboard or a mouse.

**RAM (Random Access Memory)** The working storage inside a com-

# Glossary

puter. All the information stored in the RAM is lost when the power is turned off.

**resolution** Term used to indicate the quality of image in printers and on screens.

**router** A piece of *hardware* used on a *network* to keep track of where all the computers on the network are so that it can send information to them efficiently.

**scanner** An optional *hardware* extra that plugs into a computer and allows it to copy photographs and other images from paper on to the screen.

**SCSI (Small Computer Systems Interface)** A system used to connect *hard disks* and other extras to a computer. It is slightly better but rather more expensive than *IDE*.

**serial port** The socket (or sockets as there are usually two) on the back of a computer that is used to connect a *modem* and certain other extras.

**server** A computer that 'serves up' information on demand, for example *database* records or *web pages*. It is often a large, powerful computer used in *networks*.

**software** The non-physical part of a computer which turns the hardware into a useful tool. It comes in the form of a very long set of simple instructions used to perform a useful task.

**spell checker** A facility, offered in many *word processors*, that checks spelling throughout a document, either as the user types or later.

**spreadsheet** A *software* tool for various financial and scientific calculations which can work with formulae as well as numbers.

**SQL (Structured Query Language)** A popular system for extracting useful information from a *database*.

**TCP/IP (Transmission Control Protocol/Internet Protocol)** The language used to exchange information by computers on the *Internet*.

**UltraDMA** The most recent and fastest standard for *IDE* hard-disk drives (which connect *hard disks* to the rest of the computer).

**UNIX** An *operating system* which predates *Windows*, but is popular for serious scientific and business use.

**URL (Uniform Resource Locator)** The *World Wide Web* equivalent of a postal address, used to define a unique *web page*.

**USB (Universal Serial Bus)** Used to connect hardware extras such as printers, monitors, etc. It is much faster than a *serial port*.

**utility** A small piece of software that performs a modest but useful function.

**version** The model number of a piece of *software*. Originally it comprised two numbers, which specified major changes and minor revisions (for example, '6.22' meant the sixth major update, the second minor revision,

343

and the second sub-revision). Current version names and numbers often include references to the millennium.

**virus** A destructive piece of *software* that can hide itself inside other software. The virus can 'infect' a computer, causing it to pass on copies of the virus, perhaps lose all its information, or even stop working completely.

**voice modem** A *modem* that can work as an answering machine.

**VPN (Virtual Private Network)** A company *network* that uses the *Internet* to exchange information between offices, but hides the connection behind a secret code so that outsiders cannot hack into it.

**WAN (Wide Area Network)** A *network* containing computers that are physically separated by large distances.

**web page** A single page of text, images, and perhaps other information on the *World Wide Web*.

**web site** A collection of many *web pages*, created by a single author or organisation, on the *World Wide Web*.

**Windows 2000** The latest version of *Windows NT*.

**Windows 3.1** The first successful version of Windows. It lacks certain advanced features and is now obsolete, although it is still widely used in some businesses.

**Windows 95 (Win95)** The updated version of *Windows 3.1*, released in 1995. More advanced than its predecessor, it was radically different both internally and externally.

**Windows 98 (Win98)** An updated and slightly controversial version of Windows 95, with cosmetic improvements and slightly better reliability.

**Windows NT** The business version of Windows. Designed to be more reliable, efficient and secure internally, it has the same outward appearance as Windows 95 and Windows 98.

**Wintel** Term used to describe computers that are built with *Intel* chips and use the Windows *operating system*.

**word processor** *Software* that provides an electronic typewriter facility with a computer. Words appear on the screen, where they can be changed before being printed out. Word processors usually include extras such as *spell checkers* and *mail merge*.

**World Wide Web** One of the facilities available on the *Internet*. It comprises text, pictures and other information presented on pages, with *links* that lead to other pages of related information.

**XML (eXtensible Markup Language)** An addition to *HTML* that makes it possible to display almost any type of information on a web page.

**Zip drive** A smaller version of the *Jaz drive*, suitable for keeping safety copies of up to 100 *megabytes* of information.

# Index

accounts packages 12–13, 21–2, 63–4
    balance sheet 20, 64
    bank statement reconciliation 64
    credit control 64, 66–7
    customer details 63–4
    fixed assets listing 66
    invoicing facility 64, 66
    networked accounts packages 48
    nominal ledger 64
    order processing 66
    payroll facilities 13, 22, 65–6, 92
    profit-and-loss account 64
    reports 64, 67
    supplier details 64
    'undo facilities' 67
    VAT report 64
    versus databases 86–7
Actinic Catalog 233, 239
address books and diaries 13, 14, 25–6, 25
    *see also* contact managers (CMs); personal information managers (PIMs)
address finders 83–4
addresses 319–26
    domain country codes 324–6
    domain name registration 203–5, 207
    email 203–5, 215, 220–1, 319–20
    international codes 323
    names and trademarks 205–6
    newsgroups 322–3
    UK-specific codes 323
    US codes 323
    web addresses 320–2
Adobe 108
    Acrobat 109, 121
    Illustrator 101
    Photoshop 104, 293
advertising
    banner ads 235, 236
    email mailshots 236–7
    on-line advertising 236
    Link Exchange 235
    partnership schemes 236
    press releases 234
    on the web 234–7
    your web site 233–4
    *see also* promotion
America Online (AOL) 28, 183, 184, 190, 199, 206, 216
anatomy of a computer 258–9, 260–1
Apple 139, 140, 314–15
ARCnet 59
Asynchronous Transfer Mode (ATM) 59

backup systems 30, 124, 166–70
    backup software 168
    CD-based systems 167
    DVD-RAM system 167
    full backups 168–9
    incremental backups 169
    removable systems 168
    safeguarding backups 170
    schedules 169–70
    tapes 167
    working with 168–9
balance sheets 20, 64
Barclay's Endorse card 73–4
base unit 259
BeOS 315
beta testing 130–1
boilerplate contracts 15–16, 83
book-keeping 20–4
    accounts packages *see* accounts packages
    on-line banking 12–13, 23–4, 70
    personal finance managers 20–1
    spreadsheets *see* spreadsheets
    tax calculators 24
books, electronic 219
bugs 132
bulletin boards, electronic 49
business plans 74, 83
buying a computer system 112–35
    advice from friends 31
    buying decisions 11–12
    buying extras 33
    consultants 8, 126–32, 257
    consumer issues 132–5
    DIY buying 114
    finance options 125–6
    hard-disk transplants 119
    hardware *see* hardware, buying
    installation costs 124–5
    planning and managing the project 112–14
    product information 114–16
    research 32–3
    running costs 124
    service contracts 118–19
    software *see* software, buying
    training and technical support 119–24
    very small businesses 31–9
    warranties 116–17
    working life 136

cabling systems 59–60
    10Base-T network 59
    10Base-TX 59
    Coax 59–60
    fibre-optic cables 60

345

RJ45 cables 59
ThickNet 60
ThinNet 60
unshielded twisted pair (UTP) 59
wire-less systems 60
cache memory 266
Canon Starwriter 500 40
CD-related drives 293–5
   CD-rewritable drives (CD-RW) 294–5
   CD-ROM drives 258, 259, 260–1, 276, 293
   CD writers 293–4
CD-ROMs 107, 108, 109, 260–1
cheque and invoice printing 13, 20, 21, 281
clip art 99, 111
clip music 106
clock circuit 262
commercial information, pre-packaged 82–3
Compaq 141–2
compression tools 154–5
CompuServe 28, 190, 196, 217
computer-aided design 257
computer magazines 8, 32, 115, 333–6
Computer Services and Software Organisation (CSSA) 127
consultants 8, 126–32, 257
   consultancy skills 126
   contracts 131–2
   fees 126
   finding and choosing 127–8
   formal qualifications 128–9
   web consultancy 226–7
   working with 129–31
contact managers (CMs) 25, 78, 81–2
   data-integration facilities 82
   features 81–2
   key products 43–4
   network facilities 81
Corel Draw 101, 268
cover disks 34, 37
crash-recovery systems 154
credit-card equipment 248
credit-card payments 221, 224, 237–8
crippleware 35
HM Customs and Excise 13, 63, 158

Data Protection Act 91–3
databases 14, 26, 86–90, 257
   database engine 88
   flatfile databases 87–8
   forms 88
   information summaries 89
   key products 44
   programming facilities 89
   queries 86, 89
   relational databases 88
   reports 86, 89
   scalability 88
   set-up process 86–7
   Structured Query Language (SQL) 89
   versus accounts packages 86–7
   Y2K problem 247–8
desktop computers 137
   price ranges 137, 145
desktop publishing (DTP) 15, 20, 96–104
   images 99–104
   key products 43, 96
   Postscript support 97, 284

sample-page layouts 15
and printers 96–7
Digital Audio Tape (DAT) 289–90
digital cameras 103, 295–6
digital money systems 237
Digital Versatile Disk (DVD) 107, 296–7
disk capacity 33, 267–8
disk-copying tools 155
Disk Defragmenter 165–6
disk drives
   connection systems 269–70, 276
   DVD-RAM drives 296–7
   floppy-disk drives 258, 259, 275–6
   hard-disk drives 33, 166, 258, 288
   Integrated Drive Electronics (IDE) 269, 276, 293, 302
   LS120 drives 275–6
   Redundant Array of Inexpensive Devices (RAID) 269–70
   Small Computer Systems Interface (SCSI) 269, 276, 291–2, 293, 302–3
   speed 276
   *see also* CD-related drives
disk-management tools 155
document creation *see* word processing
document and data filing 49
document management 16
document sharing 48–9
DriveCopy 166

e-commerce 7, 17, 214–39
   connecting to the Internet 215
   delivery systems 225
   email addresses 203–5, 215, 220–1, 319–20
   frequently asked questions (FAQ) document 221
   getting on-line 220–6
   getting noticed 215, 226–37
   information, selling 217–19
   necessary skills 214–15
   payment systems 215, 221, 224, 225, 237–9
   pitfalls 225
   preparation 215–20, 225
   successful on-line products 216–20
   system creation 222–3
   unsuitable products and services 219–20
   web sites 221–5
   Y2K problem 249
electronic mail *see* email
electronic meetings 16, 50–1
Electronic Point-of-Sale (EPOS) systems 14
electronic promotions 107–11
   audio and video 110–11
   hypertext markup language (HTML) 107, 108, 231, 232, 235
   multimedia tools 109
   portable document format (PDF) 108–9
electronic publishing 19
electronic texts and summaries 83
email 10, 14, 26, 28, 48, 177–83, 195
   addresses 203–5, 215, 220–1, 319–20
   attachments 178–9
   autoresponders 182–3, 221
   business uses 178
   digital signatures 181
   drawbacks 178–9
   encryption 180–1

# Index

forgeries 180
forwarding service 206–7
interception 179
key escrow system 181
mail server software 200
mailshots 236–7
mailing lists 181–2
message deletion 179
non-text information 178–9
PGP (Pretty Good Privacy) 180–1, 221
POP3 (Post Office Protocol) system 196, 207–8
prompt response to 177
scheduling 202
security 179–81
SMTP (Simple Mail Transfer Protocol) 196
software 44
two-key system 180
viruses 165
emergency data recovery 170
enterprise systems 16–17
Ethernet 58, 59
Euros 90
   Euro-ready software 72–3
expansion slots 258, 305
extenders 106–7
ezines 218

family multimedia software 34
Fast Ethernet 58, 59
fax modems 29, 277
   modem-sharing software 46
faxes 9–10, 29–30, 297
Fibre Distributed Data Interface (FDDI) 58–9
finance options 125–6
   leasing options 125–6
   loans and credit cards 125
   outright purchase 125
financial software
   accounts packages *see* accounts packages
   compatibility with other software 72
   direct-banking access 70
   Euro-ready software 72–3
   foreign-currency support 70, 73
   multiple company support 71
   spreadsheets *see* spreadsheets
   stock management 67–8
   upgradeability 71
   Y2K issues 72
floppy-disk drives 258, 259, 275–6
floppy disks 164, 275
floppy locks 164
fonts 19
foreign-currency support 70, 73
form letters 16, 19
free software 34–5
   crippleware 35
   shareware 34–5
   trial versions 35

games 11–12, 33, 34, 257
Geocities 201, 234
Gigabit ethernet 59
Gigabytes (Gbs) 265, 268
global positioning system (GPS) receiver 85
graphics cards 258, 274–5, 303–4
graphics tablets 100, 300–1

groupware 16, 48–51
   bulletin boards 49
   centralised network management 51
   conference and discussion groups 49–50
   document and data filing 49
   document sharing 48–9
   electronic meetings 50–1
   email 48
   meeting scheduling 50
   products 52–3
   project scheduling 50
   researching products 53–5
   workflow management 51

hacking attacks 173, 174, 209, 210, 238
hard-disk drives 258, 260
   adding 33, 302–3
   Jaz drives 288
   second drive 166
   transplants 119
   Zip drives 288
hardware 10
   BIOS upgrade 250
   fixes 250
   motherboard replacement 250
   networks 57–8
   optional extras 280–305
   specifications 257–79
   Y2K problem 243–5, 249–50
hardware, buying 32–3, 136–47
   advanced hardware 141–2
   customising a computer 147
   desktop computers 137, 145
   laptops 40–1, 82, 142–5
   luggables 142
   Macs 139–41, 243
   makes and models 138–42
   network servers 137–8, 145–6
   palmtops 41, 44, 82, 142
   PCs 138–9, 141, 163, 166, 243, 268
   PCs versus Macs 140
   portable computers 142–5
   portables 142
   price ranges 32, 145–6
   workstations 138
hardware failure 30, 133–4, 161–3
   fault-tolerant hardware 137, 163
   power problems and solutions 161–2
Hewlett Packard 141–2
'home productivity' software 34
home workers *see* very small businesses
hypertext markup language (HTML) 107, 108, 227–8, 235
   Dynamic HTML 231, 232

IBM 141–2
illegal activities 172–3
iMac 140, 275
image libraries 103
images, working with 14–15, 99–104, 257
   3D-design 101–2
   art packages 100
   bitmap editing 101
   clip art 99
   digital cameras 295–6
   DIY design 100–1
   drawing packages 101

347

graphics tablets 100, 300–1
illustration packages 101
illustrations and artwork 99–100
image libraries 103
image licensing 104
photographs 102–4
photomontage 104
scanners 102, 290–3
vector drawing 101
information
  losing 158
  management 14, 155
  removeable storage 287–90
  searching facilities 83–4
  security 166–70
information sharing 9–10, 45–62
  *see also* networks
Inland Revenue 63, 158
installation costs 124–5
insurance 160–1, 255–6
Integrated Services Digital Network (ISDN) 194, 200, 202, 212, 298–9
  facilities 97
  Terminal Adaptors (TAs) 298
Intel 262
Internet 7, 10, 115–16, 175–213
  addresses 319–26
  business use 26–9, 175–213
  email *see* email
  File Transfer Protocol (FTP) 193–4, 217, 229
  free software or shareware from 37
  getting information from 185–94
  live chat 183–4
  newsgroups 29, 191–3, 195
  newsreaders 28–9
  security 209–10
  software 28–9, 44
  spam 172, 174, 191, 195, 200–1, 236–7
  technical support, source of 124
  telephony and video 184–5
  user numbers 175
  World Wide Web *see* World Wide Web
  Y2K problem 248–9
  *see also* e-commerce
Internet connections 27–8, 194–213, 210–13
  Asymetric Digital Subscriber Link (ASDL) 213
  BT Click 196–7
  cable systems 213
  combined services 196
  connection reliability 198
  costs 28, 196, 197, 201–2
  dial-up connection 194, 201–2, 226
  domestic connections 194–202
  free services 197–8
  hosted option 194
  Internet servers 200
  Internet Service Providers (ISPs) 27, 28, 29, 195–6, 197, 199, 201, 206
  ISDN dial-back 212
  ISDN routers 200
  leased lines 210–11, 213
  on-line services 27–8, 190–1, 194–5, 196, 197, 199, 206, 217
  modem-sharing software 199–200
  network connections 199–201
  permanent connection 203, 206
  satellite links 211–12

Internet Service Providers (ISPs) 27, 28, 29, 195–6, 197, 199, 201, 206, 236
  business ISPs 210, 212
Intranets 51–6

Java 231, 232, 316–17
Javascript 231, 232
Just In Time (JIT) ordering options 71–2

keyboards 258, 261, 279
  Cherry keyboards 73, 279
  natural keyboards 279
kilobytes 268

LANTastic 316
laptops 40–1, 82, 142–5
  battery life 142–3
  dimensions and weight 144
  display quality and size 143
  Internet connections 40–1
  memory 144
  modems 144
  options and extras 144–5
  price ranges 40, 146
  processor chips and speed 144
  Thin Film Transistor (TFT) displays 40, 272
  trackpad and trackpoint systems 143
  voltage compatibility 143
leasing options 125–6
legal documents, pre-written 15–16, 83
Link Exchange 235
LINUX 313–14
live chat (Internet) 183–4
  AOL chat 183
  business applications 184
  chat rooms 183
  ICQ 183
  Internet Relay Chat (IRC) 183
  NetMeeting 183
  web-based chat 183–4
live promotion 104–7
  clip music 106
  computers at exhibitions 106–7
  Liquid Crystal Displays (LCDs) 105
  overhead projectors 105
  presentations 104–6
  S-Video 105
Lotus
  Domino Intranet Starter Pack 53
  Instant!TEAMROOM 53
  Notes 53
loudspeakers 278–9
luggables 142

machinery, buildings and plant: non-compliance 251–3
MacOS 314–15, 318
Macs 139–41, 243
mail merge facilities 15, 19
Majordomo 182
meeting scheduling 50
Megabytes (Mbs) 265, 268
memory 137–8, 258
  adding 301–2
  cache memory 266
  Extended Data Output (EDO) RAM 266

# Index

laptops 144
Random Access Memory (RAM) 260, 265–6
  requirements 265–6
  Synchronous Dynamic RAM (SDRAM) 266
mice 259, 261, 279, 300
Microsoft
  Access 44, 247
  BackOffice 52, 54, 200
  certifcation system 122
  Excel 43, 75
  Home Essentials 36
  NetMeeting 183
  Office 36, 43, 105, 268
  Outlook 44, 79
  SQL Server 89
  Visual Basic 90
  WebTV 216
  Windows 3.1 309
  Windows 95 61, 155, 166, 200, 310, 317
  Windows 98 54, 61, 73, 155, 166, 202, 268, 310–11, 317
  Windows 2000 200, 243, 311–12
  Windows NT (New Technology) Client 312
  Windows NT (New Technology) Server 61, 312, 317–18
  Word 36, 38, 43
MIDI (Musical Instrument Digital Interface) 278, 304
millennium bug *see* Year 2000 (Y2K) problem
modems 23, 27, 29, 261, 276–8
  cellular modems 144
  fax modems 29, 46, 277
  internal and external modems 278
  laptops 144
  modem-sharing software 199–200
  network modems 47
  speeds 277
  switches 47
  voice modems 30, 277
money management 16, 43, 63–77
  accounts packages *see* accounts packages
  electronic finance 73–4
  Just In Time (JIT) ordering options 71–2
  on-line banking 12–13, 23–4, 70
  sales management 68–9
  software 12–13
  time management 69–70
  *see also* financial software
monitors 259, 260, 270
  Cathode Ray Tube (CRT) monitors 270, 271, 272, 273
  dot pitch 271
  Liquid Crystal Display (LCD) monitors 271–2, 273
  monitor splitters 106
  refresh rate 273
  resolution 272, 274
  on-screen displays (OSDs) 273
  Trinitron and FST (Flat Square Tube) monitors 271
motherboards 258, 260, 267
  dual processors 267
  replacement 250
MS-DOS 308–9
multi-function peripherals 297–8
music clips 111
music, on-line 219

Netscape 49–50
network adapters 57
network cards 57, 58, 145
network operating systems 315–17
  Java 316–17
  LANTastic 316
  network features in standard operating systems 317–18
  Novell IntraNetware 61, 62, 316
network protocol 61–2
  IPX/SPX 62
  NetBEUI 62
  TCP/IP 62
network software 61–2
  network applications 46, 61
  network drivers 62
  network operating system (NOS) 61
  network protocol 61–2
  per user/per seat licensing 54
networks 42–3, 45–62
  bridges 58
  cabling systems 59–60
  centralised network management 51
  client-server networks 56–7
  hardware 57–8
  installation costs 125
  Internet, connecting to 199–201
  Local Area Networks (LANs) 56–7
  network modems 47
  network servers 57, 137–8, 145–6
  peer-to-peer networks 56
  pros and cons 45–6
  'public' areas 48
  remote-access options 46
  routers 58
  security 172–4
  sharing fax modems 46
  sharing printers 46, 47
  staff time-wasting activities 171–2
  systems 58–9
  Virtual Private Network (VPN) 56
  Wide Area Networks (WANs) 56, 57, 58
  Y2K problem 248
  *see also* groupware; Intranets
newsgroups 191–3
  addresses 322–3
  FAQ (Frequently Asked Questions) document 193
notebook computers *see* laptops
Novell
  certifcation system 122
  Netware 61, 62

office suites 34
  integration 90
  key products 43
on-line banking 12–13, 23–4, 70
on-line video 185
operating systems 306–18
  BeOS 315
  clustering 307
  command-line system 306
  Graphic User Interface (GUI) 307
  LINUX 313–14
  MacOS 314–15, 318
  MS-DOS 308–9
  multi-processing 307

349

multi-tasking systems 307
network features 317–18
network operating systems 315–17
Unix 312–13
Windows 3.1 309
Windows 95 155, 166, 200, 310, 317
Windows 98 54, 73, 155, 166, 202, 268, 310–11, 317
Windows 2000 200, 243, 311–12

palmtops 41, 82, 142
  key products 44
passwords 80, 107, 173–4
payment systems 237–9
  automated payments 239
  credit-card payments 221, 224, 237–8
  Open Trading Protocol (OTP) 239
  Secure Electronic Transactions (SET) 239
  secure server system 238–9
payment tracking software 13, 64
payroll calculations 13, 22, 65–6, 92
PCs 138–9, 141, 163, 166, 243, 268
peripherals 261
personal data, abuse of 173–4
personal finance managers 20–1
personal information managers (PIMs) 25, 78–80
  data integration facilities 82
  features 78–80
  key products 43–4
  network facilities 80
Personal Navigator 84–5
platform independence 108
pointing devices 299–300
  mice 300
  trackballs 300
  trackpads and trackpoints 143
portable document format (PDF) 108–9
portables 142
ports 304–5
  Firewire IEEE1394 ports 304
  MIDI and joystick ports 304–5
  parallel ports 304
  PS/2 ports 304
  serial ports 304
  Universal Serial Bus (USB) ports 304
post code summaries 82
Post Office Address File (PAF) software 83–4
power problems and solutions 161–2
presentations 104–6
print promotions 94–104
  desktop publishing 96–104
  using word processors 94–6
printers 259, 261, 281–7, 297–8
  CMYK printing 97
  colour printing 97, 282, 285
  compatibility with operating systems 287
  dot-matrix printers 281–2
  dots per inch (dpi) 282, 283
  Graphical Display Interface (GDI) models 284
  ink-jet and bubble-jet printers 282–3
  label printers 285
  laser printers 95, 283–5
  line printers 285–6
  memory requirements 284, 286–7
  microdry printers 285
  network connections 46, 47, 284, 287
  paper compatibility 286
  poster printers 286
  Printer Control Language (PCL) 284, 287
  printer supplies 124
  printer switches 47
  running costs 124, 282, 283, 286
processor chips 258, 260, 261–5
  AMD chips 262, 263
  chip speeds 264–5
  chipset 267
  Cyrix chips 262, 263
  embedded chips 240
  Intel chips 262–3
  laptops 144
  multi-chip computer systems 138
  older chips 264
  overdrive chips 303
  Pentium chips 262–3, 264, 303
  upgrading 303
  Winchips 264
product information 114–16
  computer magazines 8, 32, 115, 333–6
  high-street and trading-estate stores 115
  Internet 115–16
  newspaper advertising 115
project-management software 16
project scheduling 50
promotion 20, 94–111
  electronic promotions 94, 107–11
  live promotions 94, 104–7
  print promotions 94–104
  *see also* advertising
property marking 160
publicity *see* promotion

Quark XPress 96

Random Access Memory (RAM) 260, 265–6
recovery disks 134
reliability 12, 32, 308, 310
removeable storage 287–90
route planners and maps 15, 84–5

safeguarding your system 158–74
  computer theft 159–60
  emergency data recovery 170
  hardware failure, avoiding 161–3
  information security 166–70
  insurance 160–1
  internal security 171, 172–4
  registry problems 166
  second hard-disk drives 166
  software failure, avoiding 163–6
  staff time-wasting activities 171–2
Sage Accounting 48, 65
sales analysis 14, 21
sales management 68–9
scandisk 165
scanners 102, 290–3, 297
  colour resolution 292
  image quality 292
  image resolution 292
  optical character recognition (OCR) 290–1, 298
  size and optional extras 292
  software 293
  speed 291–2
  TWAIN compatibility 293

# Index

screens *see* monitors
serial switch boxes 47
service contracts 118–19
shareware 34–5, 37
shovelware 34
Silicon Graphics Inc (SGI) 141
software 10–11, 12
   advanced products 13–14
   backup software 168
   essential software products 12–13
   fixes 250
   Internet 28–9
   larger systems 16–17
   migration 251
   network software 61–2
   non-compliance 250–1
   patches 250–1
   problems 30–1
   product information 114–16
   sales on the Internet 216
   upgrades 251
   utilities 14–16
   Y2K problem 245–7, 250–1
software, buying 33–9, 148–57
   bespoke software 151–2, 153–4
   competitive upgrade 36
   demonstration or trial versions 37
   'free' software 33–4
   from the Internet 37
   legalities 153–4
   license to use 153
   magazine offers 34–5
   magazine reviews 32, 37
   outright purchase 35–7
   student offers 36–7
   trade-specific packages 148–51
   utilities 154–5
software failure 133, 143–4, 153, 163–6
   viruses 34, 163–5, 173
software maintenance 165–6
software manuals 121
sole traders *see* very small businesses
soundcards 261, 278
   wavetable cards 278
spam 172, 174, 191, 195, 200–1, 236–7
   spam-filtering software 174
specifications 11, 257–79
speed 261–5
   benchmarks 267
spreadsheets 14, 22–3, 74–6, 257
   3D spreadsheets 75
   calculations, handling 75
   graphs and tables 75
   key products 43
   pivot tables 75–6
   uses 74–5
   Y2K problem 247–8
stationery
   computer-generated letterheads 95
   pre-printed or customisable 71, 95
   Y2K problem 248
stock control systems 14, 22, 67–8
Structured Query Language (SQL) 89
Sun computers 141
surge suppressors 162
switches (KVM switches) 106
systems-analysis tools 154

tape drives and tapes 288–90
tax calculators 24
technical support 12, 122–4, 132
   free-support period 122–3
   on the Internet 124
   manuals and on-line help 122
   software support 122–3
   support contracts 123
   support lines 122–3
telephone
   telephone-number collections 84
   *see also* Integrated Services Digital Network
teleworking 10
terminals 57
theft, computer 159–60
Token Ring 58
training 119–22
   books 120–1
   college courses and classes 120
   commercial training 121–2
   multimedia training 121
   software manuals 121
   sources of 119, 120–2
   training goals 119–20
translation software 155
triage 252–3
tune-up tools 154

uninstallers and clean-up tools 155
Uninterruptible Power Supply (UPS) 162
UNIX 312–13
upgrades
   competitive upgrade 36
   hardware 33, 126
   software 36, 71, 251
   upgrade prices 280
Usenet 191
utilities 14–16, 34, 154–5
   backups 30, 124, 166–70
   compression tools 154–5
   crash-recovery systems 154
   disk-copying tools 155
   disk-management tools 155
   information-management tools 155
   systems-analysis tools 154
   translation software 155
   tune-up tools 154
   uninstallers and clean-up tools 155
   virus checkers 164
   voice recognition 15, 155, 156

VAT 21, 72–3
   software 13, 64
   tax calculators 24
very small businesses 18–44
   address books and diaries 25–6
   book-keeping 20–4
   buying a computer 31–9
   deciding if you need a computer 42
   Internet usage 26–9
   laptops 40–1
   messages and faxes 29–30
   palmtops 41
   word processing 18–20, 39–40
video clips 26, 109, 111
video conferencing 51
video editing 11

351

video recorders: Y2K problem 248, 253
viruses 34, 163–5, 173
　boot viruses 163
　CIH 163–4
　email viruses 165
　macro viruses 163
　Trojan horses 164–5
　virus checkers 164
　virus hoaxes 165
voice conferencing 51
voice recognition 15, 155, 156

warranties 116–17
　collect-and-return warranty 117
　return-to-base warranty 116–17
　on-site warranty 117
　voiding 118
web pages 107, 187–8, 200, 201
　autoresponders 209
　Common Gateway Interface (CGI) scripts 208
　connection speed 208
　forwarding service 201, 207
　free pages 201
　FrontPage extensions 208–9
　mailing lists 209
　Secure Sockets Layer (SSL) 209, 239
　Uniform Resource Locator (URL) 187–8
　web-caching 200, 202
　web hosting 207–10, 226, 232, 233, 239
web site design 107–8, 221–2, 226–33
　animations 231, 232
　backup 210
　basics 229–30
　Common Gateway Interface (CGI) scripts 232–3
　contact details 229
　copying pages to the Internet 229
　DIY design 226, 227–33
　features to avoid 230
　'hit counter' 230, 232
　Hypertext Markup Language (HTML) 107, 108, 227–8, 235
　image and branding 230
　intelligent applications 231
　key selling point 230
　'last modified on' line 230
　MIDI files 232, 278
　navigation bars 229
　product information 229
　special effects 231–2
　streaming video 232
　text-only option 229–30
　web consultancy 226–7
　WYSIWYG web-page editors 228–9
web sites 187, 194, 199, 215, 220, 221–5
　advertising 233–4
　directory listings 220
　foreign-language sites 189
　meta tags 235
　security 209–10
　server logs 208

Telnet and FTP facility 208
　web space 199, 207
Which? Online 108, 196
whiteboard facilities 51
Windows 3.1 309
Windows 95 155, 166, 200, 310, 317
Windows 98 54, 73, 155, 166, 202, 268, 310–11, 317
Windows 2000 200, 243, 311–12
word processing 13, 18–20, 94–6
　automated layout 19
　automated spelling corrections 19
　form letters 19
　key products 43
　letterhead design 95
　mail merge facilities 19
　special text effects 95
　text size and style 19
word processors 39–40
　desktop word processors 39
　portable word processors 39–40
workflow management 51
workstations 31, 138
World Wide Web 14, 29, 187–90
　addresses 320–2
　advertising on 234–7
　indexed searches 189
　keyword searches 188, 190
　off-line browsers 202
　portals 189–90
　search engines 188, 189, 235
　surfing the web 188
　virtual malls 234
　web browsers 29, 37, 44, 165, 195, 231
　see also index entries beginning with 'web'

Year 2000 (Y2K) problem 7–8, 240–56
　assessing the risk 242–9
　BSI compliance document 241–2
　cause for concern 240–1
　checkers 244–5, 246
　compliance 241–53
　compliance statements 245, 248
　contingency plans 241, 254–6
　credit-card equipment 248
　e-commerce 249
　financial software 72
　hardware 243–5, 249–50
　insurance and legal issues 255–6
　Internet 248–9
　networks 248
　non-compliant equipment 249–53
　resetting PCs 243–4
　sensitive dates 246–7
　software 245–7, 250–1
　spreadsheets and databases 247–8
　stationery 248
　time dilation (Crouch-Echlin effect) 244
　video recorders 248

Zip 154